D0313253

ANTHONY KING

Who Governs Britain?

A PELICAN INTRODUCTION

PELICAN
an imprint of
PENGUIN BOOKS

PELICAN BOOKS

UK | USA | Canada | Ireland | Australia
India | New Zealand | South Africa

Penguin Books is part of the Penguin Random House
group of companies whose addresses can be found at
global.penguinrandomhouse.com.

Penguin
Random House
UK

First published 2015
002

Text copyright © Anthony King, 2015
The moral right of the author has been asserted

Book design by Matthew Young
Set in 10/14.664 pt Freight Text Pro
Typeset by Jouve (UK), Milton Keynes
Printed in Great Britain by Clays Ltd, St Ives plc

A CIP catalogue record for this book is
available from the British Library

ISBN: 978-0-141-98065-2

Contents

PREFACE

This short book seeks to answer the single question asked in the title. It is not a textbook, one of those hefty tomes in which all possible questions are asked and answered, mainly in the interests of people who have to pass exams. Instead, it merely seeks to point out that the governing arrangements of the United Kingdom are not quite what they seem and, along the way, to raise some questions – some explicit, some implicit – about whether Britain's political system, as it stands, is all that it should be. The book is not yet another reformist rant, yet the reader may detect in the author a certain unease about the way we are governed now – an unease not confined to the governments of this, that or any other political party (or parties). Our grand old ship of state seems to have sprung some leaks.

What follows is about the central government of the United Kingdom: the government based in London, at Westminster and in and around Whitehall. It is not about local government, and, more important, it is not about the governments of Scotland, Wales and Northern Ireland. The author is acutely conscious that those other governments – especially the ones in Edinburgh, Cardiff and Belfast – exist and are hugely important. Their existence has changed fundamentally the UK's whole governing geometry, a fact that is frequently alluded to in the pages that follow. But the Westminster–Whitehall system is still sufficiently important – and certainly still sufficiently intriguing – to make it worth a short book of its own. The other governments are for another day.

The order in which the chapters are set out will probably strike some readers as idiosyncratic. They will be right. It is. The deliberate aim of the exercise – for example, giving foreigners pride of place in an early chapter and leaving prime ministers until towards the very end – is to disturb the order in which topics like these are customarily approached, an order that in a curious way encourages readers to think along conventional lines when new times perhaps require a less conventional approach. No chapter, or even any large part of a chapter, is devoted to the House of Lords, a body over which much ink has been spilt. The reason is simply that, as it currently stands, the House of Lords is able to vex ministers and take up their time; but – for better or worse – it is nowadays an essentially peripheral body, not a core part of this country's governing arrangements. Time spent discussing the Lords is time not spent discussing other, more important matters.

What follows is the view that one person – the present author – has of Britain's political landscape as it appears from, so to speak, the window of a passenger aircraft cruising at 35,000 feet. Snow-capped mountains are clearly visible, as are lakes, plains and wide river valleys; but enormous amounts of detail, visible and highly significant down below on the ground, are lost. Cars and lorries moving along dual-carriageway roads are only dimly visible, and it is quite hard to make out individual houses, even big ones. This is no more than a book about the landscape's most prominent features and, in particular, about those that are relatively permanent and seem least likely to change in the short term. That said, Britain's political landscape is changing – very rapidly – and this particular book, through no fault of the author's, may fail to detect the most recent seismic shifts. We live in interesting times.

Although the author's mistakes and misinterpretations are entirely his own, he was prevented from making even more of them by seven generous and patient friends who read the entire manuscript at short notice and at great speed: Ivor Crewe, Alun Evans, Peter Kellner, Penelope Phillips, Anthony Stamp and Stephen and Melinda Varcoe. They contributed much, almost certainly more than they realize. The same is true of Andrew Gordon of David Higham, Laura Stickney of Penguin Books (the two of whom first conceived of the whole enterprise) and Kit Shepherd, who copy-edited the manuscript – also at short notice and at speed – and who made still more corrections and substantially improved the overall quality of the manuscript. Valuable research assistance was provided by Katerina Balta and Rob Kemp. All of them deserve, and herewith receive, the author's enormous gratitude.

Anthony King
Wakes Colne, Essex
January 2015

CHAPTER 1

Inheritance

This book is about the United Kingdom's contemporary governing arrangements. It is about Britain today. However, if we want to understand British politics in the present, it is a good idea to begin by acquainting ourselves with a period of its history in the not-too-distant past – with the quarter-century following the end of the Second World War: the two and a half decades between 1945 and 1970. It was during those decades that the British way of doing government and politics assumed its classic form. That form was one of rugged simplicity. It was also one that was widely admired across the liberal democratic world. A French commentator wrote wistfully in 1958, 'The British political system is . . . an enviable model of democratic government. One can only regret that it could not possibly be transplanted to any other country.'[1]

What did that system consist of? An answer to that question is provided in the rest of this chapter. The answer provided here may lack subtlety and nuance, but it should capture the system's main features.

Perched atop the apex of power in that system, visible for miles, was HMG, His Majesty's Government (from 1953, for several generations, *Her* Majesty's Government). The role of the monarch him- or herself was overwhelmingly symbolic and ceremonial, scarcely at all political or governmental; for all practical purposes, the United Kingdom, despite its name, had long ago become a republic. The government of the day was most of what really mattered. It was led by the prime minister and his cabinet, the latter comprising some twenty ministers, most of them heads of government departments. Serving under members of the cabinet were some sixty junior ministers, whose titles varied. A scattering of ministers at all levels of government were peers, members of the House of Lords; but by convention most were MPs, members of the House of Commons. Apart from being peers and MPs, at that time they came from a wide variety of backgrounds. Clement Attlee's postwar Labour administration included a heavyweight trade-union leader, other trade-union officials, a prominent (and seriously rich) barrister, an economics lecturer, a school teacher, an eminent surgeon and a former leader of the London County Council. Winston Churchill's postwar Conservative administration, the successor to Attlee's, included a well-known publisher, the manager of a large department store, a research physicist, a retired army general, the managing director of a metals firm and a number of senior barristers, one of whom had prosecuted Nazi war criminals at the Nuremberg trials.

The government of the day stood at the apex of the system in almost every respect. It was in total control of foreign policy, defence, the public finances (both taxation and public expenditure) and Britain's many colonies (so long as Britain had them). The government initiated all important legislation, and it controlled completely the machinery of government – the state bureaucracy both in Whitehall and across the rest of the country. It also had effective control, although at arm's length, over the many post-1945 nationalized industries, with names such as British Railways and the National Coal Board. Moreover, the UK was then effectively a unitary state, with the UK government, dominated by the English, legislating for Scotland and Wales as well as England. The scope of the UK government's activities was wide, its effective jurisdiction within the UK immense.

The only exceptions to this general rule were Northern Ireland, whose government for historic reasons enjoyed a substantial degree of autonomy within that province, and the institutions of local government on the British mainland. Local government in Britain existed on the sufferance of national government – the government in London could in principle do whatever it liked with local authorities, including abolishing them altogether – but, in practice, local authorities had long-established, quite substantial powers and responsibilities. The creation of the National Health Service in 1948 deprived them of many of their health-related functions, but education and housing, in particular, remained largely in their hands – that is, in the hands of elected local councillors and their officials. In the field of education, there was no national curriculum. In the field of housing, local authorities after the Second World War built hundreds of thousands of houses and flats and then rented them out to tenants while continuing to own and manage them. The municipal councils of London and Glasgow were among the largest landlords in the Western world.

Government at the top – in Downing Street and across

Whitehall – was remarkably collegial. At the time, commentators usually described the British system of government as being one of 'cabinet government' – and it largely was. Postwar prime ministers believed that they should abide by the conventions of cabinet government, and by and large they did. Almost all major policy decisions were at least referred to the whole cabinet, and many important decisions were actually taken there. An elaborate structure of cabinet committees, developed after the war, was intended to make cabinet government more efficient, not to supplant it. Few postwar prime ministers were inclined to be imperious. Most depended heavily on their cabinet colleagues, especially the more senior and experienced ones. Positive prime ministerial initiatives were rare. Harold Macmillan in 1959–60 took the lead in trying to find the UK's way into what was still called the Common Market, but at the same time he went to extreme lengths to carry his colleagues with him. Few prime ministers sought celebrity status. Clement Attlee, notoriously monosyllabic, was seldom seen or heard outside the House of Commons. Harold Macmillan and Harold Wilson were more image-conscious, but even they never affected a presidential style, let alone attempted to govern as though they had presidential powers.

Men (in those days they were always men) became prime minister by virtue of becoming the leader of the majority party in the House of Commons, either because their party had just won a general election or because the incumbent prime minister had resigned. Changes of prime minister within the lifetime of a parliament – that is, between elections – occurred quite frequently. Becoming leader of one's party was entirely in the hands of one's fellow West-minster politicians. In the case of the Conservative party, party leaders until the mid-1960s were not formally elected; instead, they 'emerged' following consultations conducted by party elders among the party's supporters in parliament. The Conservatives adopted a system of choice by formal election only after the emergence in 1963 of Sir Alec Douglas-Home as party leader and prime minister had been hotly contested within the party. Labour leaders had always been elected by their fellow MPs. Once in office, prime ministers were hard to oust and seldom were ousted. Most of those who departed without their party having been defeated at a general election resigned voluntarily, though the position of several of them – notably Anthony Eden and Harold Macmillan – had become decidedly precarious.

The party system during this classic period was simple and straightforward. It comprised two, and only two, par-ties that counted for anything. The Conservative and Labour parties totally dominated British electoral politics. Both were well organized, both at party headquarters in London and throughout the country, with substantial professional staffs and large grassroots memberships. Their structures, however, were not especially hierarchical. In particular, constituency Conservative associations and constituency Labour parties selected their own parliamentary candidates, with only minimal interference from above. As party leader, Winston Churchill, for example, found it almost impossible to obtain a winnable seat for his wayward son, Randolph, who was often the worse for drink.

Because the two major parties were deeply divided

ideologically, because they appealed strongly and separately to class-based warring 'tribes' among voters and because Britain's first-past-the-post electoral system discouraged voters from wasting their votes on minor-party candidates who had no chance of winning, the vast majority of those who went to the polls at general elections backed one or other of the major parties. At the 1950 general election, nearly 90 per cent of those who turned out to vote voted either Labour or Conservative. At the 1951 general election, held a year and a half later, that figure soared to nearly 97 per cent. Until well into the 1970s, the total voting for one or other of the major parties never fell below 87 per cent. The two parties between them appeared to have a lock on the electorate as a whole. With very few exceptions, voters seemed determined – by voting for one major party or the other – to play an effective part in choosing the government of the day. Their votes were, indeed, not to be wasted.

In the British system, voters cast their votes, not directly for either of the two major parties nationally, let alone for either of the two parties' leaders, but for the local parliamentary candidate of their preferred party. Not invariably, but usually, the party winning the most votes nationally also won the most seats in the House of Commons. Either the existing government was returned to power or a new government was formed. Britain's voters at that time never voted in national referendums, and almost no one ever suggested that they should. British government was to be strictly representative government. Moreover, British voters, unlike voters in some other countries, did not elect other office holders, such as the prime minister, members of the cabinet or judges. Strictly speaking, they elected only their own local MP, but in doing so they played a part in deciding which party would form the next government. The system was rough and ready, but a skein of power linked the mass of voters directly with those who held, or were about to hold, power in London. Votes mattered. So did individual voters. As a University of Chicago professor put it:

> The line of authority between people and Government
> [in the United Kingdom] rises singly and directly;
> the line of responsibility of Cabinet and Parliament
> to the people descends singly and directly . . . In the
> British parliamentary system [the line of authority and
> responsibility] is undivided and crystal-clear.[2]

That was, to be sure, a simplification, but it was by no means an over-simplification.

Once elected as their party's standard-bearers, MPs' role in the House of Commons was essentially secondary. The job of those MPs who belonged to the majority party was to sustain that party in power, to maintain the Chicago professor's 'line of authority'. More specifically, their job was to ensure that the incumbent party was able to enact all of its legislative proposals substantially unchanged. Party loyalty was intense, party discipline tight. Backbench MPs of the governing party rebelled in any numbers only very occasionally. The government of the day quite often made concessions to placate restive MPs on the back benches; but ministers, if they insisted, almost always got their way. That was true over Labour backbench opposition to the Anglo-American Loan Agreement in 1946 and over Conservative opposition to decolonization and the Suez war during the 1950s. Only very rarely did backbench opposition stop a government in its tracks. As for MPs belonging to the main opposition party, they could make a nuisance of themselves, but they seldom counted for much. They were mostly, so to speak, noises off – raucous noises perhaps, but seldom ones that ministers listened to.

In the classic system, parliament as a whole could be effective as a forum for the airing of opinions – in effect, as a debating society – but it was generally quite ineffective as a legislative assembly. The government was in total control of the parliamentary timetable. In the House of Commons, the first reading of any government bill was a formality. At second reading, a set-piece debate usually took place, but, if the bill was voted upon, the outcome was almost never in doubt. The committee stage of a bill, following its approval in principle on second reading, should have given MPs an opportunity to discuss it in detail, with a view to their making practical improvements; but the committee stage was typically also a formality, with MPs on the government side remaining largely silent and opposition MPs, knowing that they could not possibly win, mostly just going through the motions (or dealing with their constituency correspondence). Amendments to government bills likely to be accepted by parliament were usually proposed by ministers, seldom by opposition or backbench MPs. The latter frequently knew little or nothing about the substance of what they were supposed to be discussing. The report stage in the full House of Commons, and the third reading there, were also little more than staged rituals. The House of Lords, for its part, was almost totally irrelevant. It had lost most of its substantive powers as long ago as 1911, and there was a common understanding in the Lords – known as the Salisbury convention – that the Lords would not significantly obstruct government bills, especially if the proposals they contained had been included in the governing party's election manifesto. It is only a slight exaggeration to say that by the end of the Second World War parliament had become, in Walter Bagehot's terminology, a dignified rather than an efficient part of Britain's governing arrangements.[3]

Grouped just beneath the apex of governmental power in the old system were Britain's senior civil servants: the cabinet secretary and head of the home civil service (often the same person), the twenty or so permanent secretaries of government departments and their immediate subordinates. These senior 'officials' performed two functions. Looking upward, they functioned as their minister's principal – sometimes his or her sole – policy adviser. Looking downward, they were responsible for the administration on the ground of the work of their department. To these twin tasks, senior officials were meant to bring, and usually did bring, substantial knowledge and long practical experience of the field that they were dealing with – whether it be foreign affairs, defence, health, education, pensions, transport or whatever. They were expected to bring to their tasks both substantive expertise and institutional memory. Although permanent secretaries themselves usually took command of departments that were new to them, most senior officials were 'lifers', men and women who had spent almost the whole of their careers in one department, which was commonly referred to as their 'home' department.

Officials of that generation were famed for their complete neutrality in party-political terms. The same civil servants could be, and sometimes were, deeply involved in the nationalization of industries under Labour administrations and their denationalization under subsequent Conservative administrations (and, on occasion, the other way round). Senior officials, with their long experience of working in the same department, could, of course, be set in their ways, cautious, dilatory and sometimes positively obstructive; but they could also be creative, imaginative and initiators of radical change. They worked not so much *under* their ministerial bosses as *with* them. The acute American observer Richard E. Neustadt, author of *Presidential Power* and adviser to successive American presidents, someone who had befriended many British politicians and senior civil servants, was not wide of the mark when he wrote of ministers and officials:

> Theirs is an intimate collaboration grounded in the interests and traditions of both sides. Indeed it binds them into a society for mutual benefit: what they succeed in sharing with each other they need share with almost no one else, and governing in England [as Americans then called the UK] is a virtual duopoly.[4]

Neustadt added that senior civil servants in Britain, once they had been consulted by ministers and had given them their advice, invariably implemented their decisions 'without public complaint or private evasion, even though they may have fought what they were doing up to the last moment of decision'.[5] Officials gave their advice confidentially and anonymously, but a few of them – Sir Norman Brook, Sir Burke Trend, Sir Otto Clarke, Sir Frank Lee, Sir Leo Pliatzky and Sir William Armstrong – became legends in the Whitehall world. One of the tiny band of female permanent secretaries, Dame Evelyn Sharp, was formidable both intellectually and temperamentally. The diaries of Richard Crossman, one of the half-dozen cabinet ministers she worked with, are replete with references to her. Crossman found her simultaneously daunting, infuriating and admirable. They were an uneasy duo, but a duo all the same. He was indubitably her boss – but only just.[6]

Unlike in the United States and many countries on the European continent, Her Majesty's judges were not really decision-makers in the governmental system. In the absence of a written-down, codified constitution, Acts of parliament could not be challenged in the courts; the doctrine of parliamentary sovereignty reigned supreme. Even ministers' own actions, however perverse, provided they were in accordance with the law, could not be, and were not, challenged in the courts. The judges themselves were passive, showing no disposition to act as a check on either parliament or ministers. Their job was to judge individual cases, not to make law and certainly not to second-guess the wisdom and sound judgement of democratically elected ministers. The judges deferred alike to both Labour and Conservative administrations. So anxious were they not to appear biased against Labour in the years immediately after the war that they leaned 'over backwards almost to the point of falling off the

Bench to avoid the appearance of hostility' to Attlee and his colleagues.[7] Americans spoke, and still do, of the legislative branch of government, the executive branch and the judicial branch. But Britons in the postwar period almost never used the language of three branches. After all, legislation in the United Kingdom emanated almost exclusively from the executive (that is, from the government of the day) and, so far as law and policy making were concerned, Her Majesty's judges were almost totally out of it. During the classic era in Britain, the judiciary was at most a twig of government, never a branch.

Although the government of the day remained firmly in charge, successive governments, both Conservative and Labour, drew heavily on wartime experience and, after the war, showed a willingness – even an eagerness – to consult, co-operate and even come to formal agreements with organizations outside government: for example, the Trades Union Congress, the Federation of British Industries (later the Confederation of British Industry), the National Farmers Union, the British Medical Association, the National Union of Teachers, the Bar Council and the Law Society. The British state briefly showed signs of becoming a quasi-corporatist state, with government policy no longer simply handed down from on high but instead negotiated with the government of the day's 'social partners'. In the case of economic and industrial policy, ministers of both parties frequently spoke of their desire to co-operate with 'both sides of industry' (the employers and the trade unions). Harold Macmillan's administration in 1961 even went so far as to establish a National Economic Development Council ('Neddy'), with a view to promoting co-operation between the government and both sides of industry in the interests of what was then known as 'indicative economic planning'. Along with this big Neddy came a host of 'little Neddies', based in the regions and on individual industrial sectors. This foray into corporatism never became firmly established, and bodies like the TUC and the CBI never became fully a part of Britain's governing arrangements; but it looked for a time as though they just possibly might.

Five general points need to be made about this simple and seemingly sturdy set of governing arrangements.

One is that the British system of government of that time was *highly centralized*. Local government existed, was taken seriously and enjoyed considerable autonomy; Northern Ireland was then, as it still is, a province apart. But otherwise the writ of Westminster and Whitehall ran throughout the whole of the United Kingdom. There was neither a Scottish parliament nor a Scottish government. Today's Holyrood institutions did not exist. The same was true of Wales, with no Welsh national assembly and no Welsh national assembly government. Edinburgh and Cardiff were capitals only in name. Apart from Northern Ireland, the UK system was not remotely federal. The government in London did not have to share its power with the likes of American or Australian states, Canadian provinces or German *Länder*. The UK system as a whole more nearly resembled that of France, with power concentrated in Britain's equivalent of all-conquering Paris.

The classic UK system was not only highly centralized: it was also a *power-hoarding* system as distinct from a power-sharing system. The government of the day was meant to govern – full stop. Only on special occasions – for example, during a world war or when dealing with the 'troubles' in Northern Ireland – was the government of the day expected to co-operate with the opposition parties or to involve them in any way in decision making or policy making. British government was one-party government in spirit and style, not merely in the sense that a single party was usually able to govern on its own. 'We are the masters,' a Labour minister coolly informed opposition Conservative MPs in the House of Commons in 1946. He was quite right: for the moment, the minister and his Labour colleagues *were* the masters.[8] When the Conservatives won the general election in 1951, they in turn became the masters. British governments were almost never in the business of engaging with other political parties. They were also seldom in the business of dealing on a basis of equality with organizations and bodies of opinion outside government. Governments consulted outside bodies, to be sure, but the outside bodies in question remained outside, and the final say remained in the government's hands. The title of one former cabinet minister's memoirs captured the spirit perfectly: *Ministers Decide*.[9] For a time, as we just noted, it looked as though that power-hoarding way of doing government and politics in Britain might change. But it never did.

This centralized and power-hoarding system was also a highly *establishmentarian* system. It was not, and was not meant to be, overly democratic. Rather, the business of governing was to be left in the hands of persons equipped by background, training and temperament to perform that task. In the first place, the people were to be accorded only the power to vote at general elections, and general elections were not to be held too often, ideally no more than once in every four or five years. Voters in Britain, unlike voters in U.S. primary elections, were also to have no say in the selection of parliamentary candidates – and they were certainly to have no say in deciding controversial and important issues. Attlee spoke for his generation when he said in 1945:

> I could not consent to the introduction into our political life of a device so alien to all our traditions as the referendum, which has only too often been the instrument of Nazism and Fascism. Hitler's practices in the field of referenda and plebiscites can hardly have endeared these expedients to the British heart.[10]

More generally, British politicians felt that they were under no moral obligation to be guided by public opinion. Prudence, of course, dictated that they had to pay some attention to what members of the public were thinking: general-election outcomes depended ultimately on voters' opinions and their mood. But British politicians did not regard themselves as merely the public's agents, there to do whatever the public wanted. Instead, they felt they should be guided by their consciences and their own judgements about what should be done in the national interest. The MPs who voted to abolish capital punishment in 1964 actually took pride in the fact that they knew that they were defying majority opinion in so doing. Aneurin Bevan, a leading figure in the postwar Labour party, is said to have complained that merely consulting opinion-poll findings risked 'taking the poetry out of politics'. L. S. Amery, a Conservative (and conservative) constitutional theorist, chose to paraphrase Abraham Lincoln's Gettysburg Address. 'Our system', he said, 'is one of democracy, but of democracy by consent and not by delegation, of government of the people, for the people, with, but not by, the people.'[11] His was the prevailing view, not just in his own party. Governing was for the elite, an elite of talent and experience, not the masses.

At the same time, the old two-party system was nothing if not *adversarial*. On top of personal rivalries, often intense, the differences of opinion between the two parties' leaders, not to mention their rank-and-file members, were profound. Although less so as time went on, the two parties were deeply divided along both ideological and tribal lines. During the 1945 general-election campaign, only weeks after the defeat of Germany and the break-up of the wartime coalition government, Winston Churchill insisted in a radio broadcast that a socialist administration under Clement Attlee, his long-serving and loyal second-in-command, 'would have to fall back on some sort of Gestapo'.[12] Several years later, in a speech in Manchester, Aneurin Bevan, Attlee's minister of health, was even more splenetic:

> No amount of cajolery, and no attempts at ethical or social seduction, can eradicate from my heart a deep burning hatred for the Tory Party . . . So far as I am concerned they are lower than vermin.[13]

The debates at the time of the Suez crisis of 1956 were sometimes just as rancorous. Personal friendships could cross party lines and did, but ill will, not good will, characterized postwar party politics. Whatever the other side said or did, whatever it was, must be wrong. It was during those decades that the phrase 'adversarial politics' was coined.

Finally, the system, whatever else it was, was one that had deeply embedded within it the idea of *accountability* – the idea, that is, that the system made it possible for the electorate collectively to hold the government of the day to account. The government of the day was responsible for whichever of its own actions and inactions affected the UK as a whole. Voters knew perfectly well, or else could easily find out, which political party was in power (i.e., which party constituted the government of the day). Therefore, voters collectively could either reward that government by returning it to power or else punish it by ejecting it and installing in power instead the principal opposition party. Voters might not have superordinate powers – they might not be in total control – but they could nevertheless easily identify which party was in power and collectively punish that party and privilege its opponents. The voters knew who the rascals were, as the Americans put it, and could act accordingly. The arrangement might be brutally primitive, but it could also be brutally effective. Governments knew as much and accordingly behaved responsibly and appropriately. The skein of power was taut. Power-hoarding had that simple, straightforward advantage.

The classic British political order – the one that has been described in this chapter – no longer exists in its original form. Today's system is like a very old building. Although large parts of it still stand, much of it has either fallen down or been torn down. New walls have been built and new extensions added. But, strangely, many of those who live and work in the old building – both politicians and voters – still imagine that it has not really changed in any significant way. They are wrong; but, as we shall see in later chapters, their error has already had, and continues to have, important consequences.

CHAPTER 2

Foreigners

The account set out in Chapter 1 of Britain's postwar governing arrangements was broadly accurate, but it was also radically incomplete, as are most of the accounts on offer now
of how Britain is governed in the twenty-first century. The
majority still give the impression that Britain is governed
by the British people and only by the British people – that
Britain is an island politically as well as geographically. But
that is not so. In the twenty-first century, and for many decades past, the actions and decisions of foreigners have often
had at least as great a bearing on the lives of British citizens
as the actions and decisions of British ministers, officials
and MPs. Foreigners' actions and decisions continuously
constrain the freedom of action and the room for manoeuvre
of British governments – not only in 'foreign' affairs but in
what are customarily called 'domestic' matters. Even when
their representatives are not in the room (though they often
are), the interests and opinions of international institutions,
foreign governments and foreign businesses enter continuously into the calculations of British ministers and civil servants. For many purposes, foreigners have long since become
an integral part of the UK system of government. Who

governs Britain? A large part of the answer is: foreigners, not just locals.

Britain's economy has always been far more open than that of many other countries. As a consequence, its polity has been too. In May 1931, the failure of the Creditanstalt Bank in Vienna precipitated a financial crisis which, over the course of the next few months, sucked in Germany, Romania, Hungary and ultimately Great Britain. During August 1931, the Bank of England's gold reserves rapidly drained away, and at the end of that month Ramsay MacDonald's minority Labour government, unable to agree on austerity measures to deal with the crisis, resigned. A coalition or 'National' government was formed. The British electorate had not spoken. It was foreign investors, lacking confidence in MacDonald's Labour government, who had. Nearly half a century later, in the early months of 1976, with Britain's economy already severely weakened, partly as a result of an earlier sharp rise in world oil prices, the country's foreign-exchange reserves were again rapidly draining away. On this occasion, James Callaghan's Labour government was forced to seek a massive loan from the International Monetary Fund (the first time the government of any major country had found itself forced to do so). The ensuing negotiations involved officials from the IMF, who were housed temporarily in London offices, the president of the United States, the U.S. Treasury, the State Department, the Federal Reserve and West Germany's chancellor and central bank. Although the final decision on whether or not to accept the tough terms of the IMF's proffered loan lay with Callaghan and his ministers, foreigners and foreign organizations had participated in the drama from the outset. They were not outsiders to the British system in any meaningful sense: they were insiders, influential and assertive at the very top of the 'British' system. Again, during the worldwide financial crisis of 2008, Britain's and America's decision-making processes were intertwined in much the same way.

Financial crises apart, the most intimate and intense involvement of foreigners in the making of governmental decisions affecting British citizens dates from 1 January 1973, the day on which the UK joined what is now the European Union. The original Treaty of Rome, signed in Britain's absence in 1957, created the European Economic Community and committed the states joining that body to establishing a customs union and a single common market, to allowing 'the free movement of persons' in the interests of creating the single market and, most ambitiously, to laying 'the foundations of an ever closer union among the peoples of Europe'. By the time Britain joined in 1973, agreement on the introduction of a common external tariff had created the customs union envisaged by the Treaty of Rome, but otherwise progress towards further European integration had been slow. However, in 1986 the EEC's member states, with the support of the UK under Margaret Thatcher, endorsed the Single European Act, which set in train the removal of all barriers to the free movement of goods, services, money and people across Europe. The Act gave the Community's institutions new powers to promote competition and prevent the emergence of monopolies. It also gave these same institutions new responsibilities in fields such as the environment, regional policy and research and development.

The broadening of European economic policy on this scale, together with the progressive enlargement of the Community (Britain's accession in 1973 having been followed by that of six other countries), appeared to require both a strengthening of the Community's governing institutions and a further extension of their competence. It also seemed to require a change in the Community's name. Accordingly, the treaty on European Union, the Maastricht Treaty, finally ratified in 1993, rebranded the former 'European Community'. It was henceforth dubbed, more ambitiously, the 'European Union'. The directly elected European Parliament also acquired new powers, and the remit of the EU's various institutions was extended to include influence upon, although not total control over, transport, education, consumer protection, public-health policy, policing and immigration and asylum. A new class of person was created, the European citizen, with the right to live and work anywhere in the Union and to participate in local (but not national) and European elections. The UK under John Major acceded to the bulk of the Maastricht Treaty, but succeeded in establishing the precedent that Britain (and, by implication, other countries) might be permitted to opt out of any measures adopted by the rest of the EU that it (or they) found especially objectionable.

The impact of all this on the way in which Britain is governed – and by whom – has been enormous. For many purposes, though by no means all, heads of government and other ministers from other EU countries, and members of the European Commission, are now fully integrated into Britain's governing institutions. They are no longer 'out there'; wherever they are located physically (and, in the age of electronic communications, it may not matter much), they are now 'in here'. The Foreign and Commonwealth Office no longer has a virtual monopoly over Britain's relations with other states. Its role in this regard, now relatively circumscribed, it shares with the Department for Environment, Food and Rural Affairs, the Treasury, the Home Office, the Ministry of Justice, the Department for Business, Innovation and Skills and the Department of Energy and Climate Change. Ministers and officials from these departments constantly travel to – and, on occasion, host – meetings with their opposite numbers in the rest of Europe. Because of Britain's legal obligations under the EU treaties, the actions of every British department are liable to be challenged in the European Court of Justice in Luxembourg (not to be confused with the European Court of Human Rights, which we will come to in Chapter 13).

Probably the most extreme instances in which the old-fashioned distinction between 'domestic' and 'foreign' has been largely obliterated are ocean fishing, agriculture and migration. The names of the EU's policies under the first two headings – the Common Fisheries Policy and the Common Agricultural Policy – speak for themselves. The EU, not the UK government acting on its own, imposes national quotas on the amounts of different species of fish that British fishermen are permitted to land and regulates, among other things, the kinds of nets and other gear they may use. Similarly, the EU, not the UK government alone, has been responsible in recent decades for radically reforming the CAP, continuing to subsidize EU farmers but focusing more on the environment and on food quality rather than quantity. The CAP still accounts for more of the EU's total spending than any other policy or project, but its share is now far smaller than it was. As regards human migration within the EU, all of the EU's national governments, not just that of the UK, have effectively been written out of the script. Whatever the governments of individual EU countries and their citizens may think, all EU citizens are free to move wherever they like within the Union. For the time being, the EU rules. (Whether that is OK or not is obviously a matter of dispute.)

Although those three are extreme instances, EU policy making and the policy making of national governments intersect and intertwine at points too numerous to count, with EU officials and national representatives constantly in and out of each other's offices and on the phone and iPad to one another. The fields covered include – but this list is by no means exhaustive – the mutual recognition of professional qualifications, the imposition (or not) of university fees, the distribution of aid to disadvantaged European regions, the adoption of uniform Europe-wide technical standards, the use across the EU of standardized weights and measures, the protection and extension of airline passengers' rights, the monitoring of state aid to companies in individual states, the imposition of limits on the number of hours the employees of European organizations are allowed to work, the tackling of cross-border crime and terrorism and the improvement of water and air quality (and the cleanliness of beaches) across Europe. In all of these fields and others, British ministers and officials have as their working colleagues their opposite numbers in other

EU countries. Whatever their formal designation, those colleagues are among those who govern twenty-first century Britain.

None of that, however, means that national governments, including Britain's, no longer possess any substantial 'zones of autonomy' – fields in which, as least so far as the European Union is concerned, they can do pretty much as they like. Regarding the EU, the governments of the twenty-eight member states, perhaps especially that of the UK, may no longer be as potent as they were; but they are by no means impotent. All of them are able to influence EU policy, with the largest and most stable countries, Germany, France and the UK, having the greatest clout. Moreover, the UK has succeeded in negotiating a number of opt-outs from EU arrangements it finds vexatious, most notably from adopting the euro as its national currency and from the Schengen agreement, which in 1997 abolished border controls between all the EU member states apart from Britain and Ireland. Governments in the UK – whether in London or in one of the devolved nations – still retain control over foreign policy (in the traditional sense), defence, taxation, pensions, social security, health care, almost everything to do with education, roads and transport within the UK, local and regional government and the production and distribution of energy.

If the UK were no longer a member of the EU but succeeded in entering into a free-trade agreement with it, those existing zones of autonomy would undoubtedly remain; but so almost certainly, so far as Britain was concerned, would most of the EU's effective control over what it already controls. Although no longer an EU member state, Britain would by no means be shot of the EU. On the contrary, Norway – the non-EU country whose position most closely resembles the position that the UK would probably be in if it left the EU – is bound by the great bulk of EU legislation. In order to remain part of the common market, Norway has had to subscribe fully to the rules of that market, including the free movement of goods, services, money and people. Unlike Britain, which is inside the EU, Norway, although it is outside, is nevertheless a party to the Schengen agreement, with the result that there are no border controls between Norway and the other Schengen states. A 2012 report commissioned by the Norwegian government stated bluntly that Norway's association agreement with the EU had involved 'a massive transfer of power from [the] national to the supra-national European level'.[1] The report's authors concluded that being so closely associated with the EU had benefitted the Norwegian economy and had definitely not caused serious problems. They noted at the same time, however, that:

> The basic democratic problem with the whole construction is a lack of Norwegian representation and access to decision-making processes that also impact Norway and Norwegian citizens and companies . . . In practice Norway has committed itself to adopting new policies and laws from the EU . . . without any real possibility to influence these.[2]

In other words, Norway has become what some observers call a 'fax democracy', with the EU periodically sending the Norwegians the EU's most recent instructions by fax. Foreigners are at least as much involved in the government of Norway as they are in the government of Great Britain – in fact, paradoxically, more so, precisely because Norway is not fully part of the EU.

The European Union is beyond question the international – or, better still, the supranational – organization in which Britain is most deeply embedded and the one whose decisions most closely affect Britain's national interests. But there are many others. British ministers and officials routinely transact business, usually department by department, but sometimes across the government, with the G7 and G20 groups of prosperous states and with the United Nations, the North Atlantic Treaty Organization, the International Monetary Fund (most notably in 1976, as we saw in Chapter 1, but not just then), the Organisation for Economic Co-operation and Development, the Council of Europe (custodian of the European Convention on Human Rights), the World Health Organization, the International Civil Aviation Organization, the International Maritime Organization, the Organization for Security and Co-operation in Europe and the International Atomic Energy Agency, to name only the most important. The influence on UK policy and institutions of some of these organizations is confined to a single sphere (shipping or civil aviation, for instance), but the UK is obliged to deal with all of them from time to time and with many of them all the time. To that list should be added, although it is not exactly an international organization, the U.S. Central Intelligence Agency.

In their day-to-day business, British ministers and civil servants are also obliged to deal with – and to take into account the probable future behaviour of – large private-sector firms, many of them controlled by foreign shareholders and most of them conducting their operations across national boundaries. On specific issues, negotiations between UK ministers and the representatives of multinational corporations can actually take place on a basis of equality or near-equality, with the multinational corporation sometimes having the upper hand. Motor vehicles can be manufactured almost anywhere, and it was only with great difficulty (and more than a dollop of subsidy) that the Thatcher government during the early 1980s persuaded Nissan of Japan to build an assembly plant in England's North East. Successive governments have struggled, sometimes unsuccessfully, to prevent multinational companies from taking over British firms and then closing down a substantial portion of their UK operations or transferring them overseas. The National Institute for Health and Care Excellence is constantly engaged in hard-fought battles with multinational pharmaceutical corporations – 'big pharma' – over the prices the corporations want to charge the NHS for newly developed, non-generic medicines. In general, British governments of all parties have been intent on holding out to potential inward investors the promise of a 'business-friendly' environment, one characterized by low taxes and 'light-touch' regulation.

Taxes are a continuing problem, whichever party or parties are in power. On the one hand, UK governments badly need revenue. On the other, they do not want to discourage foreign investors by taxing their profits too heavily. Their response has typically been to keep the rates of corporation tax low and not to try overly hard to collect tax from firms that have found ways of avoiding payment. Among the companies in recent years that have made substantial profits in the UK, but have found ways of paying negligible amounts of UK corporation tax, are Amazon, Goldman Sachs, Google, Starbucks, Topshop and Vodafone. The UK's cross-party parliamentary Public Accounts Committee in a report was scathing:

> The hearings we held [with Amazon, Google and Starbucks] showed that international companies are able to exploit national and international tax structures to minimise corporation tax on the economic activity they conduct in the UK. The outcome is that they do not pay their fair share. We believe that this practice is widespread and that HM Revenue & Customs is not taking sufficiently aggressive action to assess and collect the appropriate amount of corporation tax from these multinationals . . . Both HMRC and corporate taxpayers are failing to meet legitimate public expectations from the tax system.[3]

A rough estimate of the amount of tax that, collectively, firms such as those would have paid annually if they had not been able to make alternative arrangements – via Ireland, Luxembourg, the Netherlands or wherever – amounts to some £12 billion. Certainly, critics elsewhere in Europe have been known to describe Britain – which is, after all, an off-shore island – as being little more than a tax haven.

The entities described so far, both governmental and non-governmental, are corporeal. They have names, offices, phone numbers, postal addresses, email addresses, web-sites and logos. But the ability of national governments to govern is circumscribed by other factors. These factors are commonly known as 'the markets'. That way of putting it is convenient and trips easily off the tongue, but it is misleading. Phrases like 'the markets believe', 'the markets think' and 'the markets expect' imply that financial markets are human beings, or at least humanoid, and thus enjoy a degree of autonomy and the capacity to act rationally. But markets are not human beings. The outcomes of market transactions are merely the unwilled consequences of the decisions of a myriad individual human beings, and what each of those individuals does is to make decisions, not in terms of his or her own judgements, but in terms of his or her beliefs as to the judgements of others about what a myriad other human beings have done or are likely to do. In other words, the markets resemble a herd – in the twenty-first century, a herd in which each individual animal has his or her own computer terminal. Compared with 'the markets', the term 'market forces' is preferable, because it implies, accurately, a degree of relentlessness and impersonality – as in the expression 'gale-*force* winds'. It is with often unpredictable market *forces* that modern governments have to contend.

Two such forces are especially powerful from governments' point of view. Both are worldwide, owing little or nothing to national boundaries. One is the force generated by the world's multiple markets in goods, services, company shares and, not least, bonds, including government bonds. Fluctuations in the performance of British companies trading in international markets affect directly UK governments' capacity to raise revenue. In particular, the size and reach of Britain's financial-services sector means that banks and other financial institutions in the City of London and Edinburgh are highly vulnerable to external shocks. The U.S. administration's unilateral decision in 2008 to allow Lehman Brothers to go bankrupt helped precipitate Britain's worst financial crisis since 1931, possibly since the South Sea Bubble in 1720. The crisis forced the UK government to intervene in the British banking sector on an unprecedented scale. At a cost to taxpayers in the region of £50 billion, Gordon Brown's Labour government effectively nationalized or part-nationalized Royal Bank of Scotland (including NatWest) and Lloyds TSB. Much of that vast sum is unlikely ever to be recovered. The UK government's ability to borrow in order to finance its debts – and the rates at which it can borrow – are heavily dependent on the behaviour of international bond markets over which it has almost no control. In the mid-2010s, the interest on the UK government's debt (sometimes called 'the national debt') typically totalled around £50 billion annually and looked set to rise.

The other market force with which UK governments have to contend is the one generated by trading in the world's foreign-exchange markets. Britain was forced off the gold standard in 1931, and devaluations of the pound against the U.S. dollar followed in 1949, 1967 and 1972. Most spectacularly, the British government's later effort to achieve a modicum of foreign-exchange stability collapsed in a heap on 'Black Wednesday' in September 1992, when the UK was forced to exit the European Exchange Rate Mechanism in the most humiliating circumstances. In all these instances, the government of the day attempted to draw a line in the sand – that is, to defend the existing value of the pound against other currencies – only to have its line kicked over by market forces. Devaluing a currency may give a country's economy an advantage by making its exports cheaper and imports dearer (just as an overvalued currency may disadvantage a country's exporters by pushing up the price of their goods in the world's markets); but wild currency fluctuations make forward planning by firms and governments well nigh impossible. The pound has floated freely against other currencies since Black Wednesday a generation ago, and between 1992 and 2014 its value against the U.S. dollar gyrated between £1 = $1.43 and £1 = $2.01 (a difference of nearly 30 per cent) and against the euro between £1 = €1.64 and £1 = €1.12 (a difference exceeding 30 per cent). And there is precious little any British government could, or can, do about it.

The United Kingdom, like all other members of the United Nations, is often described as a 'sovereign' state, and the *Concise Oxford English Dictionary* is quite clear about what it means by 'sovereign': 'possessing supreme or ultimate power' and '(of a nation or its affairs) acting or done independently and without outside interference'. As this chapter has shown, the United Kingdom is no longer remotely a sovereign state on that definition. Nor are the other member states of the EU. Nor are the vast majority of other states in the world. Even powerful and (up to a point) self-sufficient countries such as China, Russia and the United States are far from immune to outside interference and pressures. The United Kingdom is certainly not so immune. British governments are not quite as badly placed as poor Gulliver, bound hand and foot in Lilliput; they can certainly move their limbs to some extent and have a substantial amount of wiggle room. But they do not enjoy nearly as much freedom of movement as a genuinely sovereign state would – and they definitely do not enjoy nearly as much as large numbers of Britons evidently think they do. The United Kingdom long ago lost most of its capacity to act independently. Moreover, there is no way it can regain it. We will touch on the implications of that simple fact in this book's concluding chapter.

Partisans

Some Britons enjoy political activity and are deeply committed in their minds to a political party or campaign. Some of them actually join one of the parties and pay a subscription. There used to be a lot of such people. Membership of the Conservative party peaked at 2.8 million during the early 1950s, before levelling off at about 1.2 million – still an impressive number – during subsequent decades. The Young Conservatives, with a membership at one point of 157,000, functioned as a high-class marriage market. Labour's individual membership peaked at more than a million, also during the early 1950s, and then remained steady at well over 600,000 for roughly two decades thereafter. Labour's individual membership would probably have been considerably higher had large numbers of Labour supporters not already been affiliated to the party via their trade union. Until the 1980s, it made good sense to describe Britain's two main parties as 'mass' parties.

But then the parties' memberships began sharply to decline. Growing numbers of people felt alienated from all the main parties, and even party loyalists tended not to be as intensely partisan as they had once been. Passions akin to religious fervour no longer permeated political life. Those who did feel passionately about saving the planet or saving the countryside increasingly channelled their energies, not through the political parties, but through single-issue groups such as Greenpeace and the Council for the Protection of Rural England; they engaged in politics, but not party politics. The parties' memberships suffered accordingly. They also tended to rise and fall with the electoral cycle, as people signed on and donated money when an election was imminent, but then allowed their membership to lapse once it was over.

Conservative party membership fell from 1.2 million during the 1980s – that is, during Margaret Thatcher's time in office – to half that during the 1990s, then to one-third of that during the 1990s, then to less than one-quarter of that during the 2000s; and by the mid-2010s it had imploded to about 150,000 – a fall of more than 90 per cent since the great postwar days. The Conservative party was no longer a mass party: it had become a boutique party, a party for the most ardent of the faithful. Labour fared a little better, but not much. Having enjoyed an individual membership in the order of 600,000 during the 1970s, its membership had more than halved by the 1980s and, after a brief up-tick during the 1990s, had fallen by two-thirds by the early 2000s. In the mid-2010s, it stood at roughly 190,000. That is, it had fallen by more than 80 per cent since the war. Labour's boutique at that stage was slightly larger than the Conservatives', but it was certainly not a superstore. The Liberal Democrats, with about 40,000 members nationwide, were a mere village shop. Following the 2014 independence referendum, the Scottish National Party had more members in Scotland than the Liberal Democrats had in the entire UK.

Moreover, those figures, however modest, are misleading. In the first place, having been provided by the parties themselves, they are almost certainly exaggerated. The parties have every incentive to maximize the size of their grassroots memberships, none to minimize them. Secondly, they undoubtedly give an exaggerated impression of the numbers of individual women and men actively involved in their party's affairs, notably in their internal decision making and their campaigning during elections. Not all party members are by any means party activists. It is one thing to write a cheque or make a donation online, quite another to attend dreary party meetings or knock on strangers' doors in the rain.

No one knows exactly what proportion of party members are also party activists, but the proportion is probably less than one in four and is unlikely to be as high as one in three. If the proportion actually were as high as one in three, improbable though that is, it would mean that during the mid-2010s Conservative activists across the country numbered, at most, in the order of 50,000 and their Labour opposite numbers in the order of 63,000, with the Liberal Democrats trailing far behind (though considerably more numerous in some constituencies than others). Add the number of trade unionists – say, 10,000 – who, although not individual party members are nevertheless active on Labour's behalf, and also the number of lesser-party activists, and then the total number of party activists in the country on this basis sums to roughly 125,000, or about 0.3 per cent of the UK's eligible electorate. That figure of 0.3 per cent is minuscule. Even so, it is almost certainly an overestimate.

Party leaders and their more active followers in the country are in a relationship – often an uneasy relationship – of mutual dependence. On the one hand, party leaders, MPs and candidates desperately need their party supporters to be a visible and audible presence in their constituencies, to donate money, to display posters in their windows, to plant placards in their front gardens and to provide voices over the phone and boots on the ground during election campaigns. Party leaders, MPs and candidates also badly need their activists' moral support. It is debilitating for an MP or a candidate to have to deal for months on end with vocal and disgruntled members of their local party; and party leaders, even those at or near the top, go out of their way not to alienate the people they meet at party gatherings and address at party conferences – the people whom they regard as 'their' people. Sometimes they even feel the need to sacrifice their own judgement to theirs.

On the other hand, party members in general and party activists in particular are heavily dependent on their leaders. Only their leaders are in a position to advance the causes they favour, whatever those causes may be. Without their leaders, they would be helpless. The party rank and file can contribute to the winning of elections, but only their leaders are in a position to deliver victory and then go on to deliver the fruits of that victory in the form of the kinds of policies and initiatives that the activists pine for. Most activists, even when in doubt, are inclined to give their leaders the benefit of that doubt. The leader who delivers victory – or who seems likely to deliver victory in the future – is secure. The leader who fails on that account will soon find him- or herself in trouble; many among the party's rank and file will feel let down, even betrayed. 'Never', in Robert Browning's words, 'glad confident morning again!'[1]

By a strange irony, the balance of power that exists in that relationship between leaders and followers has, if anything, shifted in party activists' favour just as the latter's total numbers on the ground have diminished. The main parties have become more internally democratic. As they have done so, the power of party members and activists within each of them has increased. Few though they are, party members and activists have substantial clout today, considerably more than they had in the past.

Party members' and activists' views are important. Except in the rare constituencies where parties have opened their choice of candidates to the wider electorate, it is party members and activists who choose parliamentary candidates, and nowadays it is they who have the power to elect their party's leader. They also help to create their party's public image on the ground, and they are often able to influence their party's rhetorical tone, its broad policy direction and sometimes even its stance on specific issues. Not a great deal is known, unfortunately, about party members' views and about how they differ – to the extent that they do differ – from the views of the parties' leaders and from those of ordinary voters. Partly because there are now so few party members, the various polling organizations find it difficult, and expensive, to conduct sample surveys relating only to them.

Even so, what is clear is that on some significant issues large numbers of active Conservative party members hold more radical views than most of their party's leaders and at the same time feel more strongly about them. In the past, those important issues included the repatriation of Commonwealth immigrants, the restoration of the death penalty and hostility to further European integration. In more recent years, they have included cutting taxes, slashing Britain's overseas aid budget, being even tougher on crime and criminals than the party's leadership, drastically reducing net immigration and, of course, not only resisting further European integration but calling for Britain to withdraw from the EU altogether. Grassroots pressure undoubtedly helps account for the fact that between 1997 and the mid-2010s four Conservative leaders in a row – William Hague, Iain Duncan Smith, Michael Howard and David Cameron – at some point abandoned the brand of 'compassionate Conservatism' that they had previously espoused in favour of something a good deal more robust.

Tensions between leaders and followers used to be far greater on the Labour side. Labour's leaders were typically moderate in their views and keen, above all, to win elections and power. In contrast, a large proportion of rank-and-file party members and trade-union activists were passionate socialists and cared far more about keeping the faith than winning the voters' support. Far from deferring to their leaders, many on the Labour side were reluctant to be led at all. In their view, only a truly socialist government was one worth having. Some militants even managed to delude themselves into supposing that Labour could win only if it advocated a fully fledged socialist programme. The split between left and right in the Labour party persisted for nearly a century, from the party's foundation in 1906 until the mid-1990s.

Labour's activists – not either backbench Labour MPs or the party's parliamentary leaders – were chiefly responsible for Labour's 'lurch to the left' during the late 1970s and 1980s, a lurch that resulted in Labour's being excluded from power for no fewer than eighteen years. Fortunately, from that party's point of view, its repeated election defeats – combined with the collapse of communism in the Soviet Union and the decline of militant trade-unionism in the UK – tore the heart out of the traditional left and united the party in again hungering for power. Better tepid Labour than the Tories led by anyone. Labour, no longer a socialist party, won in 1997, 2001 and 2005. The ancient left–right split in the Labour party was consigned to history. It has pretty much remained there.

Meanwhile, the Conservatives' internal politics, more or less by coincidence, were heading in exactly the opposite direction. For many decades, Labour had been the party obsessed by ideology. By contrast, the Conservatives were an essentially non-ideological party, less concerned with doctrine than with winning and retaining power. One of the many histories of the Conservative party was called simply *An Appetite for Power*.[2] If critics chose to dismiss the Conservatives as 'the stupid party', as many of them did, that was all right by them – so long as they went on winning. Disagreements in the party were frequent and sometimes bitter; but they came and went and never resulted in the party's splitting, unlike Labour, into two irreconcilable, deeply entrenched factions. On the contrary, enemies on one issue were liable to be staunch allies on the next. Even now, the Conservatives are not entirely a two-factions party. For all Conservatives, winning elections remains *a* paramount concern; but for many Conservatives winning is no longer *the* paramount concern. Many more Tories than in the past are true believers: more concerned, in the manner of old-style Labour partisans, with doctrine than power.

At least since the late 1970s, the Conservatives have been divided along two dimensions. One of the two divides the intellectual and spiritual heirs of Margaret Thatcher – champions of free markets, private enterprise, individual self-reliance, minimal taxation and the smallest possible state – from more pragmatic Conservatives, those that used to be labelled 'wets', who temperamentally eschew doctrine, desperately want to win and are constantly on the look-out for practical solutions to practical problems. The other dimension – with its origins dating back to the ferocious Corn Law debates of the 1840s – concerns Britain's relations with the rest of the world, notably with Europe and the European Union. Needless to say, the two dimensions overlap, with Thatcherites tending to be hostile towards the EU and pragmatists inclined to be more pro-European, or at least less hostile. Under the circumstances, and given the spirit of the present age, it is not surprising that rank-and-file Conservatives are less willing to defer to their leaders than they once were. In the past, loyalty was said to be the Tories' secret weapon. No longer. The party's divisions abide and go deep. Conservatives used to try, at least, to settle their quarrels in private. Now, less inhibited than in the past, they air them in public.

There is, however, one significant respect in which both major parties remain determinedly traditional. Despite recent efforts by the leaders of all the main parties to influence the ways in which parliamentary candidates are selected, and the kinds of people who are selected, ultimate control remains overwhelmingly in the hands of rank-and-file party members. That was true in the classic period described in Chapter 1. It still is. Unless he sobered up, and perhaps not even then, Randolph Churchill would have no more chance of being nominated as a Conservative parliamentary candidate today than he had in his father's time.

That amount of practical control in the hands of local party activists has important consequences for the way Britain is governed. Voters cannot vote for whomever they like. In practice, they can vote only for one of however many candidates the parties in their locality choose to nominate. Especially in safe seats – in recent years some 80 per cent of the total – that means that the dominant local party, in effect, decides all by itself who the local MP is going to be. Another consequence, even more important, is that in a governmental system like that of the UK, in which the great majority of ministers are drawn from the ranks of the majority party or parties in the House of Commons, local parties decide, in effect, not merely who most of the country's MPs will be but who most of the country's ministers will be; or, more precisely, the winning party or parties' local activists collectively decide which individual politicians will constitute the pool of MPs from which the prime minister will be bound to draw the bulk of his or her ministers. That is power indeed.

Unfortunately, if not much is known about the political views of local party activists, even less is known about the basis on which those same activists choose their candidates. Almost every local party organization selects its parliamentary candidate behind closed doors, in private. Decades ago, the business of candidate selection was known as 'the secret garden' of British politics. Decades later, most of the hedges surrounding that garden remain dense and impenetrable. With little detailed knowledge of the garden's shrubbery available, curious outsiders have to rely for their understanding mainly on anecdotes and on inferring the motives of local activists in choosing their candidates from the subsequent behaviour in the House of Commons of the MPs they chose. Are large numbers of a party's backbenchers in parliament highly critical of their party's leadership? If so, it may reasonably be inferred that many of the constituency parties that selected those same backbenchers were, at the time they selected them, also highly critical.

During the 1970s and early 1980s, the issue inside the Labour party of candidate selection – and deselection – was exceedingly fraught. Would-be parliamentary candidates on the moderate wing of the party, and those who supported continued British membership of the European Community, found it hard or impossible to be selected as candidates by constituency Labour parties, a large proportion of which were dominated by the party's left or far left. Many sitting MPs – no one knows exactly how many – were confronted by their local party with a choice between toeing the local party's line in public or else being prevented from standing as the official Labour candidate at the next election. Fewer than a dozen MPs were actually prevented from standing again, but many more were under pressure. One member faced with deselection, a former minister called Dick Taverne, instead resigned his seat and managed, standing as an independent, to win the ensuing by-election. Labour's left-dominated National Executive Committee eventually made it easier for constituency parties to lean on their MP by requiring all sitting MPs to be subject to a mandatory, instead of an extraordinary, reselection procedure.

Most left-wing Labour MPs were safe during this period, simply because they were on the left, and a large proportion of moderate MPs continued to enjoy the support of their local people. However, pressure on members of parliament from left-leaning constituency Labour parties almost certainly helps to account for one of the most bizarre episodes that occurred during the entire period: the election of Michael Foot as party leader in 1980. At that time, only Labour MPs were entitled to vote for the party leader, and Foot in 1980 defeated his only opponent, the moderate Denis Healey, by ten votes. A number of MPs running scared from their local parties may well have been decisive. Even though the ballot was secret, they voted for someone for whom they would not otherwise have voted. But Foot proved spectacularly inept as leader, as all but his most fervent admirers predicted. With his thick spectacles, rambling speeches, dishevelled clothes and puppet-like walk (reminiscent of Charlie Chaplin's), he was soon nicknamed 'Worzel Gummidge', after a character in children's fiction who resembled an amiable but demented scarecrow. A cartoon on the cover of *Private Eye*, headed 'Labour Leadership: New Shock', showed an elderly Foot lookalike slumped in a wheelchair with a carer leaning over him and asking, 'If you want to stay on, nod your head.' He did stay on, and led Labour to its most devastating postwar defeat (as well as to the defection of some thirty Labour MPs to form a breakaway party called the Social Democrats, one of the precursors of today's Liberal Democrats). Fortunately for Labour, Foot soon quit, the influence of the left at the party's grassroots gradually receded, and in time the mandatory reselection of MPs by party members was effectively abandoned.

The twin issues of selection and deselection have never been as contentious on the Conservative side. The most the Conservative leadership has ever tried to do is influence the demographic profile of the parties' candidates (seeking, among other things, to increase the number of female and ethnic-minority candidates) and also to exercise some degree of quality control over the party's list of approved candidates; but, even so, local Conservative associations have resisted most of such pressures, determined as always to go their own way.

It is also the case that, although rank-and-file Conservatives today are less deferential towards their leaders than they once were, they have not become noticeably readier than in the past to try to tell their MP what to do, certainly not as ready as some local Labour parties used to be. With rare exceptions, when local Conservative associations have threatened to deselect a sitting member, or have actually done so, personal rather than political differences have tended to be the root cause. Nevertheless, although the gate into the Conservatives' secret garden is still closed, it seems clear that, in choosing parliamentary candidates, a considerably larger proportion of local Conservative associations than in the past are now concerned not just with individuals' personal qualities but with their views on those political issues that most concern party members, including those that most deeply divide today's party. Just as some local Labour parties once refused to countenance the nomination of moderates or pro-Europeans, so a substantial proportion of local Conservative associations now appear unwilling to nominate either old-fashioned pragmatists or, in particular, committed pro-Europeans. As a result, Conservative leaders, whatever their own inclinations and calculations of where the party's electoral advantage lies, find themselves under constant pressure from local activists – and, even more, from MPs chosen by those same local activists – to be unbending on such issues as crime, immigration and, of course, Europe. It would seem that at the grassroots in many parts of the country, the traditional Conservative party of Harold Macmillan and Edward Heath is no more. The balance of opinion among Conservative members of the House of Commons reflects the change.

Although not much is known about the criteria that local party selectors have in mind when they pick candidates, they certainly appear to be much keener than they once were on nominating local people or at least people willing to acquire a house or flat in the constituency. In the course of a long career, Winston Churchill represented constituencies in Oldham, Manchester, Dundee and suburban Essex. He acquired residences in none of them. That could not happen today. Being female is much less of a handicap than it was. The number of women candidates adopted by the main parties has risen from fewer than one hundred after the Second World War to more than five times that number recently, and the number of women actually elected has also multiplied roughly fivefold (though women are still grossly underrepresented in terms of their proportion of the population). All parties are also far readier than they were to select candidates from ethnic minorities, including for winnable constituencies (though in arithmetical terms ethnic-minority MPs, like women MPs, are still underrepresented).

But what is striking, given that a large proportion of local party selectors are also potentially selecting government ministers, is how little attention many of them appear to pay to would-be candidates' fitness or otherwise to hold ministerial office. Leaders of all the main parties have a vested interest in recruiting into their parliamentary ranks men and women with ministerial potential. Accordingly, they try to draw up lists of approved candidates who show at least some sign of it. The Conservatives have apparently been more active and successful in that regard than Labour. But local party members and activists, of whichever party, do not share their leaders' vested interest. They may want ideally to select as their candidate someone with ministerial potential, but they have no pressing need to do that. Their principal concern appears to be with identifying someone who will be a local vote-winner and also someone they reckon they can get on with, politically and in other ways. It is almost as though dental surgeons were appointed largely on the basis of their ability to freeze patients' teeth painlessly.

Despite countless detailed amendments, the methods of choosing parliamentary candidates have remained essentially unchanged for generations; but the methods for choosing party leaders – the people at the very top – have changed out of all recognition. The prevailing passion for intra-party democracy – the democracy of the fervent few – has led to the adoption of radical new arrangements for electing party leaders, arrangements that take the election of party leaders out of the exclusive control of MPs and hands it over in large part to rank-and-file party members. The collective power of the latter is thereby hugely increased.

Upon their creation in 1988 – as the result of a merger between the Social Democrats and the long-established Liberal party – the Liberal Democrats immediately adopted the practice of electing their leader by means of a postal ballot of all party members. The Lib Dems led the way, but during the ensuing decade Labour and the Conservatives followed in the same general direction. In 1993, Labour's annual conference voted to retain the party's existing tripartite electoral college for choosing its leader (comprising, in equal proportions, members of parliament, constituency Labour parties and trade unions affiliated to the party), but for the first time required constituency parties to conduct postal ballots of their members and affiliated unions likewise to conduct postal ballots of those of their members who paid the union's political levy. (When in doubt, and even when not in doubt, Labour invariably prefers complexity to simplicity.) The effect has been to give the preponderant – but not the whole – say in electing Labour's leader to the party's members in the country; Labour's MPs, later joined by Labour members of the European Parliament, can easily be outvoted. In 1998, the Conservatives adopted a two-stage system for electing their leader, one that has had much the same effect. First, an exhaustive ballot is conducted among the party's MPs until only the top two candidates remain in contention. Then the names of those two MPs are put to all the party's members in a postal ballot. The party's MPs thus have a say, but not the decisive one.

Early leadership elections conducted under these new arrangements provide a measure of members' increased power within both major parties. Between 1993 and 2010, each of the two parties conducted three leadership elections. In both parties, one of the three elections was uncontested: Michael Howard as Conservative leader in 2003, and Gordon Brown as Labour leader in 2007. In one of the other elections in each party, the individual chosen had the support of the majority both of the party's MPs and also of its members in the country: Tony Blair as Labour leader in 1994, and David Cameron as Conservative leader in 2005. However, in the other two elections the preferences of the party's members of parliament and its membership in the country diverged radically. In other words, someone was elected over the heads of the party's sitting MPs. In the 2001 Conservative leadership contest, Iain Duncan Smith finished second, behind Michael Portillo, in the first ballot of MPs, with 30 per cent of the vote; in the second ballot he again finished second, this time behind Kenneth Clarke, with 36 per cent. On neither ballot was he ahead. But when the party's members in the country were invited to choose between Clarke and Duncan Smith, the latter won decisively, by 61 per cent to 39. No one can know who would have won if the balloting among MPs had continued – a preponderance of those who voted for Portillo might well have swung to Clarke – but, as it was, the party's members in the country, not its MPs, made the ultimate choice. (As it happens, opinion polls at the time suggested that among all voters, including Conservative supporters, large majorities thought Clarke would do a better job as Tory leader than Duncan Smith. Evidently, the party's members and activists thought otherwise.)

Much the same occurred on the Labour side in 2010. In all the rounds of balloting to succeed Gordon Brown as party leader, the top two contenders were David Miliband and his younger brother, Ed. In the end, David had a clear lead (53–47 per cent) among Labour's MPs and MEPs, and an almost identical lead (54–46 per cent) among the rank-and-file members of constituency parties. However, Ed triumphed by a margin of 60 per cent to 40 per cent among the levy-paying members of trade unions affiliated to the party, and his success in that segment of the electoral college was just enough to secure him the leadership by the hair's-breadth margin of 50.65 per cent to 49.35. The party's MPs and MEPs had thus been emphatically overruled. Nothing like that could have happened in an earlier era. But it could certainly happen again. Labour in 2014 adopted a one-member-one-vote system for electing the party leader, thus handing over even more power to the party's rank and file. (As it happens, opinion polls in 2010 indicated that among voters at large, and among Labour voters, David Miliband was preferred to his brother by wide margins; but voters' preferences seem not to have weighed heavily with a majority of levy-paying trade-union members, many of whom were persuaded to vote for Ed by their unions' leaders.)

In addition to their substantial hold over the selection of parliamentary candidates and the election of party leaders, ordinary party members, especially the more active of them, also exercise a form of 'soft power'. It is they whom both leading figures in the party and backbenchers talk to most frequently and hear the views of at fund-raising events, coffee mornings, evening socials and dozens upon dozens of more formal party meetings in their own constituencies and other parts of the country. Party members and activists are MPs' and leaders' most important – and audible – reference group. They probably spend more time talking politics with them than with any other section of the population, save possibly on the doorstep during election campaigns. Each party's annual conference is the occasion for intense interaction between a party's MPs, its would-be MPs and the constituency workers on whom they both depend. It would be odd, and would go against almost all human experience, if the views and outlook of the rank and file did not, cumulatively, come to influence the views of those above them, including those far above them, in the party hierarchy.

For all these reasons, party members and activists count for considerably more in Britain's political scheme of things than is often supposed. They influence governments as well as opposition parties. And, as we noted earlier, there is a certain irony in the fact that their power has waxed as their numbers have waned. Sometimes they resemble a small tail wagging a big dog. Whether such a state of affairs is desirable or not is another matter.

Politicians

A century ago, the great German sociologist Max Weber gave a lecture entitled 'Politics as a Vocation'. In it, he suggested that the people he called professional politicians could be divided into two overlapping categories: those politicians who lived *for* politics and those who lived *off* politics.[1] The politicians who lived *for* politics had it as their vocation – their calling, their profession to which they were dedicated, one in which they could find personal fulfilment. Those who lived *off* politics participated in political life simply, and more prosaically, as a way of earning their living. A politician who lived for politics, but did not live off it, would have to be wealthy or have some kind of independent income; a politician who lived off politics might, or might not, also have politics as his or her vocation. Of course, as Weber recognized, the two categories could overlap. Someone might easily live both for politics and off it: might be both committed to politics emotionally and psychologically and also be dependent on it as his or her principal source of income. People in that position might be called – though this was not a phrase Weber used – 'career politicians'. A career politician may, or may not, be a 'careerist' in the pejorative sense. He or she is quite simply someone dedicated to political life and who makes a living out of it: he or she may, or may not, be particularly ambitious.

Career politicians are nothing new in British politics. They have existed in significant numbers at least since the introduction of parliamentary salaries in 1911. David Lloyd George – first elected to parliament in 1890, at the age of twenty-seven, and an MP continuously for the next fifty-five years – was an archetypal career politician. He was dedicated to his craft, but also earned his living from it – at least after 1905, when he became a minister. Winston Churchill first entered the House of Commons in 1900, at the age of twenty-five, and stayed there on and off until 1964; he was undoubtedly a career politician, although by no means only that. Clement Attlee entered parliament somewhat later, at the age of thirty-nine in 1922, but pursued an exclusively political career for more than thirty years from then on. Nearer to our own time, R. A. ('Rab') Butler served continuously as MP for the Saffron Walden division of Essex from 1929, when he was twenty-six, until 1965, by which time he was in his sixties. And one could cite numerous others, a few of them well known – Arthur Balfour, Ramsay MacDonald, Sir Anthony Eden, Sir Alec Douglas-Home, Edward Heath – but most of them not. Some were not career politicians in the full sense of the term, because they had substantial private incomes, but they certainly lived for politics.

However, until quite recently, career politicians like the ones just mentioned shared seats both in parliament and around the cabinet table with men and women who, while they were certainly engaged in politics, did not, in Weber's sense, live for it. On the contrary, they had other things to do with their lives. Nearly half of those who served in the Conservative postwar cabinets between 1951 and 1957 – members of the House of Commons as well as members of the House of Lords – were in no sense careerists. The same was true of roughly one-third of the members of both Conservative and Labour governments between 1957 and 1970. A biography of Derick Heathcoat Amory, one of Harold Macmillan's chancellors of the exchequer, was entitled *The Reluctant Politician* (a title fully justified by the book's contents).[2] One of Amory's colleagues, Sir David Eccles, was quoted as saying after he left office: 'When I went out of politics, it's imagined that I burst into tears . . . I didn't. I felt I had achieved something, and I was quite happy to do something else.'[3] One of Harold Wilson's ministerial colleagues, Richard Marsh, quit the House of Commons to take up another job and wrote subsequently in his memoirs:

> The simple fact is that . . . you have to be a very special person to be a good career politician. For most senior Members of the House of Commons there is no other occupation they would willingly accept. They could not be seduced from that strange Victorian building for any other post . . .
>
> In my case this was clearly not the position. I like to have an 'in tray' and an 'out tray' and, while I enjoyed the odd debate, it doesn't appeal to me as a life's work.[4]

By now, however, the likes of Amory, Eccles and Marsh have almost entirely disappeared from the scene, certainly from the upper ranks of the British system. Recent governments – and oppositions – have been overwhelmingly dominated by career politicians, men and women who, even if they do not live entirely off politics, certainly live almost entirely for it. The Labour cabinet appointed by Tony Blair in 1997 consisted almost wholly of career politicians, the only notable exception being Lord Irvine of Lairg, the lord chancellor, a prominent practising barrister until his appointment. Similarly, the Conservative-led coalition cabinet appointed by David Cameron in 2010 comprised almost exclusively career politicians, the only notable (and possibly partial) exception being Vince Cable, the business secretary, who worked as a professional economist for thirty years before first being elected to parliament (and who excelled as a ballroom dancer). Every major party leader at least since the late 1970s, including Margaret Thatcher, has been a career politician on any definition of that term.

Career politicians now so totally dominate the upper echelons of British politics that it is fair to say that they, and those immediately around them – their special advisers and other aides – constitute a distinct and distinctive 'political class', one that is set apart from the rest of the population, even from the journalists who write about them and the civil servants who work for them when they are in luck and in office. They are the most prominent denizens of the 'Westminster village'. Those members of the political class who are also members of the House of Commons are in frequent contact with ordinary human beings living outside the village (more so than the members of the political class in some other countries); but they nevertheless have distinctive characteristics.

The great majority of them nowadays look and sound middle class, because that is indubitably what they are.

Remarkably few genuine toffs and remarkably few manual workers, or men and women of working-class origin, remain in the House of Commons. During the decade or so after the war, a substantial proportion of MPs, most of them though not all Conservatives, were posh enough to have attended a public school but had not then gone on to university. Following the 1955 general election, these public-school-only MPs accounted for 13 per cent of all MPs.[5] Following the 2010 general election, they accounted for a mere 0.9 per cent. Similarly, in 1955 roughly a dozen MPs, all Conservatives, cheerfully gave their (non-) occupation as 'private means'. In 2010, nobody did.

At the other end of the social scale, the proportion of MPs describing themselves as 'manual workers' fell during the same period by fully three-quarters, from 16 per cent to a barely visible 4 per cent. In the years after the war, it was taken for granted that a fair proportion of the cabinet ministers in any Labour government would be visibly and audibly working class. In Tony Blair's post-1997 cabinet, the boisterous former ship's steward John Prescott alone stood out. He seemed, because he was, something of a throw-back. Members of the professional and business classes totally dominate British politics today; and, merely by looking at them or listening to them, it is often impossible to tell Conservative, Labour and Liberal Democrat politicians apart. Although the number of women and people from ethnic minorities in both houses of parliament has increased substantially, most of them have also been assimilated into – or were already part of – the political class.

Although detailed evidence is hard to come by, it also

seems that fewer and fewer MPs and ministers – by now quite a small proportion – have had substantial and lengthy prior experience of the world outside politics. Postwar governments, as we saw in Chapter 1, contained considerable numbers of men – they were virtually all men – whose pre-political careers had sometimes lasted for decades: in the trade-union world, in business, as barristers and solicitors and as members of the armed forces. As late as the 1970s, a substantial proportion of senior politicians, including James Callaghan, Peter (Lord) Carrington, Tony Crosland, Denis Healey, Edward Heath, Roy Jenkins, Iain Macleod, Francis Pym and William Whitelaw, had served during the Second World War in the army or navy, where they had presumably learned a thing or two. Even if those men were career politicians, which most of them were, they brought to the table a variety of intense non-political experiences.

Few of Tony Blair's senior ministers had had any comparable experiences, whether in the armed forces or anywhere else; Alan Johnson, formerly general secretary of the Union of Communication Workers, was a rare exception. Similarly, few of the ministers whom David Cameron appointed in 2010 brought with them into government a rich body of pre-political experience, though Vince Cable, who has already been mentioned, and Philip Hammond, a successful businessman and consultant over twenty years, were exceptions. Intriguingly, the number of MPs content to describe themselves as 'politicians' or 'political organizers' has shot up in recent decades: from a mere 4 per cent in 1955 to 14 per cent following the 2010 election. Self-designated politicians and political organizers constitute one of the largest

single occupational groups in today's House of Commons –
and the true proportion is probably higher than 14 per cent,
given that not every politician or organizer wants to describe
him- or herself in those terms.

Max Weber in his century-old lecture surmised that the
future of democratic politics lay with lawyers, journalists and
the people he termed 'party officials'. At the time he wrote
he might already have wanted to add teachers to his list; and,
if he were alive today, he would almost certainly want to
add practitioners of public relations, an occupation that did
not exist a century ago. With the partial – but only partial –
exception of party officials and organizers, what these
occupations have in common is a preoccupation with the
persuasive use of words. 'To an outstanding degree,' Weber
pointed out, 'politics today is in fact conducted in public by
means of the spoken or written word.'[6] From which it followed that those trained and adept in the use of words would
be likely to prosper politically. Weber was not too bothered
by this fact (though he might have been if he had anticipated
the rise of Hitler in his own country); he simply noted that
the effective use of words had been a staple of democratic
politics since Pericles addressed the *demos* in ancient Athens
over two millennia ago. Certainly, Weber was right in his
prediction of the broad shape of any future political class in
Europe. Nearly one-third of the MPs elected to the 2010 UK
parliament came from, or were still members of, markedly
verbal professions.

However, there is always the possibility that those who
are adept at the use of words will come to believe that words
are enough, that words are just about as good as deeds and

are, indeed, all but equivalent to deeds. Some members of Britain's political class today give the impression of suffering from that particular professional deformation. It used to be said that those in opposition looked in the mirror in the morning and asked themselves, 'What will I *say* today?' whereas those in government asked themselves, 'What will I *do* today?' In the minds of some contemporary politicians, though by no means all, that distinction seems to have become blurred, even obliterated. It occasionally seemed so in the case of Tony Blair, who had briefly been a lawyer before entering parliament. It was often indiscernible in the case of David Cameron, whose pre-parliamentary experience had consisted of being a party researcher, then a special adviser to ministers and finally a full-time public-relations executive. Cameron was a man of many words.

Members of the political class are not only wholesale dealers in words: they have developed a remarkably common language and rhetorical style. Any relatively homogeneous group of people – whether a close-knit family, soldiers, sailors, farmers or barristers at one of the Inns of Court – is liable to develop a language of its own and a distinctive way of speaking. And, somewhat paradoxically, given that they are meant to be good at communicating with people beyond the world of politics, most members of the British political class have adopted a language that is instantly recognizable and largely peculiar to itself. Switch on the radio in the midst of an interview with a person or persons unknown and more often than not one can tell immediately whether or not it is a politician who is speaking. Politicians' answers to questions often sound rehearsed, stilted and declamatory, they are often repetitive and replete with 'on message' catchphrases, and they are often answers to any number of questions except the ones that the interviewer has actually asked. Politicians are exceedingly reluctant ever to say 'I don't know' or 'I'm not sure'. Even most politicians' longer set-piece speeches – at party conferences, for instance – seldom develop a sustained argument. In both interviews and set-piece speeches, ministers, in particular, often deploy numbers as weapons, boasting that they and their colleagues during the past year have increased the government's investment in state-of-the-art widgets by 100,000, when the listener or viewer cannot possibly have any idea whether that increase in widget-investment represents an astonishing achievement or an abject failure – or indeed whether the increase has happened at all. To a remarkable extent, national politicians, irrespective of party, sound and talk alike as well as looking alike.

Those who dwell in the Westminster village thus have their own argot: they also have other village-like characteristics. They have always been – since at least the eighteenth century and probably long before that – inveterate gossips. Who's in? Who's out? Who's up? Who's down? Such questions are asked incessantly and often of individuals – junior ministers and backbench MPs – whom the great majority of the people living outside the Westminster village have never heard of. No villager can walk more than a couple of hundred yards from the Palace of Westminster without bumping into fellow villagers whom he or she knows. Inevitably, feuds are frequent. The political class has its own website, PoliticsHome, its own newsletter, the *House*

Magazine, its own BBC Television slot, the *Daily Politics* show, its own slot on BBC Radio, *The Westminster Hour*, and its own parish magazine, *Total Politics* – a cheerful cross between *Hello!* and *Country Life*. For members of the political class, politics can be, and in some cases is, a complete way of life.

What are the consequences of the fact that Britain is now governed by a political class?

Today's politicians are certainly better educated than their predecessors were – or at least they have had more in the way of formal education. Roughly one in a dozen of the MPs who were elected in 1955 had never progressed beyond elementary school. Nearly half had never been to university. By contrast, almost all the MPs elected in 2010 had progressed beyond elementary school, and more than 90 per cent had attended a university, polytechnic or further-education college of some kind. Until recently, many older and retired MPs, far from harking back to a golden age of parliament, liked to point out to their younger colleagues that during the immediate postwar years a considerable proportion of members of parliament were either superannuated trade unionists, who seldom spoke and were often drunk, or ex-public-school boys, who as often as not answered much the same description. The members of today's political class are almost certainly also at least as honest and honourable as their predecessors – and at least as honest and honourable as members of the public at large. The 2009 parliamentary expenses scandal exposed the extraordinary greed of some MPs, but it also drew attention to the fact that over many years the parliamentary authorities had encouraged members to claim all the expenses they decently could in order to top up their salaries. Most members of the political class are neither stupid nor corrupt.

The work-rate among members of almost all professions has increased drastically during recent decades, and among members of the political class it has probably increased even more than among other professions. Most ministers and MPs – and many of their staffs – work phenomenally hard, far more so than their predecessors. Most MPs are expected to have a home in their constituency and therefore, unless they happen to be a London member, to have to travel back and forth frequently between London and their constituency, even if the latter is located hundreds of miles away. By the same token, most members of parliament are nowadays expected to be, and expect themselves to be, the principal point of contact between their constituents – including firms in their constituency – and every branch of government, including local government. Roy Jenkins, an up-and-coming Labour backbencher during the 1950s, visited his Birmingham constituency only one weekend and evening a month and never bought a house or flat in the city. Instead, he usually stayed with friends.[7] Gone are the days of long ministerial summer holidays, uninterrupted by phone calls and a thousand other importunate messages, except in cases of dire emergency. Ministers' red boxes have never been fuller or more pressing – and most ministers, although they grumble, rejoice in the fact. It makes them feel important.

One consequence of parliamentary and ministerial work being more demanding than it was is that only a few MPs in the twenty-first century can afford the time or have the energy to practise another profession or run a business. At most, they can act as consultants or sit on company boards as non-executive directors. The parliamentary timetable used to leave most mornings and many afternoons free, when MPs could pursue parallel careers. They did not have to be full-time parliamentarians. Barristers, in particular, could maintain an extensive practice. To take an admittedly extreme example, Sir David Maxwell Fyfe, when the Conservatives were in opposition during the 1945 and 1950 parliaments, spent most of every working day in chambers or in court, usually turning up at the House of Commons late in the afternoon and then, once he was there, frequently working all night. Meanwhile, he was shadowing the Ministry of Labour. But changes instituted during the 2000s mean that the House of Commons now meets during the morning on Tuesdays, Wednesdays and Fridays (when the House is sitting on a Friday), rendering regular morning engagements outside parliament impossible. The upshot is that most MPs, including prospective ministers, in addition to having seldom had, so to speak, coal-face jobs for any length of time before entering parliament, find it significantly more difficult than in the past to obtain relevant extra-parliamentary experience while also performing their parliamentary duties.

But perhaps the most striking feature of members of the political class is the assertiveness of a considerable proportion of them. It might be supposed that career politicians would be determined, above all else, to advance their own political careers: to obtain ministerial office, if they did not already have it, and to climb ever higher on the ministerial ladder, if they were already on it. And it probably is the case that a larger proportion of MPs than in the past do harbour such ambitions, although Ramsay MacDonald noted sadly in 1929, when he formed his second Labour government, that 'I have broken hearts – one man all but fainted when I told him he could not get what he expected'.[8] But there is no evidence that those career politicians who are ambitious are any more single-mindedly ambitious than their predecessors. On the contrary, many career politicians are also proud professionals in their way, holding views about which they feel strongly. Some of them can be pushed only so far. Although the phenomenon seems to have been overlooked, the rate of principled ministerial resignations has, if anything, increased – it has certainly not decreased – since the rise of the career politician. Michael Heseltine dramatically walked out of a cabinet meeting during the Westland affair in 1986. Nigel Lawson resigned in 1989 over differences concerning economic policy between himself and Margaret Thatcher and Sir Alan Walters, one of her principal advisers. Sir Geoffrey Howe resigned a year later over differences with Thatcher about Europe. John Redwood resigned in 1995 in protest against John Major's approach to Europe and the economy. No fewer than four ministers – including Robin Cook, leader of the House of Commons and a former foreign secretary – resigned in 2003 over the Blair government's decision to support the American-led invasion of Iraq. And Lady Warsi quit the Cameron government in 2014 over David Cameron's unwillingness to condemn Israeli military strikes on Gaza. All of those resigners were career politicians, members of the political class; but none of them, save possibly Redwood, can have imagined that by resigning they were advancing their political career. Most of them never held office again.

The assertiveness and independent-mindedness of a substantial proportion of career politicians manifests itself in other ways. Many of them are no longer content to be anonymous backbenchers. Some are eager to make their idiosyncratic views known in television and radio studios, in the press and on Twitter, Facebook and elsewhere on the web. Others are active members of parliamentary select committees, several of which have become thorns in the side of successive governments. The Public Accounts Committee – especially but not only under the post-2010 chairmanship of Margaret Hodge – became notorious for its willingness to criticize the actions of the government of the day. That committee's reports are invariably unanimous, demonstrating the willingness of at least some government backbenchers openly to criticize ministers drawn from the ranks of their own party. Moreover, in recent decades, the ability of the party whips in the House of Commons to dragoon their rank-and-file MPs has declined sharply. Backbench rebellions are increasingly common. The myth of backbench MPs' obsequiousness dies hard; but, as we shall see in Chapter 12, backbenchers are less reliable and more rebellious now than at any time since the late nineteenth century. Most members of today's political class may be content to remain biddable and on message, but a significant minority are not.

The emergence of the political class probably also helps to explain the phenomenon of ministerial activism. Yesterday's ministers were often content merely to *be*; the vast majority of today's ministers want to *do* and to be seen to be doing. They want to make their mark. They want to change the world. In practice, that means not being content to administer existing government policies, perhaps developing them incrementally: it means wanting to innovate and initiate. Ever since Margaret Thatcher's premiership, with the partial exception of John Major's years in office, ministers have typically been restless, bringers of change. They have also, more often than not, been in a hurry, wanting to see their radical initiatives reach the statute book as soon as is humanly possible – and often well before that. The ministers in the coalition government that came to power in 2010 were typical in this regard, with Andrew Lansley determined to up-end the NHS in England, Michael Gove determined to do the same to England's schools, Iain Duncan Smith bent upon revolutionizing the UK-wide social security system and successive defence secretaries equally bent upon replacing British army regulars with reservists on a vast (and doubtfully achievable) scale. Over the past four decades, the size of the UK statute book itself has expanded almost exponentially.

One abiding consequence of the political class's collective assertiveness is paradoxical. Britain's main political parties today, for all their detailed policy differences, are closer together than at any time since the 1920s in their broad ideological sweep; and ordinary voters, similarly, are in no way polarized and show few signs of becoming so. Yet British party politics, at almost all levels, remains at least as adversarial in tone and style as it ever was. Today's party leaders no longer label their opponents 'vermin' or accuse them of wanting to import the Gestapo into Britain; but they continue to bellow at one another across the floor of the House of Commons and continue to privilege disagreement over agreement. Whereas the political leaders of some other countries, including most of those in northern Europe, strive for consensus, Britain's leaders appear determined to strive for dissensus, exaggerating differences that really do exist and inventing ones that do not. Accommodation and compromise are, of course, frequently arrived at in private; but, in public, mutual abuse and eye-gouging are the norm. Opinion-poll evidence suggests that most non-politicians – that is, the great majority of the UK population – are unimpressed.

In short, members of the non-political public view from a great psychological distance what seems to them to be a remarkably homogeneous political class, comprising people who look and sound remarkably alike and who also have in common the fact that they speak a strange kind of in-house language – what might be called the Westminster dialect. Because the speakers of that dialect often give evasive answers to questions and often give the impression of promising more than they can perform, they come over as shifty and shallow. As Gordon Brown put it when he announced he was stepping down from parliament:

> Sometimes [he probably meant most of the time] politics is seen at best as a branch of the entertainment industry. There are times when political parties seem not to be agents of change but brands to be marketed to people who are seen as consumers . . .[9]

Opinion polls consistently show that a large majority of ordinary citizens do indeed believe that politicians are hucksters, people who tell lies all the time and cannot be trusted.

That said, it is worth noting that there is a long tradition in Britain of denigrating politicians as a class. Shakespeare in his time knew he could invariably get a laugh by portraying a character on stage as 'a scurvy politician'. It is also worth noting that, in the circumstances of the early twenty-first century, with Britain in chronic economic difficulties and in continuing decline as a world power, many thousands of Britons are almost certainly succumbing to the temptation to blame politicians for developments over which, in reality, they have little or no control. For anyone searching for scapegoats, politicians as a class make easy prey. They always have. Unfortunately, a large proportion of them bring it on themselves.

CHAPTER 5

Voters

A few members of parliament are not too bothered about which party wins the next general election. Life on the back benches suits them. Their only concern is to hold on to their own seat. But the great majority of MPs and candidates care desperately who wins. As keen partisans, they want their party to win; they want to further their own careers (or at any rate not to see them terminated); they are committed to their party's policies and causes; they fear the worst for the country if the other side gets into government. Which party eventually does win depends partly on the vagaries of Britain's first-past-the-post electoral system but mainly on how millions of voters cast their ballots. The views of ordinary voters matter just as much to politicians now as they did in the classic era following the war. In the age of opinion polls, focus groups and the micro-targeting of voters, they may loom even larger.

Voters matter as much as they do partly because the British system of government remains overwhelmingly a power-hoarding system. The government of the day hoards its power and is expected to use it. Governments are meant to be, and largely are, the active element in the system. Outsiders are meant to react, positively or negatively, to whatever the government in power chooses to say or do. 'Ministers', as the memoir-writer said, 'decide.' By and large, ministers relish having such a great amount of power concentrated in their hands; but it follows, at the same time, that they can never overlook the fact that this very concentration of power carries with it an enormous downside risk from their point of view. The fact that so much power is, or appears to be, in their hands means that ministers are continually left exposed – naked in the wind – to the wrath of the electorate. If things go wrong in the UK, voters know, or think they know, who to blame: possibly the European Union, but more immediately those currently in power in London (who can also be blamed for failing to stand up to the EU). Ministers are thus vulnerable to the electorate, and they know it. As a result, they are exceedingly sensitive to the state of public opinion, especially but not only during the months and years preceding the next general election. In ministers' collective insecurity lies the electorate's collective power. That power turns out to be quite substantial.

Voters' influence over government – any government – is at its maximum when certain conditions are fulfilled: when a large mass of people feel strongly about an issue, when opinion on that issue is heavily skewed in one direction (in other words, when there is something approaching consensus among the electorate) and when those in power believe that those strong feelings and that one-sidedness of sentiment could shift a critical mass of voters in their favour or against them. Ultimately, it is not what voters actually think that matters: what matters is what those in power, or who aspire to power, think they think.

Logically, ministers and opposition spokesmen can respond to strongly held and one-sided bodies of opinion in one or other of three ways, ranging from enthusiastic endorsement through reluctant acquiescence to outright defiance. It is worth illustrating each of these possible responses, beginning with enthusiastic endorsement.

During the roughly two decades from the mid-1960s onward, successive prime ministers and most of their colleagues enthusiastically endorsed the view of those voters, a large majority, who wanted Britain's trade unions to be reformed and their power drastically curbed. Public opinion and politicians' opinions largely coincided. The public wanted the politicians to do what most of the politicians wanted to do anyway. The fact that effective trade-union reform did not materialize until the time of the Thatcher government in the mid-1980s was owing to the trade-union dominated internal politics of the Labour party and manifold misjudgements by the Conservative government of Edward Heath, not at all to any reluctance on the part of the bulk of the political class. On the contrary, Labour remained unelectable for a generation after 1979 partly because of its close ties to the unions. Later, during the mid- and late 1990s, Tony Blair was able to point out to his followers in the party that, unless Labour agreed to accept the union-curbing measures introduced by Margaret Thatcher, it would probably – such was voters' hostility towards trade-union power – continue to remain unelectable for the foreseeable future. Blair won the argument, and Labour went on to win three consecutive elections. Every government then and since has retained the Thatcher laws. It may have taken a long time for voter power finally to prevail, but it certainly did in the end.

The circumstances surrounding the curbing of Britain's trade unions are well known. Less well known is an instance of voters actually initiating change – on their own volition, so to speak, and without, initially at least, politicians playing any significant part. During the Greater London Council elections of 1967, the Conservative party conducted a number of private polls on behalf of its candidates. At the pollsters' instigation, and only because the pollsters were curious, the respondents to one of these polls were asked what they thought of the idea of council-house tenants being able to buy their own homes. To the considerable surprise of almost everyone involved, it turned out that a large majority of those surveyed, including council-house tenants, thought that was a splendid idea. The message that this was so – that council-house sales might well prove a vote-winner – was passed up through the party hierarchy and three years later made a tentative appearance in the Conservatives' manifesto for the 1970 election: 'We will encourage local authorities to sell council houses to those of their tenants who wish to buy them. Thus many council house tenants of today will become the owners of their own homes tomorrow.'[1] Following the Conservatives' victory in that election, Edward Heath's government did promote council-house sales, but (for some reason) not at all enthusiastically. However, following Margaret Thatcher's electoral triumph in 1979, her government took up the cause with unbounded enthusiasm. It passed legislation absolutely requiring local authorities to give their tenants the right to buy their house or flat. Initially,

Labour was hostile to the whole enterprise; but, in the face of voters' evident enthusiasm, the party gradually, although reluctantly, admitted defeat. It believed that it had no choice. Again, voter power had prevailed.

Reluctant acquiescence of the kind Labour exhibited over council-house sales has characterized politicians' responses to other instances of voter pressure, immigration being the most important and the most enduring. Broadly, political leaders have tended to be in favour of immigration or relaxed about it; a majority of voters have typically been against it and, on occasion, not at all relaxed about it. More than a hundred years ago, Arthur Balfour's government introduced the Aliens Act 1905 in response to public pressure to limit the immigration of Russian Jews. Prior to 1962, anyone from the British Commonwealth could freely enter this country, and most political leaders, Conservative as well as Labour, defended that position; they favoured immigration on economic grounds and were desperate to retain Britain's historic links with the former Empire, now the Commonwealth. But a public opinion hostile to large-scale immigration prevailed, and a succession of statutes placed tight restrictions on Commonwealth citizens seeking to come to the UK. On every occasion, especially in 1962, senior politicians voiced their dismay at what they felt they were being forced to do in response to voters' pressure. The Labour party leader, Hugh Gaitskell, denounced the 1962 Act as 'a plain anti-Commonwealth Measure in theory and . . . a plain anti-colour Measure in practice', and many Conservatives agreed with him, some publicly, some in private.[2] But the electoral pressures were intense ('If you want a Nigger for a neighbour, vote Labour'), and when Labour came to power in 1964 it retained the Conservatives' legislation virtually intact, a few years later imposing even tighter restrictions. Many commentators attributed the Conservatives' loss of the February 1974 election to Enoch Powell's anti-immigrant and anti-Common Market propaganda following his defection from the Conservative party. By the mid-1970s, immigration had firmly established itself as being extraordinarily dangerous, at least potentially, in electoral terms. It was an issue that millions of voters cared deeply about.

Immigration then remained largely dormant as an issue – although never wholly so – until the mid-2000s, when large numbers of EU migrants, mostly from central and eastern Europe, began to move to the UK to live and work, allegedly stretching public services to the limit, forcing down wages and taking UK citizens' jobs. The Conservatives were divided on the issue, some of the party's leading figures welcoming immigration on economic grounds, others vehemently objecting to the scale on which it was taking place. As during the 1960s, Labour collectively was inclined to be relaxed on the issue. The Liberal Democrats, for their part, being ideologically pro-European, saw EU migrants as more of a blessing than a curse. But politicians at the top of all three parties, whatever their personal preferences, could not ignore the elemental fact that large numbers of voters disliked immigration (and often immigrants), felt strongly about the matter and showed increasing signs of being willing to vote for the most anti-immigration party currently on offer. The United Kingdom Independence Party (UKIP) duly arrived on the scene to play – or try to play – that role, much as Enoch Powell had nearly half a century before. UKIP and many in the Conservative party could easily blame large-scale immigration on the EU, with that organization's insistence on the free movement of labour. The major parties' leaders have responded as they were bound to do under the circumstances: they are accepting, with varying degrees of reluctance, of the idea that tighter restrictions on immigration and immigrants should, if possible, be imposed. Those in power thus find themselves in a vice, caught between the EU and its principle of the free movement of labour on the one hand and the views of millions of UK voters on the other. For now, that cruel vice shows few signs of relaxing its grip.

Immigration is unique in the scale of its capacity to alarm politicians, but it is by no means alone. Britain's continued membership of the EU finds pro-European political leaders caught between their own desire that Britain should remain in the EU and the belief of some of their followers and considerable numbers of unpredictable voters that Britain should pull out. Hence, in particular, David Cameron's promise in 2013 that, if the Conservatives under his leadership were returned to power after the general election in 2015, the government, following negotiations with the other EU member states, would hold a referendum on the issue of Britain's continued EU membership. His Labour predecessor Tony Blair made a similar compromise between his personal convictions and electoral necessity when he pledged that, before any government under his leadership took Britain into the eurozone, a yes/no referendum would be held on that issue. Blair badly wanted the UK to adopt the euro but knew that his own and his party's chances of being re-elected would be jeopardized if voters came to equate in their minds a vote for him and the Labour party with a vote for the euro. Over the euro, the electorate collectively succeeded in wielding a total veto.

In general, if large numbers of voters appear to be speaking both loudly and with one voice, politicians – and ministers in particular – will almost invariably pay close attention to them. They almost always respond, however reluctantly, to voters' clearly expressed demands. Instances of outright defiance are rare. Margaret Thatcher, although known as 'the Iron Lady', was remarkably flexible and cautious on these occasions until towards the end of her time in office. For example, she well knew that, in proposing to sell off to the private sector large segments of the hitherto state-owned public utilities, she was flying in the face of opinion-poll findings. Partly for that reason, she delayed the first major privatizations until after the Conservatives had won the 1983 general election with an increased majority. The convincing result of that election meant that she could privatize with impunity so far as the electorate was concerned. In addition, the fact that the initial privatizations proceeded smoothly and without causing public uproar meant that she could go on privatizing, confident that she would not pay a significant electoral price.

However, the poll tax was different. Here she did fly in the face of public opinion, introducing a tax that almost no one outside the Conservative party wanted and that aroused intense public hostility. But the question arises: was she knowingly and consciously defying public opinion, thereby running a serious electoral risk? The answer is that it seems most unlikely. The available evidence suggests that by that late stage of her career she was deluding herself and imagined that, if she had got away with so much in the past, she could get away with almost anything in the future. But she was wrong, and in the end the voters, not Thatcher, got their way. She was ousted as prime minister by her own party largely because a majority of cabinet ministers and Conservative MPs believed that the poll tax had made her a dangerous electoral liability. And the prime minister was not the only thing scrapped: soon the poll tax was too. Yet again, the electorate won.

One of the relatively rare instances of politicians openly defying majority opinion in the country came during the 1960s, when MPs voted by a large majority to abolish capital punishment. They did so in the full knowledge – even though some of them denied it – that the public wanted hanging retained. Speaking in the House of Commons, one MP undoubtedly spoke for most of his parliamentary colleagues when he said: 'I confess that when I entered the House . . . I did so in the hope and belief that this House will always have the courage to do what it believes to be right, even if public opinion should be against it.'[3] He himself intended to vote for what he believed to be right. Significantly, however, the bill to abolish capital punishment was not a government bill. It was a private member's bill, and the vote that took place on it was a free vote, not one that in any way committed the government. In other words, although individual MPs might suffer electorally in their own constituencies, the government as a whole could not be held to account. By insisting on a free vote on that occasion, ministers were clearly in the business of minimizing their collective electoral risks. Ministers usually are in that business.

British politicians' natural fear of the electorate – a fear intensified by the fact that Britain's power-hoarding system inevitably exposes any government to such enormous electoral risks – manifests itself in another way. It frequently inhibits ministers and even shadow ministers from tackling a range of what are sometimes known in the corridors of power as 'the wicked issues': issues on which the taking of decisive action in the country's long-term interests is accompanied by the risk of the government's suffering electorally or even being thrown out of office in the short or medium term. In connection with these wicked issues, voter power is so great that matters of great importance to the country are simply removed from the political agenda. Because ministers are reluctant to put their heads above the parapet, the issues are either not addressed at all or are addressed but in a halting and piecemeal fashion. The British system is often lauded for its decisiveness, for the freedom it gives governments to take decisive action in the national interest. In reality, the system is not nearly as decisive as it looks. It is actually a system that puts a premium on evasion.

Examples abound. Ministers in successive governments have refused to make difficult decisions on defence. On the one hand, they want Britain to be able 'to punch above its weight' in world affairs; on the other, they are reluctant to spend the money on Britain's military capabilities that would be essential if Britain were really to be able to do that. In both connections, they are inhibited by electoral considerations. They cannot bring themselves to admit publicly that

Britain can no longer rank as a world power and that defence spending can therefore be reduced substantially; but nor can they bring themselves either to raise more revenue for defence purposes or else to slash other budgets in the interests of bolstering the country's defences. Ministers fear the electoral consequences of doing either. The results are badly overstretched armed forces, aircraft carriers without aircraft and a cadre of political leaders who, since they cannot punch above their weight, talk above it instead.

That pattern is replicated in the case of Britain's ageing population and its proportionately dwindling numbers of younger, working-age people. The young show no signs of wishing either to save more for their own old age or to pay more in taxes to sustain those – possibly their own parents or grandparents – who are already old. Ministers freely acknowledge that there are problems; but they and their shadow opposites are extremely reluctant to acknowledge their severity, let alone to devise and implement the extremely expensive and onerous measures needed to deal with them. In a public lecture, the former chairman of a House of Lords Select Committee on Public Service and Demographic Change showed some sympathy with ministers' reluctance to either speak or act:

> [The] last thing you want to do if you're running up to an election is to start offering a set of really big problems and really big issues. The public do not wish to know. They want to think it's going to get better . . . At least, that's how politicians think of them and so the last thing politicians want to be saying at this point, when we've had a very

difficult seven or eight years, is, well, actually, there are some really big challenges ahead.[4]

Given the scale of the challenges and their belief that voters do not acknowledge that these challenges really exist – and would be unwilling to accept their implications even if they did – politicians naturally have every incentive to evade the issue. It would be strange if they did not.

In the cases of defence spending and the challenges posed by Britain's ageing population, almost every voter in the land is directly or indirectly implicated: high taxes are an issue for everybody. In the case of locating new airport capacity in the South East of England, the voters who matter – those likely to be adversely affected by any expansion – are clumped together in a large number of parliamentary constituencies near Heathrow, Gatwick, Stansted and other possible airport sites. The votes of people living in those constituencies could determine the outcome of a close election. Largely as a result, although most observers agree that additional airport capacity in the South East is needed, and although the question of where to locate it has been debated since 1960 (that is, for over half a century), no decision had been come to at the time of the 2015 general election. Instead, David Cameron's government in 2013 appointed a commission under Sir Howard Davies to advise the government on the best way – or the least bad way – forward. The Davies Commission succeeded the Roskill Commission, which had explored the same issue between 1969 and 1971. The Roskill Commission's recommended site was rejected by the government of the day; although an alternative site was chosen, it was quickly abandoned too. The Davies Commission was not due to report until September 2015, conveniently after that May's general election. Of course, its final recommendation may be accepted and acted upon. But then again, it may not.

Other difficult issues have similarly been 'kicked into the long grass' (as the saying goes): among them, issues relating to climate change, illegal drugs, how to finance increasingly expensive public services and the long-term future of Britain's energy and food supplies. Each of these issues is substantively difficult; there are no easy answers. But, in each case, politicians have listened to Britain's voters telling them, in effect, 'I wouldn't go there if I were you', and have acted – or rather, for the most part, have not acted – accordingly. Whether the voters really are saying what the politicians are hearing them say, or whether the voices they are hearing are actually those of the mass media, is a question we will come back to in Chapter 8.

British voters certainly do not govern the UK in the style of a face-to-face New England town meeting, but they should definitely be numbered among those who are crucially involved in Britain's governing arrangements – and not merely when they go to the polls every few years. Their presence is felt by the political class all the time, and their influence on public policy is palpable. Moreover, their behaviour in recent decades has actually had a profound effect, not just on public policy but on the entire political system. Collectively, the electorate has succeeded in destroying Britain's classic two-party system. Millions of voters' individual choices and actions, spread over many years, have had enormous cumulative consequences.

The table opposite charts the course of the collapse of the classic two-party system. As the figures show, the system remained, or at least looked, relatively sturdy and stable during most of the first three postwar decades. But then, during the two general elections of 1974, the percentage of voters opting for one or other of the two main parties suddenly fell from the high 80s to a mere 75 per cent. The number of seats won by parties other than the Conservatives or Labour in that year trebled. Part of the increase could be accounted for by the rise of the Scottish National Party north of the border and by the severing of the links between the mainland Conservative party and the Northern Ireland unionists; but the return to something more like two-party politics in 1979 was only partial, despite the SNP's heavy loss of votes and seats. Already, permanent cracks seemed to be appearing in the old party system's foundations.

Ever since 1979, with only a brief interruption in 1992, between one-quarter and one-third of all those who have gone to the polls in general elections have turned their backs on both the Conservatives and Labour and have voted for one of the lesser parties: the Liberal Democrats, one of the Northern Ireland parties, the SNP in Scotland, Plaid Cymru in Wales, the Greens, the Referendum party (briefly, in 1997), Respect (briefly, in 2010), the British National Party, UKIP or one of the innumerable, usually evanescent fringe parties littered across the political landscape. Simultaneously, several of the lesser parties – notably, the Liberal Democrats, the SNP and Plaid Cymru – have succeeded in concentrating their support in individual constituencies, so that they have been far more successful than in the past in translating their

PERCENTAGE OF POPULAR VOTE AND NUMBER OF PARLIAMENTARY SEATS, 1950–2010*

GENERAL ELECTION	% OF VOTE CAST FOR CON., LAB. CANDIDATES	% OF VOTE CAST FOR ALL OTHER CANDIDATES	TOTAL NO. OF CON., LAB. MPS	TOTAL NO. OF ALL OTHER MPS
1950	89.6	10.4	613	12
1951	96.8	3.2	616	9
1955	96.1	3.9	621	9
1959	93.2	6.8	623	7
1964	87.5	12.5	621	9
1966	89.8	10.2	616	14
1970	89.4	10.6	617	13
1974 (Feb.)	75.0	25.0	598	37
1974 (Oct.)	75.0	25.0	596	39
1979	80.8	19.2	608	27
1983	70.0	30.0	606	44
1987	73.1	26.9	605	45
1992	76.3	23.7	607	44
1997	73.9	26.1	584	75
2001	72.4	27.6	579	80
2005	67.6	32.4	554	92
2010	65.2	34.8	565	85

* Compiled and recalculated from David Butler and Gareth Butler, Twentieth-Century British Political Facts 1900–2000 (Basingstoke: Macmillan, 2000), pp. 236–9; David Butler and Gareth Butler, British Political Facts since 1979 (Basingstoke: Palgrave, 2006), pp. 108–9; and Dennis Kavanagh and Philip Cowley, The British General Election of 2010 (Basingstoke: Palgrave Macmillan, 2010), p. 353.

votes into seats. As the figures in the table also show, the number of seats won at general elections by parties other than the Conservatives and Labour has soared in recent decades. In the 1950s, the total number of lesser-party MPs typically remained in single figures. In the elections between 1997 and 2010, that same total never fell below seventy-five and once, in 2005, reached as many as ninety-two.

The collapse of the old two-party system is relatively easy to explain. Governments of both major parties were in office as Britain's power and status in the world declined and were therefore implicated in that decline. They were also in power as successive economic storms battered the country – storms that Conservative and Labour governments alike found difficult or impossible to hold in check. Millions of voters were undoubtedly alienated, many of them permanently, by Labour's 'lurch to the left' during the 1980s and the Conservatives' simultaneous sharp turn to the right under Thatcher. The long-term decline of the Conservative party in Scotland expedited the SNP's rise north of the border. Across the British mainland, the fragmentation of the historic social-class structure helped to weaken the emotional ties that bound individuals both to their class and to whichever party represented that class. This did not, however, mean that voters who no longer possessed a strong class identity were necessarily readier than they had been to switch between the two main parties. A voter who no longer thought of him- or herself as middle class or felt any affinity with the Conservatives might nevertheless be reluctant to vote Labour. Equally, someone who no longer thought of him- or herself as working class or felt any affinity with the

Labour party might nevertheless find the idea of voting Tory abhorrent. In addition, one class whom voters in large numbers increasingly did *not* identify with – indeed, felt positively antagonistic towards – was the political class. For all these reasons, the pool of voters whom the lesser parties could call on for support was far larger in the early twenty-first century than it had been in earlier generations.

Widespread alienation from the political class coincided with – and was partly caused by – the ever-growing sense that it did not greatly matter which of the two main parties was in power: both appeared to kowtow to the EU and the banks, and both, it was alleged, constantly broke their promises. Back in the late 1940s, L. S. Amery, someone already quoted in Chapter 1, was able to take the existence of the Conservative–Labour two-party system for granted and confidently assert that the rank-and-file voters' sole task was to decide which of the two main parties should form the next government: 'by the time it comes to an actual decision', he wrote, the voter's 'function is the limited and essentially passive one of accepting one of two alternatives put before him'.[5] That may have been true back then, but it is far from being true now. The great majority of those who have voted for one of the lesser parties in the general elections since 1974 cannot possibly have imagined that they were voting to choose a government. Indeed, most of them must have been conscious that that was precisely what they were *not* doing. Instead, they were turning their backs on the whole business of government-choosing. Far from voting passively, as Amery thought appropriate, they were voting actively: to express their dismay with both major parties and, quite possibly, the whole political class. Either that, or they were not bothering to vote at all.

The cumulative outcome of voters' willingness to vote for parties other than the Conservatives or Labour, and the lesser parties' new-found ability to win and often to hold onto seats in parliament, is to make it far more difficult than it was in the past for either major party to gain an overall majority in the House of Commons. That difficulty was masked between 1997 and 2005 by the Labour party's vast preponderance over the Conservatives. Labour was so far ahead of the Conservatives in each of the three general elections during that period – 1997, 2001 and 2005 – that Labour could easily gain a commanding overall majority on its own. But, when the two major parties were closer together, as in 2010, the parliamentary arithmetic caught up with both of them. In 2010, any party wishing to command an overall majority, however slim, had to win 326 of the 650 seats in the House of Commons. In 2010, that proved impossible, and the Conservatives, fully nineteen seats short of a majority, found themselves having to do business with the Liberal Democrats. For the foreseeable future, unless one of the two major parties manages to establish total dominance over the other, the UK seems bound to be governed more often than not by coalition governments, minority governments or governments with only tiny majorities in parliament.

That represents a sharp break with the governing arrangements that characterized the British system during the classic period and again between 1979 and 2005. The rise of the lesser parties also means that, whereas during the classic period voters typically elected governments, for the foreseeable future voters in some numbers will still go to the polls, but the formation of an actual government is likely to be sorted out, as it was in 2010, by politicians from different parties negotiating with each other afterwards. Putting the same point another way, the business of fighting elections and the business of forming governments will be disjoined – as the two activities customarily are on the European continent. If voters dislike that outcome, all they have to do is stop voting in such large numbers for lesser parties.

CHAPTER 6

Ideas

At any given time, Britain is governed not only by human beings but by the ideas that happen to dominate their thinking at that time. As the Cambridge economist John Maynard Keynes put it in an oft-quoted passage:

> The ideas of economists and political philosophers, both when they are right and when they are wrong, are more powerful than is commonly understood . . . Practical men, who believe themselves to be quite exempt from any intellectual influences, are usually the slaves of some defunct economist. Madmen in authority, who hear voices in the air, are distilling their frenzy from some academic scribbler of a few years back.[1]

On another occasion he wrote in a similar vein that 'a study of the history of opinion is a necessary preliminary to the emancipation of the mind'.[2] Lacking a sense of how opinion changes, one is apt to imagine that the opinions of the present moment are opinions for all time. Dominant though they may be for the time being, the political and economic ideas that prevail at any particular moment have not always prevailed and will certainly not prevail indefinitely.

The mental and intellectual world of ministers and officials during the twenty years or so following the Second World War was very different from our own, especially with regard to economics. At that time, market forces were far from being accorded the primacy they are now. Although no one ever suggested introducing a Soviet-style command economy into the UK, market forces were nevertheless dammed up in all manner of ways – usually without causing a great deal of controversy. Market forces played no role within the new and highly centralized NHS. There was no competition on British railways. Universities and schools did not compete with one another for 'customers' (a.k.a. 'students'). Local authorities controlled land-use planning tightly, and in 1955 Conservative ministers began to promote the creation of what were called 'green belts' around towns and cities. The value of sterling against other currencies was pegged, foreign-exchange controls remained firmly in place, and modern-day foreign-exchange markets scarcely existed. Competition with the BBC in the field of television was introduced only during the 1950s (and, even then, had to overcome Winston Churchill's stubborn opposition). Commercial radio did not arrive until the 1970s. Few today would dream of trying to curb market forces on that kind of scale or even of hinting that perhaps market forces should be drastically curbed. The idea that free markets are essential and inescapable is now virtually a hegemonic idea – one so firmly implanted in people's minds that they are unable to escape from it.

Before the doctrines of market economics achieved their present ascendancy, leading politicians in the Conservative party as well as on the Labour side were tempted from time to time by the idea that Britain's economy might perform better if it were 'planned', as it undoubtedly had been (better than Germany's) during the war. Hugh Dalton, Labour's first postwar chancellor of the exchequer, was an enthusiast for manpower planning and the planned allocation of other resources; but Stafford Cripps, his successor at the Treasury, was not, and the notion of economic planning fell out of fashion for more than a decade. But then, in 1961, the Conservative prime minister, Harold Macmillan, impressed by the apparent success of French 'indicative planning', established (as we noted in Chapter 1) the National Economic Development Council ('Neddy'), which a year later duly published a voluntary national plan. That plan, however, had little or no effect on the behaviour of those who were meant to be guided by it, and a similar fate befell the similar national plan published in 1965 by Harold Wilson's Labour government. The latter failure doomed the idea of comprehensive economic planning. Nothing has been heard of it since.

An economic idea that proved a good deal more tenacious than any form of economic planning was the widely held assumption that the state, on behalf of the public, should own and manage, if only at arm's length, the country's main utilities: water, gas, electricity, telecommunications, the railways, the national airline (if there was one) and so forth. Labour for many decades championed the idea of public ownership, and many party MPs and activists wanted to extend it far beyond the utilities. Although the Conservatives were always less keen on the idea, they were nevertheless content for decades to accept that the main utilities should be lodged in the public sector. Moreover, when Rolls-Royce Ltd got into difficulties in 1971, Edward Heath's Conservative government had no compunction about nationalizing the company, and the same government in the Industry Act 1972 arrogated to itself sweeping powers to intervene massively in industry, even to the point of nationalizing individual firms without the need for further legislation – sufficient powers of intervention to make even the most far-left Labour government proud. Indeed, Labour did make some use of the powers in question following the party's return to office in 1974. But Margaret Thatcher's government put a stop to all that – and then proceeded to go further. It and its Conservative successor under John Major sold off to the private sector practically all of the publicly owned utilities. In later decades, privatization continued, although on a more modest scale, during the period of Tony Blair's post-1997 Labour government. Long before the turn of the millennium, privatization was an idea (and a word) whose time had come. Nationalization was an idea whose time appeared to have gone, except that Gordon Brown's Labour government in the depths of the 2008–9 financial crisis bailed out – nationalized or part-nationalized – two virtually bankrupt banks, Lloyds TSB and Royal Bank of Scotland. But those two emergency nationalizations bucked the trend. The Labour party long ago abandoned the idea of nationalizing what used to be called 'the commanding heights of the economy'.

Between them, market forces and the trade unions certainly killed off the idea – which had a longer shelf life than anyone now alive probably remembers – that Britain could develop some kind of enduring prices and incomes policy.

Alarmed by inflationary pressures building up in the economy, the Conservative chancellor of the exchequer Selwyn Lloyd announced in 1961 that there would have to be a 'pay pause' until the rate of productivity growth had caught up. The pause, however, applied only in the public sector, had little effect, encountered stiff union resistance and was abandoned after only a year. Labour under Harold Wilson had another go, persuading parliament to pass a Prices and Incomes Act; but, like its predecessor, this measure had limited effect to begin with – despite the government's proclaiming a 'wages freeze' and later a 'period of severe restraint' – and became progressively less effective as time went on. The Conservatives in opposition inferred that incomes policies, whoever introduced them, were doomed to failure, and accordingly promised in their 1970 election manifesto not to repeat any such attempt. But once back in power, they did repeat it – between 1972 and 1974 – with similarly little success. Undeterred, and confronted with inflation rising at an accelerating rate, Harold Wilson's second Labour government also repeated the attempt. This particular exercise in pay restraint – agreed voluntarily in 1975 between the government and the largest trade unions – began by succeeding beyond anyone's wildest expectations, helping in three years to drive down the annual rate of inflation from nearly 30 per cent to less than 10 per cent; but, with prices still running ahead of wages, the unions eventually rebelled, and widespread industrial disputes during the 1978–9 'winter of discontent' soon brought down both the policy and the government. Incomes policy in the end proved a chimera. No one has sought to introduce such a policy since.

The idea of prices and incomes policy was destroyed by market forces, the trade unions and much bitter experience; but it was also destroyed by the emergence of a rival economic theory. The principal aim of prices and incomes policy was to damp down inflation; but, except temporarily, it had never succeeded in doing that. The increasingly influential monetarist school of economists maintained that this was no accident. They argued that prices and incomes policy was fundamentally misconceived because it assumed that inflation resulted from an upward pressure on wages. In reality, they insisted, any upward pressure on wages in a country could lead to inflation only if accompanied by an over-large increase in the quantity of money circulating in that country. Control rigorously the rate of growth of a country's money supply and the problem of inflation would simply go away – or at least be substantially mitigated. By 1979, when the Conservatives returned to power under Margaret Thatcher, monetarism had become a core part of the party's economic orthodoxy.

That idea – an old idea but newly fashionable – then went for a bumpy ride. One problem, endlessly discussed, was how to measure the money supply and its rate of growth. Without coming to any agreed conclusion, ministers, their specialist advisers and economists debated at length which of the various quantities known as M0, M1, PSL2 or £M3 was the most appropriate measure. Another problem was how actually to set about controlling the supply of money, however measured. Even more serious was the fact that, as the Thatcher government quickly discovered, inflation had sources other than over-rapid increases in the money supply. The price of oil shot up on world markets shortly after the Conservatives came to power, and the government's own decision to shift the burden of taxation from direct to indirect taxes, notably VAT, also forced up the cost of living. Although the Thatcher government bore down on inflation, it never succeeded in bringing it totally under control, and control of the money supply gradually became only one element in the government's – and subsequent governments' – economic thinking, instead of being its key element. Monetarism as an idea never died, but it signally failed to fulfil its initial promise.

Monetarism initially established its intellectual credentials in opposition to Keynesianism, a body of theory gradually developed by John Maynard Keynes during the 1930s. Writing during the Great Depression, Keynes addressed the issue of the prolonged unemployment that characterized that decade, unemployment that persisted in defiance of classical economists' insistence that in time, and if the government were fiscally prudent, the economy would right itself, that the trade-cycle mechanism was self-correcting. Keynes argued instead that the trade cycle was not self-correcting and that, in times of economic downturn, governments should be prepared to cut taxes and increase public spending – that is, to run deficits – in order to increase consumer demand and stimulate economic activity. Keynesianism as a body of ideas took hold rapidly in Britain, more so than in many other countries, and was the economic orthodoxy of most of the postwar period.

By the 1970s, however, the economic problems that Keynes had addressed were no longer the ones pressing in upon British governments. Growth was sluggish, and the supply side of the economy – as distinct from the demand side – was not one that Keynes had had much to say about. Understandably, in the circumstances of the 1930s, Keynes had also been far more concerned about combating deflation than about combating inflation. But as time went on the UK economy increasingly showed signs of suffering from the malaise that came to be known as 'stagflation', an unhappy combination of slow growth, mounting unemployment and rapidly rising prices. Keynesian counter-cyclical measures could help deal with the problem of unemployment, at least in the short term, but they scarcely addressed the problem of slow growth and they looked certain to ratchet up the rate of inflation. It was as much the irrelevance of Keynesian ideas as their intrinsic defects that caused policy-makers to turn to alternative nostrums such as monetarism and privatization. It was far from easy to revive Keynesian thinking during the early years of the twenty-first century, when governments were already running unsustainable budget deficits.

One fashionable idea has only recently resurfaced although, unlike monetarism and Keynesianism, it has an ancient lineage. Nowadays, it is known as 'outsourcing': the idea that the delivery of services once provided directly by central government or local authorities should, wherever possible, be contracted out to private companies. But two millennia ago – and in some jurisdictions more recently than that – it was known as 'tax farming': putting out to tender the collection of taxes in a region or province, then awarding the contract to the highest bidder and allowing him to keep the difference between the revenues he was obliged to hand over to the state and the amount he actually collected.

Tax farmers could easily abuse the system, and often did. The first Roman emperor, Caesar Augustus, put an end to the practice in ancient Rome.

In modern Britain, outsourcing on a substantial scale began during the time of John Major's government and became common practice during Tony Blair's time in office. Local authorities were required to outsource services where it was shown that private firms could provide best value. Private companies built and managed a significant proportion of the prisons in England and Wales. Substantial parts of the probation service were outsourced. The NHS in England made increasing use of privately owned hospitals and contracted with private firms to conduct a wide range of clinical procedures. By the time the post-2010 coalition government came to power, outsourcing as a mode of operations was endemic, the government's default position. A service should be outsourced unless an overwhelming case could be made for not doing so (and sometimes not even then). One private company assessed the medical condition of benefits claimants. Another maintained the UK's stock of nuclear weapons. The public sector was no longer responsible for a majority of the residential care homes for children. The delivery of adult social care was also largely in private hands.

No one has yet produced an independent and comprehensive review of the experience of outsourcing, setting out when outsourcing delivers value for money and an improved service and when it does not. But there have certainly been difficulties, as tends to happen when an *idée fixe* drives policy. One private supplier signally failed to supply enough security personnel for the London 2012 Olympics. Another was found to have defrauded the Ministry of Justice by claiming it had delivered remand prisoners to the courts in time when it had not. Another failed to provide adequate translation services to the courts (or, sometimes, any services at all). Yet another failed horrendously to conduct proper assessments of men and women claiming disability benefits (for example, summoning to an assessment one individual who was lying in a coma). Some of the difficulties arose out of the fact that, far from operating in highly competitive markets, four of the biggest outsourcing firms – Atos, Capita, G4S and Serco – were effectively oligopolists. In one report, the National Audit Office noted that the government might be overly dependent on those four providers, adding acidly, 'There is a sense that some may be "too big to fail" – and difficult to live with or without.'³ The idea that outsourcing was a panacea for most of the public sector's ills was certainly an idea that came. It is probably yet another idea that, in the fullness of time, will go.

No British government now seeks to control prices and incomes or plan the economy in the manner envisaged by Harold Macmillan and an older generation of Labour politicians. No government now adheres exclusively to monetarist ideas. Large-scale nationalization has also been written out of the script, with the result that matters once hotly debated are no longer debated at all. The intellectual climate has changed utterly. For now, advocates of the idea that competitive markets are the road to economic salvation are in charge. For now, the onus is on those who are sceptical about the universal desirability of markets to show why they may *not* always produce optimal outcomes.

Overall, the result of the changing zeitgeist has been to create a generalized prejudice in much of the political class, not just within the Conservative party, in favour of the private sector and against the public sector – the reverse of the prejudice that existed in previous generations. Under the new intellectual dispensation, it is largely taken for granted that the private sector can almost invariably be counted upon to function more effectively and efficiently than the public sector. Firms in the private sector have every incentive to drive down costs, to hire the best people (and to fire the worst) and continually to innovate. Moreover, unless they are monopolists or quasi-monopolists, they are certain to have competitors breathing down their necks. By contrast, it is alleged that public-sector organizations typically have no competitors, have no incentive to contain costs and almost invariably become institutionally sclerotic. The private sector is thus dynamic, the public sector sluggish. That, at any rate, is the predominant view early in the twenty-first century. No competing view has yet risen to challenge it.

Changing economic ideas have a profound effect on the policies that governments adopt, but there are other ideas that affect the conduct and institutions of government itself. One such is the idea, pervasive in modern British society, that the aim of every individual in the society probably already is – and certainly should be – to advance his or her own career, to get on in the world. Associated with that idea is the notion that the best way to get on in the world is to change one's job frequently, perhaps every two or three years, whether within the same organization or by means of moving from one organization to another. The emphasis is on the individual, not the organization. Institutional loyalty is at a discount. The individual who puts institutional loyalty and a desire to engage in disinterested public service ahead of the advancement of his or her own career is apt to strike others as being somewhat eccentric, perhaps even a bit of a mug. Not wishing to appear to others as either an eccentric or a mug, individuals in that kind of moral environment more often than not adapt to their environment and become preoccupied with their own careers. The consequences for British government of the current careerist orientation we shall come back to later, in the chapters dealing with ministers and officials.

Since the postwar period there has been a sea change in British ideas about nothing less than democracy itself, a change that has already had all manner of practical consequences. For generations, politicians and citizens alike seemed to accept that a simple and straightforward division of labour existed in the British system between the government of the day on the one hand and the electorate on the other. The job of the government was to govern. The job of the voters was to pass judgement every few years on the quality of that government's performance. Government was permanent. Democracy was periodic. In the years between general elections, ministers typically paid attention to public opinion (it was electorally prudent to do so), but they were in no way bound by it. There was no institutional means by which the public at large could impose its will on a government. Government in Britain was not *by* the people – and almost no one ever suggested that it should be.

But ideas about democracy have changed. Millions of

people claim to want more democracy, and the bulk of the political class is clearly minded to give it to them, at least on some occasions and under some circumstances. The change began with 'the romantic revolt' of the 1960s, when an altogether new assertiveness displaced the deference to their elders and betters that had previously led most people in Britain simply to accept the idea that governments should, except on very rare occasions, be left to get on with it:

> Millions of ordinary Britons, and not just radical student leaders, decided that they wanted their voice to be heard and to be heard all the time, not just once in every four or five years. They wanted to be asked their views, to be consulted. They wanted, or said they wanted, to participate more actively in public affairs . . . They demanded that government at all levels be more responsive to their concerns.[4]

It was against that background that Harold Wilson and the Labour party agreed that the first-ever national referendum in Britain should be held in the mid-1970s, on the subject of whether or not Britain should continue to be a member of the European Common Market. The 1975 referendum's purpose was certainly not the idealistic one of a government's being more responsive to the people: it was to resolve an intractable internal dispute within the Labour party. But the idea of calling a referendum would probably never have occurred to Labour's leadership if the climate of opinion in the country had not already changed.

Once one referendum had been held, it was inevitable that more would be called for. Before 1975, referendums were virtually unknown in the UK and seldom advocated. From

1975 onward, they were an accepted part of Britain's political arrangements. The late-1970s Labour government held two more, in Scotland and Wales, on the issue of devolution. John Major, in 1996, announced that a Conservative government would hold a UK-wide referendum before joining the euro. Tony Blair did likewise on the Labour side and then went on to join the Conservatives in pledging to hold a referendum on any proposed new European Union constitution if it radically expanded the EU's authority. The Blair government after 1997 organized referendums in Scotland, Wales and Northern Ireland on the devolution of powers to those three countries, another in London on the creation of a new Greater London Authority and yet another on a proposal to introduce a tier of regional government in the English North East. The post-2010 coalition government reiterated that a referendum would be held before Britain joined the eurozone and in 2011 actually held a UK-wide referendum – only the second – on the adoption (or, in the event, the non-adoption) of the Alternative Vote in general elections. It subsequently encouraged the holding of a referendum in Scotland on whether or not that country should become independent. In 2013, as we noted in the last chapter, David Cameron announced that, if a Conservative government were returned to power following the 2015 general election, it would hold a nationwide referendum on Britain's membership of the EU.

At the same time as the idea of referendums was taking hold, so was the idea that the people's voice should be heard in other contexts. Leaders of all the main parties had apparently come round to the view that Britain was suffering from a profound democratic deficit. They also seemed to imagine that the voters themselves were famished and had an insatiable appetite for ever more democracy. The late-1970s Callaghan government instituted direct elections to the European Parliament. Parent governors of English schools were henceforth to be elected. Towns and cities were encouraged to decide in referendums whether or not they wanted to be presided over by an executive mayor; and, if they did decide to establish such a post, to hold direct elections to decide who should fill it. David Cameron's coalition government went on to create regional police and crime commissioners in England and Wales, and they were, of course, to be directly elected by the people of the various regions.

The British people, via the ballot box, do now have a more substantial role to play in the British system of government than they used to have. Because both Conservative and Labour governments, for their own reasons, promised to hold a referendum on adopting the euro as the UK's currency, and because the leaders of both parties knew that such a referendum would be lost, the British people effectively vetoed Britain's adoption of the euro – for good or ill, a substantial achievement. However, two points about the seemingly onward march of democracy should be noted. The first is that, in Britain, politicians, not the people, decide when the people's voice should be decisive; there is no provision in Britain, as there is in many American states, for allowing the voters, by means of petitions, to take the initiative in calling for a popular referendum to be held on a given issue. The second is that voters may not be quite as hungry for more democracy as they seem and as some of them claim. On occasion, voter turnout in referendums is high: in Scotland's independence referendum in September 2014 the turnout was a prodigious 84.5 per cent. But sometimes it is quite low – in the 2011 Alternative Vote referendum it was only 42.2 per cent – and the turnout in other kinds of elections is often low to the point of being risible. In local elections, it hovers just above 30 per cent, in European Parliament elections it has never exceeded 40 per cent and once fell to 24 per cent, and hardly anyone bothered to vote in the first round of elections for police and crime commissioners held in 2012. The average turnout across England and Wales in those elections was a paltry 15.1 per cent – the lowest turnout in any comparable round of UK elections since the Great Reform Act of 1832. Perhaps more democracy is not what the people really want after all.

If referendums have partially dented the old power-hoarding structure of the British system, the devolution of power to Scotland, Wales and Northern Ireland has given the system's formerly centralized character a severe knock. The idea that different parts of the United Kingdom should be governed in different ways and by different people dates back to the 1880s. But the notion that the UK should be governed as a more or less undifferentiated whole – or at least governed in its entirety from central London – has been slow to fall into disrepute. In the English portion of the UK, although pressure for radical change has been mounting, highly centralized government remains the norm, with local government allowed only limited room for manoeuvre.

W. E. Gladstone tried hard to grant Ireland a measure of home rule during the last two decades of the nineteenth century but was thwarted first by the House of Commons, then by the House of Lords. The Conservative and Unionist party and the Liberal Unionists were adamantly opposed throughout ('Unionist' in their names referring to the union with Ireland). Gladstone's Liberal successors made more headway in the years leading up to the First World War, and Ireland might have gained home rule but for the outbreak of that war. By the time the war ended, the majority in Ireland had decided to go their own way, and the island was left divided between what eventually became the Republic of Ireland in the south and most of the predominantly pro-British province of Ulster in the north. By an irony of fate, the Protestants of Ulster, hitherto opposed to home rule, found themselves in 1920 the only inhabitants of the UK to possess it. It took the form of a Northern Ireland prime minister and parliament, with almost total control over Northern Ireland's domestic affairs (an arrangement that left the Protestant majority free to oppress the nationalist, Catholic minority). Following a period of direct rule from London during the 'troubles' of the late twentieth century, Northern Ireland regained its home-rule status following the 1998 Good Friday agreement. The governmental arrangements of Northern Ireland have always been anomalous and still are.

Many Gladstonian Liberals advocated not merely home rule for Ireland but what they called 'home rule all round', meaning that any measures of autonomy granted to Ireland should also be made available to the peoples of Scotland and Wales. Strangely, however, the idea of home rule all round – or what we now call devolution – was exceedingly slow to catch on. Until quite late in the twentieth century, most Scots and people in Wales, although possessed of strong national identities, nevertheless seemed content with the UK's existing England-centred arrangements. And of course the English were content with them too. However, for reasons that are still not entirely clear but that undoubtedly owed much to the discovery of North Sea oil, to the Conservative party's implosion in Scotland and to the spread of small-nation nationalism across much of western Europe, more and more Scots during the last three decades of the last century came to favour home rule for Scotland or even outright independence. After some lapse of time, a majority of the people of Wales came to feel much the same.

The Labour party – and at first only the Labour party, along with the Liberals – acknowledged the force of the Scottish claims and attempted during the 1970s to enact legislation providing home rule for both Scotland and Wales. That legislation failed, but in 1997–8 the New Labour government under Tony Blair granted a large measure of domestic autonomy – among the largest measures of autonomy ever ceded by a central government to any nation or region – to a new Scottish parliament and Welsh national assembly and their respective executives. The voters of the two nations ratified the Blair government's proposals in their referendums. The Westminster regime's stranglehold on the government of the entire UK had thus been decisively broken. It only required the Scottish and Welsh governments to wrench still further powers from Westminster and Whitehall, notably over taxation, for the process of dismantling the UK's centralized governing structure to be complete. The grandly named secretary of state for health in the government of the United Kingdom of Great Britain and Northern Ireland is no longer that. He or she today is merely the health minister for England.

Ideas are transient; many of them go in and out of fashion. Often they give the impression of having a life of their own. But they can be immensely powerful, especially when they take hold of the minds of politicians and senior civil servants. Devolution to Scotland, Wales and Northern Ireland is here to stay. So, at least for the time being, is the idea that the most efficient and successful economy is invariably one almost wholly in the hands of private companies and subject to the maximum amount of free-market competition. Early in the twenty-first century, one idea seeking to make its way is the idea that the most successful societies are relatively egalitarian societies, ones marked by the absence of extremes of wealth and poverty. But the idea that greater economic and social equality would be a good thing for Britain is an idea whose time has not yet – and may never – come.

Interests

Ideas are important, but interests are too. Sometimes the two point an individual or an organization in the same direction. Sometimes they conflict. People may develop or seek out ideas to rationalize or justify their interests. Equally, they may assess their interests in terms of ideas that they already hold. An individual may believe passionately in free-market economics but at the same time fight like a tiger to prevent houses being built on the green belt adjacent to their house. Someone else may believe passionately in the importance of state education but at the same time send their children to a fee-paying school because they believe it would be in their children's best interests to do so. If ideas and interests conflict, ideas win on some occasions, interests on others. The importance of interests certainly cannot be discounted. Few politicians make that mistake.

What are 'interests'? Words become important here. The adjective 'interested' has two antonyms: 'disinterested' and 'uninterested'. A disinterested person is someone who has no personal stake in the outcome of a trial or dispute; whatever the outcome, he or she will be neither better off nor worse off as a result. An uninterested person is someone who – whatever his or her personal stake (or lack of one) in the outcome of a trial or dispute – takes no interest in it and may well be bored by it; he or she would rather be at home watching television. Most of us hope that the judge at our own trial will be disinterested – that is, will not stand to gain or lose by whether or not the jury finds in our favour – but we also hope that he or she will be sufficiently interested not to fall asleep on the bench or try to complete *The Times* crossword. The convenient shorthand term 'interest group', although often used, has the disadvantage that it can refer simultaneously to groups with selfish interests, such as high-street retailers, multinational oil companies and trade unions, but also to entirely disinterested groups such as the Royal Society for the Protection of Birds, which has no actual birds among its members. To further complicate matters, interest groups in either of these two categories are sometimes referred to collectively as 'pressure groups', even though many of them do not actually bring 'pressure' to bear on anyone, perhaps because they lack the means or simply choose not to. To confuse matters still further, the individuals who work for interest groups, of whichever type, are often referred to as 'lobbyists', even though most of them never go anywhere near the lobby of the House of Commons or indeed any lobby outside a hotel. As though all that were not enough, while many interests are organized, some are not. People may have interests in common but lack the will or the means to pursue them collectively. 'Interests' for the purposes of this chapter are simply people, or groups of people, who have a stake or cause in common, irrespective of whether or not they are organized formally into a group.

Although it still exists, one very large organized interest

has suffered an almost total eclipse since the postwar decades. The trade unions were once virtually an estate of the realm, consulted by governments and feared by them in equal measure. The leaders of some of the biggest unions – Frank Cousins, Jack Jones, Hugh Scanlon, Joe Gormley, Arthur Scargill – were household names, as were the names of most of the biggest unions – the Amalgamated Engineering Union, the General and Municipal Workers' Union, the National Union of Mineworkers, the National Union of Public Employees and the Transport and General Workers' Union (the 'T&G'). The annual Trades Union Congress was a major political event, covered extensively in the media. General secretaries of the TUC – George Woodcock, Vic Feather, Len Murray – were famous men, and governments of both major parties constantly sought to engage with the unions, in the interests of achieving wage restraint and preventing strikes and also, for a time, with a view to promoting indicative planning. That era, long gone, now has a musty smell about it, like a damp room that has not been aired for many years.

The unions' power, when they had it, rested on the largest unions' enormous size (during the early 1970s, the T&G alone boasted more than two million members), on their ability to claim plausibly that they spoke for the great mass of the country's manual workers, on their considerable wealth, on their close links with the Labour party and, above all, on the ability of several of them to disrupt badly the workings of the economy. Several of the big unions not only spoke loudly – they carried big sticks, which they were happy to wield. Strikes in the motor industry were endemic. Frequent strikes by dockworkers disrupted vital imports and exports.

The railways were sometimes shut down for days on end. A miners' strike in 1972 led to a grossly inflationary wage settlement and, more significantly, showed 'that the miners had the power to bring the nation to its knees'.[1] In the winter of 1973–4, the threat of another miners' strike, followed by an actual walkout, resulted in electricity shortages, the imposition of a three-day working week and the holding of an early general election, which the incumbent government, that of Edward Heath, lost. Across-the-board industrial disputes during the 1978–9 'winter of discontent' helped terminate the life of the Callaghan government. Even Margaret Thatcher backed off on the first occasion the miners threatened to strike during her premiership.

But that was then. Less than a decade later, the unions' power had effectively been broken, and at the beginning of the twenty-first century their ability to influence governments, let alone destroy them, is minimal. Most non-trade-union members would be hard pressed to name a single trade-union leader, and the membership of unions affiliated to the TUC has fallen by 40 per cent, from more than twelve million at the end of the 1970s to less than seven million today. Names of unions like Unite and Unison convey little (and make them sound more like choral societies than industrial organizations). Undoubtedly the unions contributed mightily to their own downfall. Their serial and seemingly selfish acts of industrial militancy during the 1960s and 1970s fuelled inflation, did nothing to increase real wages and alienated large swathes of the general public. The alienated members of the public included a substantial proportion of the unions' own members, who frequently objected to being called out on strike themselves and resented the adverse effects that strikes by other unions were having on them. By large majorities, voters welcomed the Thatcher government's tough union-curbing legislation (the most significant elements of which are still on the statute book). Thatcher and her government's hard-fought but ultimately overwhelming victory in what proved to be the last of the miners' strikes (that of 1984–5) showed that even the most powerful-seeming union could be beaten in the end. The Thatcher government's victories not only weakened the unions but made them look weak and led many potential members to wonder whether a union was really worth joining. Simultaneously, the size of the manual working-class – the trade unions' core constituency – was gradually shrinking and, along with it, such feelings of pan-working-class solidarity as still existed. The labour movement was no longer, as it had once been, a genuine movement. It had become just one interest among many.

The unions' decline has had one significant, purely political consequence. All along, the unions have been by a very wide margin the Labour party's most generous financial backers. Labour as a party could scarcely exist without the unions, and during the whole of the postwar period – up to and including the 1980s – it was scarcely too strong to describe the Labour party as a wholly owned trade-union subsidiary. But as time went on, the unions' seemingly unbridled aggression and their unpopularity increasingly rubbed off on the party. Whereas the link between the unions and the party had previously benefitted the Labour party, that same link had now become a liability, a grievous one. The party needed to distance itself from the unions, and under Tony Blair's leadership it did just that. Unlike his Labour predecessors, Blair had few personal links with the unions and their leaders, and he shared Thatcher's distaste for the way in which they threw their weight about and sought to influence party policy. 'The trade union movement', he told an interviewer, 'is a tremendously important, integral part of British society, *but* it's important that Labour speaks for the whole community.'[2] The significance of the remark lay in the 'but'. As party leader and prime minister, Blair made it clear that he regarded the unions as merely one among the many interests that had a claim on his attention. His two immediate successors as party leader, Gordon Brown and Ed Miliband, made friendlier noises towards the unions than Blair had, but their attitude was fundamentally the same: civility and some sympathy, but no obeisance. The post-Blair relationship between the party and the unions resembles less an intimate marriage than a somewhat uneasy civil partnership. Although the unions and their members still provide the party with the bulk of its income – they continue to prefer Labour to Conservative governments – they do not appear to expect, and they certainly do not get, a great deal in return.

The loosening of the links between Labour and the unions during the 1990s finally brought down the curtain on the postwar era, during which organized interests and government departments often saw themselves as partners engaged in a common enterprise: the National Farmers' Union and the Ministry of Agriculture, Fisheries and Food; the National Union of Teachers and the Ministry of Education; and the British Medical Association and the various royal colleges and the Ministry of Health. Margaret Thatcher, in this as in so much else, was inaugurating a new era when she boasted on television: 'I can give you a check list now of the way in which we have tackled vested interest.'[3] Thatcher disliked vested interests – she disliked intensely their cosiness and complacency, regarding most of them as no more than obstacles to change – and the trade unions were by no means the only items on her list. Tony Blair's and David Cameron's governments perpetuated her broad approach.

Today, there is a far larger number of organized interests than there was in Thatcher's time. One scholar points out that what he calls today's 'pressure-group politics' is not the same as it was 'in the Establishment dominated era of the 1950s'. Society has changed, and the political process is far more open than it was:

> After the end of the Second World War, most pressure groups were organized around one of the great 'Estates' that represented the pillars of society: business, labour, agriculture and the professions. The exceptions were a number of cause groups supported by reformist members of the middle class, often with their own Establishment connections. Today, there is a far greater number and wider range of pressure groups, reflecting a more fragmented society in which personal identity does not derive from a social class or professional grouping, but from a much wider range of possible identities.

He adds that supporting a particular group 'can almost be a lifestyle choice'.[4]

The trade unions in their heyday ultimately thrived on

raw power, with strategically placed unions in a position to disrupt the entire national economy by withdrawing their labour. Today, few organized interests, if any, are able to do anything like that. Most groups, if they are to succeed in exerting influence, need to be more subtle. They also need to make sure they are addressing the particular people and institutions they need to address. Unfortunately, there are no yardsticks – and probably never could be any – against which to measure precisely the power and influence of different organized interests or any means of accurately assessing when their influence has been crucial in affecting specific government decisions and policies. Even so, educated guesses are better than nothing.

As we saw in Chapter 5, the views of voters are continually factored into politicians' and ministers' calculations; any organized interest, however powerful-seeming, is unlikely to get its way if a substantial majority of voters are convinced that something should be done or, equally, are convinced that something should definitely not be done. Business interests, with the Confederation of British Industry in the vanguard, have long advocated the free movement of workers into Britain from the rest of the EU and elsewhere. Writing in 2014, the CBI's director-general was emphatic that immigrants were vital to the health of both the British economy in general and its social services in particular, and that 'Across the political spectrum, there [was] a mismatch between rhetoric and reality'.[5] However, majorities of British voters over several generations have been more impressed by the rhetoric than by the reality, and politicians of all parties, whatever their own views, have felt obliged to respond.

The tobacco industry failed to prevent the introduction of a ban on smoking in public places, because voters as well as ministers were overwhelmingly in favour of it. But it did succeed in preventing (or at least delaying) the requirement that cigarettes be sold only in plain packets, because most ministers and the public seemed indifferent. In the face of public outrage following the Dunblane massacre of Scottish schoolchildren in 1996, the gun lobby failed totally to prevent the introduction of a ban on handguns. As luck would have it, a general election was due to be held a few months later.

Unsurprisingly, given the potential importance of voters to their causes, organized interests do their best to try to influence public opinion, usually via the media, including social media. For the most part, they are probably wasting their time, effort and money. Campaigners campaign to show that they are campaigning, and possibly because the competition is campaigning, not because they have any realistic prospect of activating people or changing their minds. In the case of self-interested groups, such as individual firms and industries, the propaganda that emanates from them is almost always transparently self-interested, in practice serving mostly to reinforce the views that those who sympathize with them already hold. Disinterested propaganda is more likely to be effective, precisely because it is disinterested; the campaigners are campaigning for others, not themselves. ASH (Action on Smoking and Health), founded originally by the Royal College of Physicians, played some part – no one knows how large – in promoting the cause of a total ban, the one that was eventually adopted, on smoking in public places. There can be little doubt that environmental issues, including climate change, have risen on governments' agendas, largely as a result of accumulating scientific evidence, but also thanks to the media-oriented activities of such organizations as Greenpeace, Friends of the Earth and the World Wide Fund for Nature.

In their relationships with ministers and civil servants, one of the most useful single tools in the toolkit of any organized interest is knowledge that it possesses and that the ministers and civil servants do not possess but desperately need. Organized interests can benefit hugely from the asymmetry that often – indeed typically – exists between their knowledge, expertise and experience and that of the government with whom they do business. Except by coincidence or happenstance, ministers and civil servants in the Department for Environment, Food and Rural Affairs are unlikely to know as much about farming as farmers and the National Farmers' Union. Similarly, ministers and civil servants in the Department for Work and Pensions are unlikely to know as much about non-state pensions as people in the private pensions industry. Compared with police officers, few in the Home Office really know a great deal about on-the-ground policing. Compared with relevant outsiders, most ministers and officials in the Department for Business, Innovation and Skills know precious little about the economics of supermarkets, the postal service and scientific research, let alone about outer space (which is listed among its responsibilities). Experience certainly suggests that those procuring defence equipment or IT systems are consistently at a disadvantage when dealing with arms manufacturers or IT suppliers. Officials admit they are often not in a position to be 'intelligent purchasers' of whatever is on offer. Their ignorance is organized interests' power – a power that can be used honestly or, alternatively, exploited.

A good deal depends on an organized interest's public standing, if it has one, and the quality of its professional reputation. The National Union of Teachers, having once been virtually in a partnership with the Department for Education, came to be seen both by a substantial section of the general public and by departmental ministers and officials as a bastion of self-interested conservatism. There were few votes to be lost in combating the NUT's occasional militancy, more to be won. The NUT and its members could therefore be trampled upon with impunity. For similar reasons, the Thatcher administration found it easy to deprive solicitors of their lucrative monopoly of property conveyancing. The Law Society could only protest. (She failed to deprive black-cab drivers in London of their monopoly because they were well liked and had 'the knowledge', because they might – and probably would – cause considerable disruption and also because, as it happened, they constituted a fair proportion of her own constituents in Finchley.) In a nation of animal-lovers and birdwatchers, the Royal Society for the Prevention of Cruelty to Animals and the Royal Society for the Protection of Birds both enjoy privileged positions. They profit from their standing with the public – enormous numbers of whom belong to one or other of the two organizations – and also from their expert knowledge of animals and birds. The RSPCA even has some legal powers. The alcohol lobby meanwhile has to tread warily, fighting a rearguard action against minimum pricing and unable to fend off either tough drink-driving laws or the swingeing taxes levelled in the UK on alcoholic drinks. The Independent Schools Association benefits from the prestige of several of its member institutions, from the fact that closing them down would infringe on people's rights, from the aspiration of many parents to send their children to such schools – and, of course, from the fact that so many MPs, ministers and senior officials already educate their own children privately. But, at the same time, the association's members are aware that their status as charitable institutions is precarious and that they must adapt their behaviour – and also try to adapt their image – accordingly.

The medical profession might be thought to enjoy privileged status. Doctors are generally held in high esteem, and their professional expertise is almost universally acknowledged. Certainly the professional and scientific views of the Royal College of Physicians, the Royal College of Surgeons, the Royal College of Nursing and so forth carry enormous weight with ministers and officials in the Department of Health, the National Institute for Health and Care Excellence and elsewhere. However, at the same time, those same bodies – along with the British Medical Association – are also regarded by ministers and officials, if not by anyone else, as self-interested trade unions, eager to protect their existing ways of practising as well as their sectional interests. The medical profession's all but unanimous opposition to the Cameron government's sweeping reorganization of the NHS in the early 2010s certainly gave ministers, including the prime minister, pause – literally as well as figuratively – but it did little more than that. Parliament adopted the government's proposals virtually intact. Since the implosion of the trade unions, a British government with an adequate parliamentary majority and one that is determined to get its way is very hard to halt in its tracks – at least in purely domestic matters.

Organized interests usually exist and operate outwith (as the Scots say) the machinery of government. They and those whom they seek to influence keep each other, at least publicly, at arm's length. However, some organized interests are themselves actually organs of the state but nevertheless actively engage in pressure politics. Insiders pursue outsiders' strategies. Most notable under this heading in recent years have been the armed forces and the police. During a period of tight government spending, both the armed forces and the police believe that they are hard done by and as a result feel entitled to resort to the traditional methods employed by outside groups. More and more overtly, they seek to influence ministers via backbench MPs and, failing that, to influence both ministers and backbench MPs via the media. In doing so, they expect to enjoy, and probably do enjoy, substantial public support. Active and recently retired army officers publicly deplore cuts to the size of the army, and admirals and air marshals complain that the UK is reducing both the size and the capabilities of all three of its armed forces without reducing the scale of the country's overseas commitments. Conflicts of interest among the services only intensify the lobbying and publicity-seeking activities of all three of them. Meanwhile, police chiefs insist in public – on radio and television and in newspaper interviews – that further reductions in police budgets and the size of police forces can only result in a reduced quality of policing and in corresponding threats to the public's safety.

Lobbying of that kind is highly visible. The very fact that it is visible almost always means that the organized interest in question has failed to achieve its objectives in private. The most effective lobbying is almost always the least obtrusive. Intensive but little noticed lobbying by the insurance industry during the 1980s helped persuade the Thatcher government to promote the sale and marketing of personal pensions (often with disastrous consequences for those who bought them). Private-sector transport companies helped persuade the Major government, probably not to adopt the principle of privatizing British Rail, which ministers were minded to do anyway, but to fragment and embed franchising in the railway industry in the way that it did. The alcohol lobby, although by no means always successful, was almost certainly responsible for causing the Cameron government in 2013 quietly to abandon its own pledge to introduce the minimum pricing of alcoholic beverages. Private-sector accountancy firms are often deeply involved in the writing of tax legislation, which they themselves then set about circumventing. In the words of a parliamentary Public Accounts Committee report, 'we have seen what look like cases of poacher, turned gamekeeper, turned poacher again, whereby individuals who advise government go back to their firms and advise their clients on how they can use those laws to reduce the amount of tax they pay.'[6] Most of the business transacted between organized interests and government departments is humdrum, of advantage to both parties and would withstand any amount of parliamentary or public scrutiny. But not all of it would.

Corruption on all but the pettiest of scales is virtually unknown in British government. Unlike in some countries, ministers and civil servants in Britain do not expect as a matter of routine to receive backhanders from construction firms to which they award lucrative contracts; and as a matter of fact they never do ask for backhanders or receive them. Nevertheless, money counts. The financial transactions between politicians and organized interests are often made public – most notably in the House of Commons Register of Members' Interests – but they are transactions all the same. At any given time, a substantial proportion of both MPs and members of the House of Lords are acting as consultants and advisers, sometimes to charities and other pro bono organizations, but more often to private-sector firms, a large proportion of which are already doing business with the government or aspire to in the future. Considerable numbers of sitting MPs, and even more serving ministers, cannot help but be conscious that, as they take decisions in the present, their decisions may affect their employment prospects in their post-parliamentary or post-ministerial futures. How often ministers' decisions are thus affected is an open question. Probably not very often. But probably not never. Specific decisions apart, ministers – even Labour ministers – are liable to want not to develop a reputation for being hostile to business interests. In time, any such reputation might cost them dear. Several members of Tony Blair's cabinet made small fortunes on leaving politics. Blair himself made a large one.

Money also matters to the parties themselves. Labour, as we have already noted, still depends heavily on donations from trade unions and their members, although a scattering of private individuals also give large sums. (A major donor for a considerable time was Lord Sainsbury of Turville, scion of the supermarket family.) The Liberal Democrats also depend on receiving a few large donations. For their part, the Conservatives during the postwar period depended mostly on the relatively small amounts of money subscribed by their many thousands of individual members. Now, however, they rely largely on the largesse of the rich: wealthy firms and individuals. In an age of rising political costs, the leaders of all parties are required to spend far more of their time fund-raising than in the past. On one occasion, the Conservatives were embarrassed to have it revealed that the combined worth of their guests at an especially posh fund-raising dinner exceeded £11 billion. Present at the dinner were David Cameron, six of his cabinet colleagues, half a dozen billionaires and, apparently, Vladimir Putin's judo partner. Although no bribes were offered, and almost certainly no deals done, substantial donations to the party's coffers followed.[7]

The trade unions and their levy-paying members who donate to the Labour party must sometimes wonder whether they get good value for money. Donors to the Conservative party, at least when that party is in power, probably do better. As one of them candidly told the *Financial Times* in 2011, 'There probably aren't many votes in cutting the 50p top rate of tax, but among those that give significant amounts to the party, it's a big issue, and that's probably why it's a big issue for the party too.'[8] A few months later, the Conservative-led government announced that the top rate of tax would be cut from 50p to 45p. There may not have been some causal connection; but, then again, there may have been. The ties that bind together politicians and vested interests are often knotted by threads of gold.

The interests discussed so far in this chapter have mostly been organized interests, but not all interests are organized. Some of them consist of completely unorganized sections of the population which, whether they are like-minded or not and whether they know it or not, have common interests. The well off – defined by the dictionary as people 'in a favourable situation or circumstances' – have always constituted one such interest, with the seriously rich being those individuals who are in the most favourable situations or circumstances, in purely material terms at least. They have interests in common. They know it. They typically, though not invariably, have common values and a similar outlook on life. They see a good deal of each other. They are disposed to look after one another. Their children go to the same or similar schools. They drive, or are driven, in similar cars. Even if they never meet, they recognize each other at a distance. The well off are clearly, by a wide margin, the dominant interest in Britain today, even though there is no formal organization that unites them and uniquely represents their interests. They also benefit at the moment from the fact that they have no real competitors, whether in the form of a counter-culture with widespread appeal (as distinct from sporadic and short-lived protest movements), or in the form of an explicitly egalitarian ideology with widespread appeal (socialism being intellectually dead), or in the form of a political party or other political organization with widespread appeal prepared to challenge directly the well off's social, economic and cultural dominance. The well off live in a larger comfort zone than many of them perhaps realize.

Britain's other large unorganized interest occupies the other end of the social scale. It comprises people with little or no capital wealth, on low incomes, with uncertain job prospects, who may be living on state benefits, are badly housed and who probably have few if any paper qualifications – in short, the poor and disadvantaged, including lone parents in large numbers. The poor, like the rich, include both the deserving and the undeserving; but the undeserving rich have the advantage of more money. The less well off may be organized locally and, if they are lucky, in tight family units, but they are in no way organized for the purposes of pressing their interests on the government at Westminster. They are in no position to attend fund-raising dinners with cabinet ministers. The trade unions, even at the height of their power, never took much interest in the unemployed and the desperately poor; their principal, almost their only, concern was with the welfare of their own members, the men and women who chose their own union's top leadership. The Labour party, however, did once act as a kind of proxy interest group on behalf of the least well off, urged on by such disinterested organizations as Shelter and the Child Poverty Action Group. But Labour no longer plays that role to the extent that it once did, the party in recent decades having become reluctant, for understandable electoral reasons, to appear overly keen on the redistribution of income from the well off to the less well off or to allow itself to be presented as being in any way hostile to the interests of business. The result is that the great bulk of interest-group activity in Britain, as in most other developed countries, is tilted heavily in favour of the well off and scarcely takes into account the interests of the less well off, especially the very poor. In this case, the material and moral interests of the dominant section of British society and the prevailing ideas of the age go comfortably hand in hand. In the words of the old soldiers' song:

It's the same the whole world over,
It's the poor wot gets the blame,
It's the rich wot gets the gravy.

The last two of those lines are certainly true of Britain today, but views obviously differ about whether or not they also amount to 'a bleedin' shame'.

Media

It is not merely picky to point out that 'media' is a plural noun – the plural, in English as well as in Latin, of the singular noun 'medium'. There is no such thing as 'the media'. Instead, there are all kinds of media – newspapers of all sorts, magazines in profusion, television, radio, the World Wide Web, blogs, Twitter, Facebook and many more besides, with undoubtedly still more to come – and it is seriously misleading, as well as lazy, to lump them all together, as though they constituted a single corporate entity. In a book about British government, the question that needs to be asked is not one about 'the media'. Instead, and more precisely, it is: which particular media influence political leaders, especially those in government, in what ways and to what extent?

Important parts of that three-part question are not easy to answer, because the relationship between those media that really are influential and those top politicians whom they seek to influence is a garden every bit as secret as what goes on in the course of selecting parliamentary candidates. Almost all the media are not just media organizations: they have other interests and are no more anxious than other organized interests to reveal to the outside world how they set about exercising their influence. News-gathering organizations gather and report news about everything except their own relations with party leaders and government ministers. A few of them boast about their own more successful public campaigns – the *Sun* even claimed to have handed the Conservatives victory in the 1992 general election ('It's The Sun Wot Won It!') – but they are more reticent about most of their own activities. Still, as in the case of the selection of parliamentary candidates, one can pick up clues and draw inferences.

It goes without saying that a wide variety of media reports and campaigns can influence the conduct of government or at least perturb ministers. The findings of a BBC investigation on *Panorama* or a Channel 4 investigation on *Dispatches* can jolt ministers into taking action; and during the 2010s the *Guardian*'s publication of Julian Assange's WikiLeaks documents and the same paper's phone-hacking revelations caused disruption and dismay, ended careers and ruffled feathers on both sides of the Atlantic. In an earlier generation, the *Sunday Times*'s campaign to demonstrate and expose the horrifying birth defects caused by the drug thalidomide played a pivotal role in having the drug withdrawn in the UK and its victims compensated.

Despite the rise of the electronic media and their own declining circulations, the most powerful media in Britain are almost certainly still the national newspapers – that is, the newspapers published in London and distributed across the country. Politicians read those papers, even if fewer and fewer others do, politicians believe that the views of newspapers influence the views of voters, and the news agendas of many of the other media, including those of the main television and radio broadcasters, are influenced by the papers' agendas. Newspapers in like fashion feed off each other. It is very hard for one paper to ignore another's big story. A big story does sometimes emanate from one of the social media, but not often. The social media, in so far as they share common interests and concerns, feed off newspapers and the other traditional media far more often than the other way round. Newspaper proprietors, editors and journalists remain influential outriders of the political class – and some of them do not ride all that far outside.

In political terms, then, newspapers matter more than other media, certainly more than television and radio, which are legally constrained to be impartial. Also in political terms, some newspapers matter more than others. The two that matter most are undoubtedly the *Daily Mail* (and its Sunday twin, the *Mail on Sunday*) and the *Sun* (and its Sunday twin, the *Sun on Sunday*, formerly known as the *News of the World*). Far more people read them than read any other papers. The large amounts of time and energy that senior politicians devote to courting them provide a good indicator of just how influential politicians believe they are capable of being.

During the run-up to the 1997 general election, the newly elected leader of the Labour party, Tony Blair, flew more than twenty thousand miles to Australia and back to address a meeting of executives of Rupert Murdoch's News International organization, owners of the *Sun*. He subsequently attributed Labour's victory in that election to that paper. A journalist named Hugo Young, someone who observed Blair closely at that time, wrote after the election:

> Mr Blair's gratitude to the *Sun* has been evident ever since. The messages of recognition were followed by a stream of articles ghost-written by his press secretary, Alastair Campbell, a master of this tricky craft . . . The hallmark of all these exercises has been their collaborative spirit. We get the sense of a Prime Minister and editor who are in this thing together, with the proprietor [Murdoch] lurking benignly alongside – and the next election already in the sights of an unquestionably far-sighted political leader.

Young added that 'Downing Street seldom makes a big move without weighing carefully what the *Sun* will think.'[1] Another of Blair's press aides later said of Murdoch:

> His presence was almost tangible in the building [10 Downing Street] and it was as if he was the 24th member of the Cabinet. In fact more than that. In some areas of policy, [he was] more influential on the Prime Minister and on the direction of the Government's policy than most of the other 23.[2]

Gordon Brown, Blair's successor, was just as keen to keep on Murdoch's good side; as prime minister, he even dropped in on the wedding of Murdoch's favourite editor, Rebekah Brooks ('he had to be [t]here, to show respect'[3]). Unfortunately for Brown, Murdoch, under pressure from his son James, decided to switch sides. The *Sun* was soon as passionate in David Cameron's support as it had once been in Blair's.

The personal relationship between Cameron and the

Murdoch family began by being, if anything, even closer than the one between Rupert and Tony Blair had been. First as Conservative leader of the opposition, then as prime minister, Cameron attended Rupert on board his yacht among the Greek islands, appointed another Murdoch editor, Andy Coulson, as his communications chief, cast himself (or was cast) in the role of Rebekah Brooks' confidante, held at least one secret meeting with Rupert in Number 10 (the visitor arrived through the rear entrance via a back alley), entertained Rebekah Brooks at Chequers and dined with Rupert in New York. Above all, Cameron took a formally detached but nevertheless benign view of the Murdochs' proposed purchase of all the shares they did not already own in the satellite broadcaster BSkyB. Only with the collapse of that transaction in the midst of the 2011 phone-hacking scandal did the relationship cool. Fortunately for Cameron, there was never any real chance that the *Sun* or the *Sun on Sunday* would desert the Conservatives for a Labour party led, not by the emollient Tony Blair or even the cantankerous Gordon Brown, but by the allegedly left-leaning Ed Miliband (inevitably known to the *Sun* as 'Red Ed').

Courting the *Daily Mail* was both easier and more difficult: easier because the *Mail*'s strong-minded editor, Paul Dacre, was based in London and not New York; more difficult because, although the *Mail*'s enthusiasm for the Conservatives occasionally wavered, it was never anything other than a Conservative newspaper. Nevertheless, leading figures on the Labour side did go out of their way to try to mute its hostility, even to win it over. Tony Blair tried to win it over prior to the 1997 general election and was said to be 'heartbroken' when he failed.[4] More even than Blair, Gordon Brown was determined, at the very least, not to become a hate figure for the *Mail*. He befriended Paul Dacre, spent a weekend with him at one of the editor's homes in the country and in 2003 even addressed, via a video link, the guests at the Savoy Hotel celebrating his ten years as editor of the *Mail*. On that occasion, Brown insisted that Dacre had 'devised, developed and delivered one of the great newspaper success stories of any generation'.[5] In the end, however, although the *Mail* conceded during the 2010 election campaign that Brown had been 'basically good' as prime minister, he had also been misguided.[6] The paper advised its readers to vote Conservative – i.e., to eject Brown from office.

Why do party leaders take newspapers – especially the *Mail* and the *Sun* – and some other media so seriously, sometimes to the point of appearing craven in their dealings with them? Unsurprisingly, much of the answer, though not all, lies in the most basic calculation that they make: that newspapers – on their own and via their influence on other media – influence voters in large numbers, possibly in sufficiently large numbers to determine the outcome of general elections, especially close ones. Whether that calculation is well founded in reality is another question – the findings of academic researchers are inconclusive – but what matters is that political leaders believe it is. Moreover, even if they did not believe it and doubted whether newspapers could actually influence how large numbers of their readers voted, they would still be well advised to take newspapers seriously. After all, their doubts might be misplaced: newspapers might have that capacity. Better safe than sorry. It may appear – and be – undignified, but party leaders reckon they have no option but to do their best to keep the various papers as sweet, or at least as little sour, as they can. The downside risks they would run if they did otherwise would be enormous.

Beyond doubt, that simple calculation is the single most important influence on the thinking of the parties, but the hopes and fears of individual politicians also come into play. When David Cameron finally decided to stand for the Conservative leadership in 2005, of course he set about wooing Conservative MPs and rank-and-file party members – the men and women who would ultimately decide his fate – but he also set about wooing the *Daily Mail* and the *Daily Telegraph*, the two papers most read by Conservative activists. One of his first meetings as candidate was with Jonathan Harmsworth, proprietor of the *Daily Mail* and the *Mail on Sunday*, and he spent much of the rest of the campaign 'struggling to win over the key newspaper executives'.[7] In the course of his years-long campaign to oust Tony Blair as prime minister, Gordon Brown leaned left towards the *Guardian* and its leading columnists but also right towards Rupert Murdoch and the *Sun* and his friend Paul Dacre and the *Mail*. The *Guardian* would reinforce his support within the Labour party. The *Sun* and the *Mail* might, with luck, improve his chances of leading Labour to victory at the next election. (Unfortunately for him, he had no such luck.) In the 2010 contest to succeed Brown as Labour leader, both leading contenders, David and Ed Miliband, hoped they could secure the backing of the *Guardian* and the *Daily Mirror*, the two papers with the largest Labour readerships.

Politicians have a strictly political stake in not falling foul of newspapers, especially the mass-market tabloids, but they also have a personal stake. Negative coverage and exposés in the tabloids can make their lives hell. An apt verb has been invented to describe the behaviour of some papers: 'to monster'. The politician who is monstered may, or may not, have done anything wrong. If he or she has done something wrong, the revelation of the wrongdoing may, or may not, be in the public interest. But, either way, the politician in question suffers intense personal embarrassment, possibly physical harassment and sometimes total public humiliation. He or she is made to look foolish – or worse – in the eyes of both colleagues and constituents. His or her political career may come to a juddering halt. The reasons for monstering can range from a desire to expose criminal wrongdoing to a straightforward dislike on the part of a newspaper of someone's political opinions. The scope and intensity of the monstering can, of course, vary widely.

The catalogue of recently monstered politicians is long (and the list that follows, in strict alphabetical order, is far from complete): Paddy Ashdown ('It's Paddy Pantsdown' according to the *Sun*), John Bercow (disliked by many fellow Conservatives and with a much-publicized Labour-supporting wife), Tony and Cherie Blair (especially over Cherie's purchase of flats in Bristol and her relationship with her fitness adviser Carole Caplin, whose boyfriend turned out to be a convicted Australian conman), David Blunkett (revealed by the *News of the World* to have had a three-year affair with an American magazine publisher), Chris Bryant (revealed to have posted a photo of himself clad only in underpants on a gay dating site), Robin Cook (threatened by imminent press exposure into acknowledging that his marriage was at an end and that he was having an affair with one of his aides), Liam Fox (who resigned as defence secretary when the *Guardian* drew attention to his habit of travelling abroad with a dodgy-looking character who gave those they met the impression that he was one of the minister's official aides, which he was not), Chris Huhne (forced to resign his cabinet post and eventually imprisoned in the wake of revelations to the *Mail on Sunday* by his estranged wife), Tessa Jowell (when she and her husband separated amid accusations that he had accepted bribes from the Italian politician-tycoon Silvio Berlusconi), Neil Kinnock (subjected as Labour leader to sustained ridicule by sections of the Conservative-supporting press, with a *Sun* front page in 1992 depicting his head inside a light bulb, with the headline 'If Kinnock wins today will the last person to leave Britain please turn out the lights'), Ed Miliband (subject, like Kinnock, to sustained ridicule, with the *Daily Mail* describing his father, a Jewish refugee, as 'The Man Who Hated Britain'), Brooks Newmark (who resigned as a minister and announced he would not stand at the next election after sending explicit photos of himself to an undercover *Sunday Mirror* reporter posing as a woman), Mark Oaten (revealed by the *News of the World* to have hired male prostitutes), John Prescott (found to have been having an affair with his diary secretary), Clare Short (vilified as a 'killjoy' and 'fat and jealous' by the *Sun* for campaigning against its daily topless Page 3 girls), Tom

Watson (hounded by News International newspapers for his part in a plot to oust Tony Blair as prime minister and replace him with Gordon Brown at a time when the Murdoch press still backed Blair) and Tim Yeo (forced to resign as a minister after tabloid papers revealed he had fathered a child outside wedlock). It subsequently emerged that several of the monstered had had their phones hacked by tabloid journalists.

All of those episodes caused the individuals caught up in them – indirectly as well as directly – much distress, some of it undoubtedly deserved, some of it not. However, those episodes are only part of a larger picture. For every politician exposed or ridiculed in this manner, how many others have adjusted their behaviour, including their political behaviour, out of a fear of being exposed or ridiculed? How many, in other words, have been blackmailed either implicitly or even – probably on rarer occasions – explicitly? The number cannot be zero; but how large it is, and who exactly have been affected, is unknown and also, as is the nature of blackmail, unknowable. Those who have been intimidated are most unlikely to acknowledge the fact. Even if they have done nothing wrong, they are unlikely to want to present themselves as supine or vulnerable. Just as bullies seldom admit to being bullies, bullies' victims are usually reluctant to admit to having been bullied.

While he was still prime minister but after it was known that he was about to resign, Tony Blair gave full vent to his exasperation at and hostility towards the media. He gave a speech, written in his own hand, in which he described the media as hunting in packs 'like a feral beast'. He admitted that

Labour had 'paid inordinate attention in the early days . . . to courting, assuaging and persuading the media', adding:

> I am going to say something that few people in public life will say, but most know is absolutely true: a vast aspect of our jobs today . . . is coping with the media, its sheer scale, weight and constant hyperactivity. At points it literally overwhelms . . . People don't speak about it because, in the main, they are afraid to.[8]

But Blair himself went on in the same speech to bear witness to that very fear. Instead of singling out the *Daily Mail* and the *Sun* for criticism, he picked on the inoffensive *Independent*, the weakest daily newspaper and the one least able to hit back effectively. He subsequently confessed to a reporter why he had done so: 'His real target had been the *Daily Mail* but he feared what the paper would do to him and his family should he have targeted it.'[9]

Later, two members of the House of Commons Culture, Media and Sport Select Committee confessed that in the opening stages of the phone-hacking scandal they had been too intimidated by the Murdochs' News International organization to dig deeply enough. Adam Price, a Plaid Cymru MP, said:

> I was told by a senior Conservative member of the committee, who I knew was in direct contact with executives at News International, that if we went for her [Rebekah Brooks], they would go for us – effectively that they would delve into our personal lives in order to punish us.

The other MP, Labour's Tom Watson, recalled the time when he had openly called for Tony Blair's resignation despite News International's still supporting him:

> A very senior News International journalist told me that Rebekah would never forgive me for what I did and that she would pursue me through Parliament for the rest of my time as an MP . . . It led me to consider seriously leaving Parliament, because the pressure and the stress were so great.[10]

Those two MPs in the end refused to be intimidated. Other MPs, including ministers, have almost certainly not been so tough.

Precisely how far newspapers' campaigning and pressure have influenced the actual content of successive governments' policies is impossible to gauge. Newspapers often go with the flow of public opinion, a flow that would have moved on unabated even if all the papers had simultaneously gone on strike. Similarly, in exerting pressure on ministers, newspapers may merely be urging them to adopt courses of action that they would have adopted anyway. In 2003, prior to the American-led invasion of Iraq, Tony Blair and Rupert Murdoch spoke on the phone several times, with Murdoch urging Blair to stand by – and invade with – the Americans. Apparently, there are 'serious people who live and breathe Westminster politics who believe that Tony Blair's decision to back the invasion of Iraq . . . was crucially influenced by his fear of Murdoch'.[11] But it is at least possible, indeed highly probable, that Blair would have gone along with the Americans anyway – without any urgings from

Murdoch – given his deep commitment to the Atlantic alliance, his abhorrence of Saddam Hussein's cruel regime and his belief, already publicly proclaimed, in the desirability, on occasion, of humanitarian intervention.

Even so, it is hard to believe that relentless campaigning and carefully calculated reporting on the part of widely read newspapers does not have the power under some circumstances to create a climate of opinion, one in which it is hard and unfashionable to advance some causes and, by a wide margin, easier and more convenient to conform to the prevailing consensus – or at least to what the newspapers succeed in convincing their readers and the wider world is the prevailing consensus.

In the case of this country's relations with Europe and the EU, it seems possible that the latter-day climate of opinion in Britain, preponderantly dubious about the whole Brussels enterprise, might be quite different if the balance of opinion in the press today were the same as it was at the time of the referendum on the Common Market in 1975. Forty years ago, the bulk of the press was broadly pro-European. On 6 July 1975, the British people voted by a two-to-one majority to remain in the Common Market, and the next day the bulk of the British press responded with something like jubilation. 'Yes!' trumpeted the *Daily Mail*. 'Good! Now let's all get cracking!' the *Sun*'s headline read.[12] Today, most newspapers – including those with by far the largest readerships, notably the *Mail* and the *Sun* – are either hostile to the EU in all of its manifestations or else critical of it at every opportunity (from bendy bananas through crooked cucumbers to headlines such as 'Fun areas shut in "safety" move: EU bans play time').[13] Rightly or wrongly, the EU itself is monstered. Much has changed over the past four decades, and the EU is now a far more intrusive presence in British life than it was then, but it is not beyond the bounds of possibility that a ferociously hostile press has contributed to the change in the political climate that, for good or ill, has undoubtedly taken place.

The influence of the press has probably been less great in the case of immigration. 'Brussels' for most Britons is a verbal abstraction. But hundreds of thousands of immigrants, a large proportion of them from other EU countries, are an immanent reality – visible and audible across the land (though more visible and audible in some parts of it than others). Given that the numbers are so large and that most of them have arrived relatively recently, it was inevitable that millions among the indigenous population would in time come to resent the presence of so many foreigners in their midst and also, in some communities, their negative impact on local housing, schools and other public services. The bulk of the tabloid press has undoubtedly played upon people's resentments and fears and may, up to a point, have intensified them; but it is hard to maintain that it created them. They would exist even if the tabloid press did not. The same, however, was not true of asylum-seekers, both those already in the country (whether legally or otherwise) and those attempting to enter Britain (also legally or otherwise). As a matter of routine, the *Daily Mail*, the *Sun* and the *Daily Express* referred to asylum-seekers as 'parasites', 'scroungers', 'asylum cheats' and 'illegals' (even when they were not). One paper managed to publish a story – which, although it was false, it retracted only slowly – to the effect that 'callous asylum-seekers' were catching, cooking and eating the Queen's swans.[14] Government ministers found it hard to cope. They coped mainly by making life harder for asylum-seekers.

The tabloid newspapers' influence on policy in the field of law and order has undoubtedly been more substantial. They have helped keep crime and criminals even nearer the top of the political agenda than they would otherwise have been. Two politicians in the early 1990s, Tony Blair, as Labour shadow home secretary before he became leader, and Michael Howard, the real home secretary under John Major, started the bidding war between the two major parties on crime and punishment, with each party claiming to be tougher on crime and criminals than the other. However, the tabloids and the *Daily Telegraph* – with their reporting and commentary often echoed on television and radio – helped ensure that the war continued, with scarcely ever a truce. Lance Price, after he left his post as a Downing Street press officer in Blair's government, complained of 'the number of hours I spent with ministers planning new "crackdowns" on drugs, asylum seekers and benefits cheats'.[15] Magistrates and criminal court judges responded to the political and media pressure by imposing more custodial sentences and longer ones, with the result that Britain's prison population soared above that of other European countries and even many American states. Kenneth Clarke, as justice secretary, attempted to halt the war in 2010 with a series of proposals aimed at reducing both the prison population and the rate of reoffending; those who pleaded guilty early could have the time they spent in prison drastically reduced. But Clarke's colleagues, including the prime minister, took fright, and after five months David Cameron announced that the plans were to be abandoned and replaced by even sterner measures than before. The *Daily Mail* was delighted, heading its leading article, 'Finally Mr Cameron acts like a Tory PM'. The *Sun*'s splash headline read: 'Can we claim victory over Justice Secretary? – YES WE KEN'.[16] The Labour opposition, having initially welcomed the end of the war, immediately resumed hostilities, evidently believing it had no option.

The political reach of the tabloids goes even wider. The best-selling papers, in addition to being hostile to the European Union in general, have also been hostile to the single currency in particular. Even if Gordon Brown as chancellor had not effectively vetoed British entry into the eurozone, the opposition of such a large section of the press would probably have made it impossible for Tony Blair to have held and won a referendum on the issue. The same newspapers that have applauded the war on crime have also applauded the war on drugs, making it all but impossible for successive governments to rewrite – as almost all authorities in the field believe they should – the ancient Misuse of Drugs Act 1971.

As well as affecting general issues, tabloid pressure can sometimes also be brought to bear in individual cases. In 2007 a small child, known at the time only as Baby P, died of physical abuse and neglect in the London borough of Haringey. The *Sun* called for the borough's head of children's services, Sharon Shoesmith, to be sacked. The relevant minister, Ed Balls, did not respond at first, whereupon

Rebekah Brooks phoned him repeatedly to press the *Sun*'s case. According to an official who listened in on some of the calls, 'She was pretty blunt with him. She was telling Balls he had to sack her [Shoesmith], and it was quite threatening – "We don't want to turn this thing on you."'[17] Balls did sack her, only for the Court of Appeal to rule that she had been unfairly dismissed. In the end, Shoesmith received a payout for her unlawful dismissal in the region of £600,000. If Brooks' phone calls to Balls were decisive – they may not have been – they cost Haringey Council, but not either Brooks or Balls, a great deal of money.

Those in control of media empires are, of course, especially likely to bring pressure to bear on government ministers and opposition leaders when their own interests are threatened. The 1992 Labour election manifesto promised that an incoming Labour government would 'establish an urgent enquiry . . . into the concentration of media ownership' and would consider introducing laws to protect individuals' privacy against press intrusion.[18] As Labour leader between 1994 and 1997, Tony Blair was, as we have seen, desperate to win the support of Rupert Murdoch's media empire. By the time of the 1997 general election, those two pledges had been quietly dropped. Later, with David Cameron's coalition government in power, when the Murdochs, father and son, were anxious to buy the shares they did not already own in BskyB, their bid raised serious competition issues. Nevertheless, it seemed all but certain to be waved through until the phone-hacking scandal erupted. Prior to the scandal, the Murdochs certainly lobbied hard on the bid's behalf, and they enjoyed, in effect, privileged backchannel access to Jeremy Hunt, the minister for culture, media and sport latterly in charge of the bid. In that case, their lobbying probably made little difference since Hunt, for political and ideological reasons, was already on their side. They would have found Vince Cable a tougher nut to crack – and knew they would.

Uncensored media are essential to the health of any liberal democracy. A liberal democracy lacking such media would be unworthy of the name, and a whole volume could be devoted to describing and applauding media reportage, investigations and exposés that have been in the public interest and have unsettled and even deposed those in power. But this is not a book about the media. Its title is *Who Governs Britain?*, and an important part of the answer to that question is that a subsection of the British media, notably national newspapers and even more notably several of the tabloids, have substantial though by no means unlimited power within the political system and are capable, on occasion, of influencing and constraining the actions of democratically elected political leaders and governments. In 1931, the then Conservative leader, Stanley Baldwin, finding himself under constant attack by the two most prominent press barons of his day, Lords Beaverbrook and Rothermere, denounced them publicly for – as he contemptuously put it – aiming at 'power without responsibility – the prerogative of the harlot throughout the ages'.[19] Would a modern-day party leader dare utter such sentiments in public? Alas, that question must be left hanging.

CHAPTER 9

Ministers

Ministers decide. That continues to be the bedrock doctrine underlying the whole of Britain's governing arrangements. Other institutions, people and forces may influence and constrain what ministers of the crown can do, but otherwise ministers are free, within the law, to do pretty much whatever they like – and, if they dislike the law enough, they can usually change that, too. In the British system, the executive branch of government is by a wide margin the dominant branch. As we shall see in later chapters, parliament and the judiciary certainly count for something – but less than ministers do. It is the ministerial ladder, above all others, that ambitious British politicians seek to climb.

However, although the British system still remains a power-hoarding system, as it was during the classic era described in Chapter 1, it is a considerably less centralized system now than it was then. To be sure, the central government in Whitehall exercises far greater control over English local government than it used to; but, against that, there now exist in Scotland and Wales, as well as in Northern Ireland, real governments with substantial legislative and executive powers – powers that are all but certain to be increased rather than diminished as time goes on. To an extent largely unrecognized among the benighted English, the writ of many UK government ministers and ministries no longer extends throughout the UK. The Whitehall-based ministers responsible for agriculture and fisheries, the arts, education, health, housing, law and order, local government, personal social services and transport are all, in effect, England-only ministers, a fact of which they themselves are well aware, even if many (most?) of the English are not.

Still, England accounts for nearly 85 per cent of the UK's population, and the government of the UK still has many UK-wide responsibilities, so it is worth knowing something about these ministers, especially in view of the dominant role – because of power-hoarding – that they still play in the English and UK-wide political systems.

One oddity about the holders of UK ministerial office is the minute size and the strange composition of the 'gene pool' from which the great majority of them are drawn.[1] Since at least the middle of the eighteenth century, it has been custom and practice in this country for ministers of the crown to be drawn from – or, if not drawn from, then quickly made members of – either the House of Commons or the House of Lords. That is, all ministers have been expected to be parliamentarians. Both the custom and the practice are reinforced by the fact that British ministers are expected to be able to give an account of themselves and to answer questions in parliament, and for the time being only parliamentarians are allowed to do that. The Ministerial and Other Salaries Act 1975 simply assumes, without saying so explicitly, that ministers will be members of one or other of the two houses. Custom and practice in Britain also assume that the great majority of ministers, including almost always the holders of the most high-profile government posts, will be members of the governing party or parties in the House of Commons, not the Lords. The number of government supporters in the House of Commons is usually about 350 to 375, and seldom rises above 400. Sometimes it can be well below 350.

That number, whatever it is, is the maximum size of the gene pool from which some ninety House of Commons ministers, sometimes more, are typically drawn. But of course the maximum size of the pool is not also the realistic size. At any given time, a substantial proportion of government supporters in the House of Commons will be, in the eyes of the prime minister (and quite possibly in other people's eyes too), unfit to hold ministerial office. While most MPs nowadays are sensible, sane and reasonably articulate, not all are. Some are old and frail, some are ill, some are lazy, some drink too much, some have skeletons in the closet (of which the whips have been made aware), some are wildly unpredictable, some are likely to have proved failures as ministers already, some are too nervous to perform competently at the dispatch box, some are too dim to do the same, some are impossible personally, some will inevitably not be to the prime minister's political taste, and one or two of them may conceivably be foreign spies. (One postwar Labour backbencher was rumoured to be a Soviet agent. He was also an exceedingly ugly man, of whom Churchill is said to have remarked, 'He's not as nice as he looks.') In short, the number of *ministrables* from whom the prime minister of the day can choose in forming his or her government is likely to be nearer 200 than 350, and even that lesser figure is probably stretching it a bit.

The ministerial gene pool in Britain is far smaller than in most other countries, including almost all other European ones. In some member states of the EU – in France, the Netherlands and Sweden, for example – there is an absolute rule of incompatibility: a government minister may not also be a member of parliament. An MP who accepts appointment as a minister is required to resign his or her parliamentary seat. However, in a majority of the member states – including, most notably, Germany, Italy, Poland and Spain – the prevailing rule is more relaxed: a government minister is not required to be an MP, but he or she may be. In all of those countries, whatever the precise rules in any one of them, the country's president, prime minister or chancellor is free to appoint to ministerial office whomever he or she pleases. The persons appointed may be drawn from any walk of life – minister-presidents of German *Länder*, local mayors, lawyers, academics, bankers, industrialists, trade-unionists, whoever – and often are. The Republic of Ireland is the only other EU member state that requires ministers also to be parliamentarians, although Britain did succeed in exporting this requirement to its original overseas dominions, Australia, New Zealand, Canada and South Africa.

The gene pool from which the majority of British ministers are drawn is thus tiny by international standards. It is also composed in a distinctive manner. Apart from the minority of ministers who are drawn from, or parachuted into, the House of Lords, it consists entirely of individuals who happen to have been selected as parliamentary candidates in seats subsequently held or gained by the party or parties in power. As we saw in Chapter 3, there is no reason to think that the local activists who choose parliamentary candidates are especially interested in their ministerial potential as distinct from their other qualities. Even if they were interested, it is not clear that they would have the means, in the time available, of ascertaining which if any of the shortlist of prospective candidates before them actually possessed such potential. Party activists are seldom experts in the field of personnel recruitment. Although the fact is not desperately significant in itself, it is true – to take only one example – that the twenty-six members of the House of Commons recruited to the cabinet by David Cameron and Nick Clegg in May 2010 had probably been selected as parliamentary candidates by a total of no more than about four thousand individual party members. All but one or two of them represented safe seats. Their ultimate endorsement by their local electorates was largely a formality. Selection by the few was more important than election by the many.

More significant is the fact that, as we saw earlier, in recent decades the great majority of ministers in all parties and at all levels of government have been more or less direct entrants into the political class. That is, they have overwhelmingly been career politicians, without any substantial prior experience in walks of life wholly or largely unrelated to politics. Although appointed to the executive branch of government, they have brought with them into office almost no real-world executive experience. The kinds of heavyweights who served in the Attlee and Churchill administrations are scarcely to be seen.

When Tony Blair became prime minister in 1997, his only experience of non-political working life had been eight years spent practising as a junior barrister. Before being elected to parliament, Gordon Brown, Blair's chancellor of the exchequer, had spent roughly the same amount of time working as a politics lecturer and television journalist. Robin Cook, Blair's first foreign secretary, worked for only four years as a school teacher and as a tutor-organizer for the Workers' Educational Association, before becoming an MP (having already spent time as a local councillor). Jack Straw, Blair's first home secretary, took only a little longer before he, too, was elected to the Commons. He practised briefly at the criminal bar, before spending five years as political adviser to two Labour cabinet ministers and then two more years working as a researcher on Granada Television's *World in Action* programme. Almost all the other members of Blair's 1997 cabinet, comprising nearly two dozen members, were also career politicians. The three notable exceptions were Alan Johnson, the former trade-union leader, John Prescott, Blair's deputy prime minister, who had spent some time working as a steward on board ocean liners (not an executive position but certainly a worldly one) and Derry Irvine (Lord Irvine of Lairg), a prominent barrister and judge before becoming lord chancellor. But they *were* exceptions.

In terms of its members' pre-parliamentary backgrounds, the cabinet assembled by David Cameron and Nick Clegg in May 2010 was very similar to Blair's, especially in its upper reaches. Cameron worked for a time in the Conservative Research Department after leaving university, and then as a special adviser to two Conservative cabinet ministers before taking up a post in corporate communications. Apart from a few post-university odd jobs, his chancellor, George Osborne, devoted the whole of his working life to politics before entering parliament: first as a researcher in the Conservative Research Department, then as special adviser to a cabinet minister and finally as an aide to successive Conservative party leaders. The pre-parliamentary life of the foreign secretary, William Hague, was similarly steeped in politics and, when first elected to the House of Commons, he became its youngest member. In the case of Theresa May, the home secretary, her pre-parliamentary working life was less exclusively political. She spent a full decade in the world of banking and finance before becoming an MP. Otherwise, the great bulk of Cameron's cabinet colleagues were career politicians, although a larger proportion than in Blair's first cabinet could boast of at least a modicum of pre-political executive experience. Only three members in a cabinet of twenty-nine were clearly outliers – members of the political class, but only just. Before being elected an MP at the age of fifty-four (compared with Cameron's thirty-six, Osborne's thirty and Hague's twenty-eight), Vince Cable had had a varied career as an economics lecturer, finance officer in the Kenyan government and chief economist at the Royal Dutch Shell oil company. Cameron's Liberal Democrat deputy, Nick Clegg, wrote for the *Financial Times* (he was one of the cabinet's three former journalists) before joining the staff of the European Commission, where he dealt with governments across central Asia and helped negotiate Russia's and China's entry into the World Trade Organization. Before entering parliament, Philip Hammond had built a substantial business career in manufacturing, housing, health care and oil and gas, with consultancies extending as far as Latin America and sub-Saharan Africa. But those three individuals, like Johnson, Prescott and Irvine in Tony Blair's government, were atypical of the whole.

There is no reason to denigrate career politicians as a class. Over the past hundred years or so, their distinguished ranks have included David Lloyd George, Winston Churchill, Neville Chamberlain (as both housing minister and chancellor, if not as prime minister), R. A. Butler, Herbert Morrison, Aneurin Bevan, Hugh Gaitskell, Harold Macmillan, Iain Macleod, Edward Heath, Roy Jenkins, Denis Healey, Tony Crosland, Margaret Thatcher, Michael Heseltine and Geoffrey Howe. More recently – and in some cases more controversially – they have included Kenneth Clarke, Douglas Hurd, Tony Blair and Gordon Brown. Politics as a way of life attracts some extraordinarily able men and women, and many of them bring to their ministerial posts stamina, energy, creativity, determination, political nous, good judgement, fluency with words and a good lawyer's ability to absorb and process vast amounts of new information speedily. Many of them, though by no means all, are capable of being inspiring. Perhaps above all, the best of them are able – more able than most people in other walks of life, including business and academia – to cope with and respond positively to the multidimensional dilemmas that uniquely characterize politics at the top.

But the gene pool in Britain *is* very small, it consists predominately of people without much in the way of previous non-political experience, and there is no necessary fit – and there may even be a misfit – between the wide variety of jobs that need to be done at ministerial level in any government and the availability of people equipped with the requisite knowledge and experience to do those particular jobs. Not all career politicians are of the highest quality, and even the most gifted of them are likely to be able to perform better in some posts than in others. The same individual may well not possess both diplomatic and organizational skills. Someone with an instinctive feel for educational issues may not have the same feel for issues relating to international trade. Holding a first-class degree in philosophy, politics and economics (PPE) from Oxford does not guarantee that its holder will be a politically adept and multi-skilled polymath.

Moreover, there is a growing body of evidence suggesting that people who have worked for a long time in specific industries tend to perform better as leaders in those industries than people who lack that experience and have been imported from elsewhere. They know more – and are more realistic – about the issues and the kinds of people they are dealing with. Thus, football teams whose managers have excelled as players on the field tend to outperform those whose managers have not; hospitals led by first-class clinicians commonly outperform those that are not; the most research-productive universities typically have, or recently have had, as their vice-chancellor (in the UK) or their president (in the U.S.) men and women who themselves are, or recently have been, active researchers. 'Experts and professionals need to be led by other experts and professionals, those who have a deep understanding of and high ability in the core-business of their organization.'[2] Technocrats with no feel for the realities of politics are useless (or worse) and may merely import into politics the predilections and biases of their previous profession; but politicians devoid of specialist knowledge may underperform in fields that require – or at least would profit from – such knowledge. At the moment, British prime ministers' range of choice in this regard is severely restricted – far more than is commonly the case elsewhere.

Turnover among the ministers drawn from Britain's small gene pool is also high. At any given time, a UK minister doing any given job is unlikely to have been doing that particular job for very long. Some of what are called 'reshuffles' – as though ministers were merely playing cards in a pack – are triggered by events largely or wholly beyond a prime minister's control: deaths, scandals and unexpected resignations. Others occur because the prime minister of the day wants to sack incompetent or awkward colleagues and/ or to reward genuine talent and satisfy junior ministers' and backbenchers' hunger for place and promotion. Either way, the removal or promotion of one person is almost never followed by the appointment or promotion of only one or two other persons. Reshuffles are usually on a substantial scale, largely because the gene pool is mostly confined to government supporters in the House of Commons. Sacking one MP usually means replacing him or her with another MP, which in turn usually means replacing him or her with yet another MP, which in turn usually means . . . And so forth. Always in the background is the prime minister's need to keep his parliamentary party happy or at least not too dangerously unhappy.

Almost everyone in Britain is at least vaguely aware of the phenomenon of reshuffles, but most are probably unaware of their full extent or cumulative consequences. Tony Blair held the office of prime minister for just over ten years. Gordon Brown, his chancellor of the exchequer, remained in the same post for all of those ten years (mainly because he was dangerous, and Blair much preferred to have him inside the tent pissing out rather than outside the tent pissing in). Blair's deputy, John Prescott, also served for the full ten years. But otherwise the rate of turnover among cabinet-level ministers, notably among heads of government departments, was prodigious. During the ten Blair years, there were four foreign secretaries, four home secretaries, four defence secretaries, eight ministers in charge of transport, seven secretaries of state for trade and industry, six ministers responsible for local government, six ministers responsible for pensions and social security, five education secretaries and four health secretaries. Their average tenure of office was little more than two years. Most of them had had no prior ministerial experience of working in the same or a nearby field. Needless to say, almost none of them had brought with them into office experience in the same or a nearby field from the world beyond politics.

Gordon Brown, during his brief tenure of the premiership, carried on in the Blair tradition, sacking or reshuffling roughly a third of Blair's cabinet on his first day in office and conducting three further reshuffles during the three years that remained to him. David Cameron came to office determined to slow down the rate of ministerial churning, and up to a point he succeeded, aided by the fact that he could not wilfully and on his own initiative sack or move his Liberal Democrat ministerial colleagues. But even he was only partially successful. After nearly five years, only ten of the twenty-nine members of his original cabinet still held the same post they had held at the outset. There had already been three secretaries of state for defence, three secretaries of state for culture, media and sport and another three at the Department for Transport. Government by neophyte remains broadly the rule.

Strangely, in view of the fact that no one seems eager to do anything radical about it, it seems to be almost universally agreed that perpetual motion among ministers is not at all a good idea. The former Conservative prime minister John Major was adamant that 'moving ministers around too quickly is not conducive to good government', and Jack Straw, who held four senior cabinet posts under Blair and Brown, felt so strongly about what he called 'the constant churn' of ministers that he devoted a whole passage to the topic in his memoirs.[3] The churn of individual ministers, he wrote, 'led to them, and government as a whole, functioning far less well than they could have done if they'd had the time and security to learn their jobs and get on with them'.[4] The London-based Institute for Government, in 2010–11, asked current and former ministers, senior civil servants and well-informed outsiders a simple, open-ended question: 'What makes an effective minister?' Heading the list of factors cited by respondents as making for ministers who were *not* effective was 'rapid turnover of ministers'.[5] The Institute's subsequent report, entitled *The Challenge of Being a Minister*, concluded that 'a real constraint on ministerial effectiveness is that many ministers do not stay in their posts long enough'.[6] Constant reshuffling of the pack may also reinforce the widespread public impression that Westminster politicians are a class apart, content to go on playing abstruse political games among themselves.

Although a good deal has changed, with more ministers nowadays than in the past having little in the way of a pre-political or non-political hinterland, their formal job description remains essentially the same. Officials advise. Others may do the same. But ministers decide. However, several decades ago, ministers' informal job description began to change subtly but quite fundamentally. Ministers were no longer there merely to decide: they were to initiate, command and drive forward. Resistance was not any longer to be accommodated: it was to be overcome. The age of the macho minister had dawned.

Unusually, the beginnings of this process, though it was not seen as such at the time, can be dated quite precisely. Although Margaret Thatcher as education secretary during the early 1970s had not had an especially fraught time with her departmental officials, she nevertheless had, in the words of her most recent biographer, 'a temperamental and ideological suspicion of the Civil Service', and on becoming prime minister in 1979 she was determined to dominate the official machine, not by changing its formal structure but by bending it to her will:

> She used every remark, every memo, every meeting as an opportunity to challenge existing habits, criticize any sign

of ignorance, confusion or waste and preach incessantly the main aims of her administration.[7]

In May 1980, she somewhat reluctantly hosted a Number 10 dinner meeting between herself and the permanent heads of government departments. She hated every minute of it. She was bent on change, halting Britain's seemingly inexorable long-term decline. Collectively, they came over as supercilious, sullen, resistant, resentful and, worst of all, defeatist. At one point, she whispered to her cabinet secretary, Robert Armstrong, sitting next to her, 'They are all against me, Robert. I can *feel* it.'[8] Later, she described the occasion as 'one of the most dismal occasions of my entire time in government'.[9]

The word soon went out, via the Whitehall grapevine if not directly. The prime minister was determined to be the boss in her sphere. Her ministers had also better make sure they were the boss in theirs. Ministers who were patently in charge of their departments and who brooked no opposition from officials could expect to be promoted. Ministers who hesitated, buying into the ingrained caution of their senior officials, could expect to have their careers terminated. What had once been expected to be a collaborative relationship between ministers and officials – though with officials, of course, ultimately deferring to ministers – was now expected to be more strictly hierarchical, with ministers boldly asserting their authority and being rewarded by the prime minister for doing just that. Ministers came to see their senior officials as one, but only one, source of policy advice and as having as their primary responsibility executing in full their minister's will, ideally enthusiastically, however perverse they might think that will to be. By the time Thatcher left office, the doctrine of the constitution had not changed in any material way, but the feel of it certainly had. Although there was a partial reversion to type during John Major's premiership, and although the ways in which ministers operate inevitably vary from department to department and from individual to individual, the conception of the minister's role established by Thatcher has remained the prevailing conception ever since. Government in Britain is no longer the duopoly it was when Richard Neustadt wrote.

The ideal post-Thatcher minister – and many of them *are* nearly ideal – has a number of attributes. He or she is well educated, articulate and confident and works hard. Most of them can cope reasonably satisfactorily at the dispatch box in the House of Commons and in television and radio studios. Most of them want to do good and are convinced that that is precisely what they are doing. To be sure, they are competitive, especially in relation to other members of their own party, but there is nothing new in that. Similarly, they are anxious to be popular with members of their own party, but there is nothing new in that either.

However, most of them differ from the bulk of their pre-Thatcher predecessors in three significant respects. In the first place, as we have seen, they are keen to innovate and to be seen to be innovating. Few of them are content to do a good job of administering – and, where necessary, tweaking – their department's existing policies. They believe, and are probably right to believe, that if they are to impress their colleagues in general, and the prime minister in particular, they must constantly be seen to be taking initiatives, never to be resting on their oars. As one former minister, himself a serial innovator, put it in an interview, ministers these days arrive in their departments under intense pressure to innovate, not just to administer whatever policies they find in place: 'You get brownie points for the former, none for the latter.'[10]

Second, if change is desirable, and it often is, then it is desirable *now*, not at some unspecified time in the future. One of the principal characteristics of Margaret Thatcher's ministerial heirs and descendants, in all parties not just hers, is the desire to have their innovations fixed firmly in place as soon as is humanly possible – ideally much sooner. Post-Thatcher ministers are characterized by their impatience. They want to make their mark and to make it now. A line of policy that takes a long time to develop is apt to have been fully developed only after the minister who first proposed it has long since moved on. Similarly, a line of policy that does not produce results for a considerable period of years is also almost certain to deliver them only long after the minister-innovator has moved on. The career politician who wants to advance his or her career can only do that in the here and now.

The third way in which post-Thatcher ministers differ from their predecessors is closely related to the second. It concerns how ministers think about time: their place in it and how it relates to the future. Ministers, especially if they are career politicians, have every incentive to concern themselves with the present – or at least with the next two or three years – and have no incentive at all to think about the longer term future. They may 'think long'; but, if they do, it is because they choose to do that, not because they must. Their time horizon is typically bounded, if not by the next reshuffle, then by the next general election. Getting innovative legislation onto the statute book trumps ensuring that the policy embodied in that statute achieves its stated purposes. If it succeeds at some time in the distant future, no one is likely to attribute the success to the person who introduced it. If it fails, no one is likely to have a good enough memory to recall who the long-gone miscreant was. Time marches on. The time for ministers and officials to raise their champagne glasses in celebration is now. The future can take care of itself.

We will return to the implications of ministers' changed role in the final chapter of this book. In the meantime, having looked at the relationship between ministers and officials from ministers' point of view, it is time to look at it from the point of view of officials.

CHAPTER 10

Officials

There is an often told and widely believed story about who governs Britain and how it is governed. It concerns the relationship between democratically elected ministers and unelected officials, and it is quite an attractive story in its way. Ministers, according to the story, come and go. They provide their department with broad political direction and are responsible for taking the most difficult and contentious decisions; but they are not, and cannot reasonably be expected to be, deeply knowledgeable about the varied and complex matters that their department inevitably deals with. For that deep knowledge and experience, they rely on their senior civil servants, the permanent officials with whom they work most closely and who are their principal advisers. Between them, ministers and officials are the two mighty pillars of the British state, easily its two strongest human supports.

Some of what is said about the British civil service is still true. Ever since the late nineteenth century – in the decades following the gradual implementation of the so-called Northcote–Trevelyan reforms – the quality and integrity of the British civil service have stood comparison with any similar body in any other country in the world and have been manifestly superior to most of them. Progressive reformers in the United States at the turn of the last century sought to create a federal civil service modelled on Britain's, and the Indian civil service is still regarded today as one of the most enduring and valuable legacies of the British Raj. British civil servants served governments of different political persuasions impartially. They still do. They were, and still are, recruited and promoted strictly on merit. They were, and remain, uncorrupt and incorruptible. Not least, they are still a largely self-governing cadre. They themselves take most decisions about themselves, largely free of the constraints and temptations of both personal patronage and political favouritism. The 'old corruption', for which British public life was once notorious, has long gone.

The traditional British civil service, however, was more than honest. It was also dynamic, or at least capable of being dynamic. Generations of senior civil servants regarded it as part of their mission, not merely to serve their ministerial masters, but to promote causes. One of them, Sir Rowland Hill, founded the modern Post Office. Sir James Kay-Shuttleworth, a pioneer of Victorian public health, laid down the foundations of England's state elementary school system. Early in the twentieth century, Sir Robert Morant played a central role in the expansion of secondary education in England and Wales. Sir Eyre Crowe was a dominant figure in the Foreign Office long before he became its permanent secretary in 1920. Following the Second World War, Sir Frank Lee, a formidable Treasury mandarin, pushed hard in Whitehall for British membership of the Common Market and later for the abolition of what was then known as 'resale price maintenance', a legally enforceable anti-competitive device that enabled manufacturers to determine the prices at which shops sold their goods. Lee, as one commentator put it, 'had strong views on policy . . . and did not bother to hide them'.[1] He was not untypical of his time.

However, although some mandarins were dynamos, the great majority were not. Their essential role was to serve ministers by helping them to promote their chosen causes and – probably equally important – by doing their best to prevent them from making mistakes. L. S. Amery, whose views about the role of the electorate we noted in Chapter 1, was equally clear in his own mind about the role of officials. He likened each of Britain's great departments of state to a ship. The ship's captain, the minister, might have lots of bright ideas, but the crew, the permanent officials, knew far more than he did about navigation. The ship's crew, he wrote, 'has an accumulated knowledge of wind and weather, of reefs and shoals, by which a new captain is inevitably guided'.[2] The captain had a perfect right to set the ship's course, but the crew had a corresponding duty to warn him of any perils that might lie ahead. It was also perfectly acceptable for members of the crew, who had probably been on departmental deck for far longer than he had, to suggest which course the ship should take, even if it was not the one the captain initially preferred. Indeed, it was their bounden duty to present the captain with a range of options.

Writing soon after the war, Amery was expressing the conventional wisdom of his time, and it was a wisdom that prevailed for several decades after that. Central to his conception was his understanding – his belief – that the senior officers among the ship's crew, and probably many of the junior ones too, would have been sailing in the same ship for a considerable period of time, perhaps for most of their careers. Several years later, a former head of the home civil service, Sir Edward Bridges, saw as the essence of a civil servant's work the 'slow accretion and accumulation of experience'. Civil servants should have discovered what worked and what did not and what aroused public criticism and what did not. It was 'the duty of the civil servant to give his Minister the fullest benefit of the storehouse of departmental experience; and to let the waves of the practical philosophy wash against ideas put forward by his ministerial masters'. The very first quality that a civil servant needed, according to Bridges, was 'long experience of a particular field'.[3] In short, civil servants should know a lot. Although perhaps generalists as administrators, they should be specialists in the work of their own department. And they should also have seen a lot. They should be the custodians of their department's institutional memory. In Bridges' view – and that of many of his generation – having seen a lot was all but equivalent to knowing a lot. Learning on the job trumped learning from books – or, heaven forfend, from non-civil servants.

It almost goes without saying that, especially as the British economy slowed during the late 1950s and the early 1960s, and as Britain declined as a world power, that view of the training and role – the whole mind-set – of senior civil servants became anathema to a growing number of sceptics and critics. On the left, the mandarinate was seen as complacent, elitist and, above all, ignorant – ignorant especially of statistics, the social sciences and life as it was actually lived in council houses and on the shop floor. On the right, the mandarinate was seen not only as complacent but, worse, as a formidable obstacle in the way of radical change. Bridges' successor as head of the home civil service, Sir William Armstrong, was heard to say wanly that Whitehall's role was to 'manage the decline of Britain in an orderly fashion'.[4] Margaret Thatcher was extreme but by no means alone in being deeply affronted. 'I preferred', she wrote in her memoirs, 'disorderly resistance to decline rather than comfortable accommodation to it.'[5] It was in that not-to-be-messed-with frame of mind that she met her permanent secretaries at their dismal dinner in May 1980, the one recounted in the previous chapter.

As we also saw in the last chapter, ministers were from now on to be cast in the role of activists and initiators. They were to be, and to be seen to be, the top dogs in Whitehall, not merely formally but in reality. But that change of role meant a corresponding change in the role and mind-set of officials. From now on, officials were to be civil *servants* in reality, at their master's beck and call, eager to do their master's bidding. By no means all the senior officials then in place were happy with the new dispensation; probably most of them were not. But, if they were sufficiently senior, they were already on the verge of retirement, and within a few years most of Thatcher's uncomfortable dinner guests, even if they had stayed on for a while, had quit the scene. By the time New Labour came to power in 1997, there were few, if any, of the old-style mandarins still in place. Most of them had been washed out by time and by Edward Bridges' 'waves of the practical philosophy'.

Some among officialdom were lucky. They found themselves working for – but also with – ministers who valued those brave enough to speak truth to power. Michael Heseltine, one of the ablest and most committed departmental ministers of modern times, much preferred officials who acknowledged that he was their boss but at the same time could be counted upon to say what they thought. 'The civil servants who worked with him saw Heseltine as an exceptional motivator with an unusual ability to inspire and enthuse.'[6] Not all officials in the early days of the rebalancing of the relationship between ministers and civil servants were so lucky. During the mid-1980s, Norman Fowler, the secretary of state for social services, led a review of the social security system that questioned some of the assumptions that had underlain the system ever since Attlee's time. A senior official in the department recalled what happened next:

> We had a very traumatic final meeting, which was meant
> to be no holds barred, but where one senior official . . .
> suffered greatly. He gave Fowler a lecture on the fact that,
> since 1948, the social security system had been governed
> by consensus, that this was immensely valuable and should
> not be thrown away. You could hear Fowler, a Thatcherite
> minister, almost spitting at this . . . Not surprisingly, the
> official's speech went down like a lead-balloon.[7]

The careers of officials like him also went down like lead balloons. Their colleagues could not help but notice.

Many ministers, with much expected of them and suspicious of their officials, turned for help and advice to a new breed of quasi-officials: the so-called special advisers, now fashionably called 'spads'. Special advisers work in Whitehall and are paid out of public funds like other civil servants, but they are licensed to play a more overtly political role. Ministers appoint their own special advisers, and those they appoint are strictly political appointees: when their minister goes, they go. Some special advisers are policy experts and see their main role as providing their boss with politically congenial policy advice. Some are chiefly concerned with communications, trying to ensure that their boss and his (or her) doings get a good press (a role that can easily extend to bad-mouthing the boss's rivals). Some provide their boss with an extra set of political antennae, warning him of impending trouble and reminding him who his friends and enemies really are. Most play some combination of these roles, and many provide their boss with someone whom he or she can confide in – or blow off steam at – over a drink late at night. The number of special advisers across Whitehall has expanded almost exponentially, from a mere handful or fewer in the mid-1960s to between ninety and a hundred half a century later.

Although special advisers are still far fewer in number than the many hundreds of senior officials, their mere presence inevitably complicates career officials' lives. Some spads are brighter than others, some more emotionally intelligent, some more collegial than their colleagues in their approach to working with officials. At their best, they can discourage officials from pursuing lines of policy that have no chance of finding favour with their minister, and they can also reconnoitre the political ground before either ministers or officials advance too far into it. Knowing the mind of their minister, as they usually do, spads are also in a position to establish firmly their minister's priorities, as well as his or her personal likes and dislikes, in officials' minds. Those special advisers who bring genuine policy expertise to the table are often more creative in their thinking than career officials and readier to challenge departmental orthodoxies. They are also likely to have useful policy-relevant contacts in the world beyond Whitehall. Against that, only a minority of spads can actually lay claim to genuine policy expertise, many of them are exceedingly wet behind the ears – wetter than they probably realize – and almost all of them reinforce ministers' disposition, which would be present anyway, to force the pace of whatever they are doing and to accommodate it continually to the timetable of politics and to purely political exigencies. A large proportion of spads are drawn from, and then become charter members of, the political class. Whatever else they do, they certainly reinforce the dominance of ministers vis-à-vis officials.

In the new dispensation, ministers at all levels also draw on ideas and advice emanating from think tanks, some of them studiously non-aligned, most of them politically committed in one way or another. Civil servants make formal submissions to ministers. Think tanks and their senior executives make informal ones, frequently at seminars and working dinners, commonly in the form of published books and pamphlets. Thatcher and her ministers, unimpressed by what they saw as officials' rigidity and timidity, drew heavily in opposition and government on the work of radical free-market think tanks such as the Institute of Economic Affairs and the Centre for Policy Studies. Pro-market think tanks with names like Policy Exchange and Reform, many of them generously funded, have proliferated ever since. For their part, Labour and Liberal Democrat politicians mingle with researchers at bodies such as Demos, the Institute for Public Policy Research, the Resolution Foundation and the Social Market Foundation. More detached, less partisan, are bodies such as the Institute for Fiscal Studies and the Institute for Government. All these organizations carry on a brisk trade in people as well as ideas, with think tankers morphing into spads and spads into MPs and ministers. Senior officials, who once virtually monopolized the giving of policy advice, now find themselves sharing their influence on ministers with an amorphous swirl of what Americans (for some obscure reason) call 'policy wonks'.

More than two decades after the fall of Margaret Thatcher, the vast majority of officials, including the most senior, give the impression of having settled into their new, more subordinate role. Most of them have, of course, known no other. Undoubtedly there are still some ministers (an unknown number) who, like Heseltine, like to have their propositions challenged and who become uneasy when their officials appear over-anxious to oblige. John Hutton, a successful departmental minister under Tony Blair and Gordon Brown, is clear that a minister's chances of getting things right are likely, even now, to be compromised 'if the civil servants round your table won't tell it to you as they really believe it to be'.[8] But, whatever ministers may say, that would appear to be a minority view, especially when the civil servants in question are made aware that their ministerial boss is hell bent on a specific course of action. During the 1980s, civil servants appear to have mounted no or very little resistance to the introduction of Margaret Thatcher's ludicrous and ultimately self-destructive poll tax. At an early stage, it became clear that plans for the 2000 Millennium Exhibition were lapsing into chaos; but, in the words of one official speaking of himself as well as his colleagues, 'No one had the balls to say, "Look, let's stand back and reassess."'[9] After nearly two decades of Conservative rule, officials felt the need in 1997, and for several years thereafter, to prove to New Labour ministers that they were not covert Thatcherites and could therefore be trusted. 'We wanted', one of them said, 'to avoid a Sir Humphrey image. We became afraid to say "No, Minister".'[10] In 2010, a similar fear of being thought obstructive apparently gripped Department of Health officials, who appear not to have objected strongly when they were confronted by a newly installed Conservative health secretary clearly determined to overhaul – hastily as well as radically – the entire NHS in England. Contemplating the overall change in outlook that began in Thatcher's time, a long-serving civil servant was pretty sure of the reason:

> I think what happened during the 1980s is that the Civil Service moved to recognising their job as delivering what ministers wanted. Can-do man was in and wait-a-minute man was out. Ministers not only knew what they wanted, but often how to get there. The Civil Service role as ballast was sidelined. There was no room for it.[11]

And can-do man (and woman) has been in, and wait-a-minute man (and woman) has been out, ever since. Fortunately, can-do man (and woman) is quite often able to do. The British civil service continues to recruit some of the best and brightest among the country's university graduates, a large proportion of them are as dedicated to public service as they ever were, and a considerable proportion of them remain in the civil service for the bulk of their working lives. When they succeed, their successes, precisely because they are successes, typically go unremarked. They are not reported on television or in the press, and ministers seldom go out of their way to give credit to their officials, rather than themselves, for whatever it is that has been accomplished. Ministers prefer to claim the credit for themselves. In particular, ministers are most unlikely to praise officials publicly for having dissuaded them from doing something stupid.

Nevertheless, there are good reasons for believing that the civil service as a whole, and certainly large parts of it, is increasingly no longer capable of providing ministers with the knowledge, the long experience and the 'ballast' that they require – in other words, that cracks are beginning to appear in one of the two mighty pillars of the British state. To change the metaphor, the British civil-service machine used to be likened to a Rolls-Royce. That grand old car undoubtedly still looks good on the outside; its minders take care to polish it lovingly. But closer inspection suggests that rust is beginning to corrode the wheel arches, that the clutch is slipping and that the brakes may be dangerously faulty.

One ages-old and long-recognized problem has become more acute. Just as ministers no longer – in so far as they ever did – bring with them into ministerial office substantial practical experience of the world outside politics, so the great majority of civil servants are likewise amateurs in that sense. Most arrive in Whitehall straight from university and then learn mainly on the job. They quickly become experts in the highly specialized field of Whitehall politics but not in fields such as defence procurement, higher and further education, prisons management, transport, health-care delivery or local-government finance. Successive governments have promoted all manner of in-service training programmes, although most of them are of short duration. They have also recruited increasing numbers of officials, including senior officials, from the private sector and local government – one head of the home civil service during the 2010s had previously been chief executive of Sheffield City Council – but reports from the National Audit Office and parliamentary select committees routinely point out that senior civil servants' knowledge of the subject matter they are dealing with can often be thin and that shortages of some specialist skills are endemic. Few civil servants know much about information technology (although governments are increasingly IT-dependent and IT-demanding); few are skilled project managers; and fewer still have the skills needed to manage IT projects. As one official put it, civil servants in his own department were not in a position even to act as 'intelligent customers'.[12]

The most serious skills shortages are often ones that go unrecognized. A minister may imagine that his (or her) officials have both the ability and the resources to carry out his wishes when in fact they lack one or other or both. And in the present can-do age they may be reluctant to tell him so. The minister lays down the policy, and his officials are left to get on with it, in the full expectation, at least on the part of the minister, that they actually can get on with it. For generations, ministers have often developed policies without giving due consideration to how they might be implemented in practice; but today's can-do culture greatly increases the chances of that happening – that is, of the gap between policy and implementation widening further. 'Yes, minister' is so much easier to say than 'I don't know, minister' or 'I'm not sure, minister'. Officials have every incentive to try to implement the minister's wishes; but they largely lack incentives to express doubts about whether or not what the minister wishes to happen can in reality be made to happen. They may not be sure one way or the other: speaking truth to power demands, in addition to self-confidence, a knowledge of where the truth lies, and that knowledge is not always available. Some ministers evidently suffer from the Owen Glendower complex: 'I can call spirits from the vasty deep.' But not all officials have Hotspur's chutzpah and feel able to reply:

> Why, so can I, or so can any man;
> But will they come when you do call for them?

It is civil servants' job to make sure that their minister's spirits do come when he or she calls for them, and often they succeed. But not always. They could not make the 1980s poll tax work. In 1992, they could not prevent sterling from falling out of the European Exchange Rate Mechanism. A decade later, they were unable to deliver Tony Blair's over-ambitious and ultimately aborted scheme for instantaneous information-sharing across the NHS in England. A decade after that, there was no way in which they could deliver on the Conservatives' 2010 manifesto pledge to reduce annual net migration into the UK to tens of thousands (compared with hundreds of thousands in the past). In any or all of these cases, did officials warn ministers that they were being asked to attempt the impossible? In the fullness of time, historians may – or may not – be able to answer that question.

Another sign that something may be amiss relates back to L. S. Amery's remark about civil servants' 'accumulated knowledge' and to Sir Edward Bridges' insistence that the first quality a good civil servant needed was 'long experience of a particular field'. The traditional story about how British government works – still widely credited – holds that transient ministers, whatever the limitations of their personal knowledge, are able to rely on the accumulated knowledge and experience of their officials. In the nature of the case, ministers are often ignorant because a subject is new to them. According to the story, civil servants, having been around for a long time, are able to compensate for their masters' ignorance. However, there are good reasons for thinking that that part of the traditional story – essential to its attractiveness – is probably no longer true or, at any rate, is certainly less true than it was.

Comprehensive quantitative evidence is lacking, but anecdotal evidence – of which there is by now a great deal – suggests that officials, once the embodiments of departmental continuity, are now at least as transient as their political masters and therefore at least as liable not to have a very firm grasp of what they are doing. Civil servants move

from post to post for career-related rather than policy-
related or implementation-related reasons, and they seldom
remain in any one post, or in any one group of related posts,
for more than two or three years. Moreover, when departments and agencies shed staff – which is most of the time –
it is often the most knowledgeable and experienced staff
who leave first. They, being more experienced, typically earn
more than their juniors, they are often near to retirement
in any case, and the best of them can usually find jobs elsewhere. In one of its reports in the mid-2010s, the House of
Commons Public Accounts Committee, having noted that
the Home Office was failing to deal with an enormous and
growing backlog of asylum cases, commented contemptuously: 'This is partly as a result of a botched attempt by the
[UK Border] Agency to downgrade staff that resulted in 120
experienced caseworkers leaving.'[13] Reports from that committee as well as from others frequently draw attention to
that kind of haemorrhaging of staff.

Anecdotes relating to the rapid rate of turnover among
officials are too numerous to list, but here is a sample.

- A senior figure in the world of higher education went to
  see officials at the Department for Business, Innovation
  and Skills. He went because ministers were floating the
  idea of a major innovation in his field. He mentioned to
  the officials that the idea being floated was actually being
  refloated: it had already been discussed in detail, and
  rejected, in a government-commissioned report published
  several years earlier. Not only had none of the officials ever
  read the report: none of them had ever heard of it.

- A well-known solicitor went to see officials at the Ministry of Justice about proposals affecting solicitors emanating from that department. It turned out that none of the officials he met had ever practised as a solicitor and that none of them showed any signs of being able to take in what he was talking about.

- A minister had a pet project that he was promoting with the support of his ministerial colleagues. No major political issues were involved. Most of the matters that remained to be dealt with were legal and technical. He reported that during the three years he had been involved with the project he had had six different officials working on it under him, one after the other, that only one of the six had ever really got his head round the project and that that official had recently applied for and won promotion to a more senior position in another, unrelated department. As soon as he had become useful, he moved on.

- A rumour – it may be only that – is widely credited to the effect that the annual rate of turnover among Treasury officials approaches 50 per cent and that many of the economists and others recruited to the Treasury are not really interested in working for the Treasury but merely want to have the fact that they once worked there appear on their CV. They regard service in the Treasury as nothing more than a box to be ticked.

- Business people and the heads of charities frequently report that they are supposed to have regular six-monthly (or thereabouts) meetings with officials from the government department that they work most closely with. The regular meetings do take place, but on each occasion a different phalanx of officials almost invariably turns up. As a result, the meetings go round and round in polite circles, with real progress seldom made. Institutional memory has been replaced by institutional amnesia.

· The cabinet minister in charge of a large department was once asked how his efforts to deal with a sudden crisis were being affected by his officials' knowing more about the relevant issues than he did. 'Know more about them than I do?' he retorted. 'I've only been here two years, and I already know more than any of them.'

Another cabinet minister voiced similar complaints. He reckoned that his own department's collective memory was so short and that its records were so poor that:

you end up in a situation where only a handful of people ever remember what has been said or done . . . people deal only with the instant they are living in, rather than drawing on any kind of history or knowledge of the detail and background to a particular issue.[14]

One particular episode, much publicized at the time, provides a vivid illustration of what can happen when an important decision is taken by a combination – by no means an unusual one – of ill-informed ministers and ill-informed officials.

In January 2011, the Department for Transport initiated the process for awarding a new franchise for operating passenger trains on the West Coast Main Line between London Euston, Manchester, Liverpool and Scotland. A few months later, the department announced that four firms and consortia had been invited to bid for the franchise, and in mid-August 2012 it declared that the winning bid had been submitted by a firm called FirstGroup. However, a rival firm, the one that held the existing franchise, Virgin Trains Ltd, appealed against the decision, claiming that the department had made material errors in the course of the bidding process. After weeks of public controversy, parliamentary debate and legal argument, the secretary of state for transport announced in early October 2012 that the award of the franchise to FirstGroup was to be cancelled and that for the time being Virgin Trains would continue to operate the line. Although innumerable details remained to be sorted out, the franchise was finally awarded, in effect, to Virgin in December 2012, almost two years after the whole bidding business had begun. The cost to taxpayers of the chaos amounted to not less than £40 million, probably a lot more.

What had gone wrong? It may be relevant that during the two years in question the Department for Transport had two secretaries of state and three permanent secretaries (though the latter three were not exactly 'permanent'); but the high rate of turnover at the top may not have mattered all that much because it seems clear that no one anywhere near the top had the faintest idea what was going on in any case. They did not know because no one told them, until it was too late, that a number of middle-ranking officials harboured doubts about crucial details of the franchising process. The author of a subsequent inquiry into the fiasco considered it 'appropriate to draw out certain cultural aspects' of the affair:

> The Inquiry has been provided with consistent evidence
> from interviews to suggest that DfT officials felt inhibited

from escalating [i.e., informing their superiors about] significant risk areas. This inhibition may in part be attributed to the fact that, when attempts were made to escalate such issues, in some instances senior officials were perceived to be unreceptive or not willing to give due attention to the concerns raised.[15]

Power seems not to have wanted to face the truth. It was also the case that, as the inquiry pointed out, the department, largely as a result of government cuts, had recently lost a large number of its most experienced staff, including many of those who had previously worked on rail franchising. The department in the process lost both 'corporate memory' and relevant commercial experience. Several of those who departed went to work for private-sector organizations, including the West Coast Main Line franchise bidders. One result was that 'many of the DfT's full-time . . . Project Team were relatively junior and did not have experience comparable with those of their counterparts' in the bidding companies.[16] These junior officials were also under pressure to complete the whole franchising operation in a great hurry. As in so many other instances, the traditional story of how Britain is governed was not the true story.

The message of this chapter and the preceding one is – or should be – clear. Whatever the constraints upon them, ministers still stand high among those who govern Britain, or at least in those aspects of British government that have not been devolved to Edinburgh, Cardiff or Belfast. But, although individual civil servants can still be highly influential, the collective influence of the British civil service is now scarcely a shadow of what it used to be. Someone once described the two decades after the Second World War, accurately, as 'a mandarins' paradise'.[17] Since then, the mandarins have been all but expelled from their former Garden of Eden. Ministers' spads have not replaced them.

Prime Ministers

It is easy to overestimate the importance of the prime minister in the British system of government. Indeed, it is hard *not* to overestimate his – or, once upon a time and undoubtedly again in the future, her – importance. By a wide margin, the prime minister of the day is the best-known politician in Britain. He appears on television all the time. His face constantly features in the newspapers and on social media. He regularly exchanges insults with the leader of the opposition in the House of Commons. He travels widely in this country and abroad. He hobnobs with foreign leaders such as the German chancellor and the American president. Not least, an enormous proportion of everything that his government does is attributed personally to him. There is even a good chance that his wife will achieve minor-celebrity status. Small wonder, then, that the prime minister of the day, whoever he is, comes to be regarded as the United Kingdom's prime mover and shaker, the boss, the man in charge, the man who really makes things happen (or conspicuously fails to). The occupant of 10 Downing Street today seems to embody in his person the entire power of the British state.

As usual, the truth is a good deal more complicated. The former Liberal prime minister H. H. Asquith's saying from the 1920s – 'The office of the Prime Minister is what its holder chooses and is able to make of it'[1] – still holds good. But, while the matter of personal choice remains largely in the hands of the prime minister himself, the matter of his ability to make something of his position relates at least as much to the nature of the office itself and to the political circumstances in which he finds himself. The position of a prime minister who is able to work in close harmony with his chancellor of the exchequer obviously differs sharply from that of a prime minister whose chancellor hates him, covets his office and is determined to wrest it from him. Furthermore, the constraints on every prime minister's ability to act are far greater than usually appears from the outside.

On taking office, every prime minister acquires a number of useful power resources – resources that are his to take advantage of during the whole of his time in office and irrespective of what kind of person he happens to be. They are institutional, not personal. They come with the job. They help define the prime ministership as a political institution.

The British prime minister's best-known institutional resource is also, beyond doubt, his single most important: his total control over the hiring, firing and relocating of every minister in his government. He can appoint whomever he likes to whatever ministerial posts he likes, and similarly he can sack anyone he wants to sack or move them sideways or downward in the ministerial hierarchy. His freedom in this respect is total, except when there is a coalition government and he has no option but to negotiate with the leader or leaders of the other party or parties in the coalition. Even then, he is usually free to dispose of the members of his own party as he sees fit. The only constraint on him – referred to in Chapter 9 – is the need to choose the great majority of his ministers from among the MPs of the governing party or parties. It goes without saying that, in the age of the career politician and with a large proportion of MPs aspiring to ministerial office, the implications of the prime minister's power to appoint (and disappoint) are immense. Any minister who incurs the prime minister's displeasure, for any reason, is liable to find his career abruptly truncated or terminated. A prime minister almost never needs explicitly to threaten. Implicit in the prime minister's power of appointment is a threat that never needs to speak its name.

The prime minister's power under this heading, while immense, is obviously not unconstrained, even when a government is a single-party government. When Nigel Lawson resigned as chancellor of the exchequer in October 1989, Margaret Thatcher replaced him with John Major, whom she presumably thought would be more pliable. But Major – like Lawson, but unlike her – was convinced that Britain should join the European Exchange Rate Mechanism, and he spent the next twelve months working hard at persuading Thatcher to agree. She finally capitulated in October 1990. During the year in question, the arguments over the wisdom or unwisdom of joining the ERM were political and economic; but a significant unstated premise underlying all of them was the fact that Margaret Thatcher, already weak politically, could not afford to lose a second chancellor. If Major resigned, she would be done for (which she soon was anyway). A few years later, Major himself, by now prime minister and beset by criticism of his European policies among Conservative MPs and within his own cabinet, vented his frustration at being unable, in practice, to exercise his nominal power to hire and fire. He told a television journalist:

> Just think it through from my perspective. You are the prime minister, with a majority of eighteen, a party that is still harking back to the golden age that never was and is now invented. I could bring in other people. But where do you think most of this poison is coming from? From the dispossessed and the never-possessed. You and I can think of ex-ministers who are causing all sorts of trouble. Do we want three more of the bastards out there?[2]

Tony Blair, Major's successor in Number 10, would have loved to sack his chancellor, the obstreperous and obstructive Gordon Brown, but always felt it would be politically too risky to do so. Brown in turn was so keen to remove Alistair Darling from the Treasury that 'He ended up offering me just about every job that was going – including the Foreign Office', but Brown backed off when Darling threatened to resign from the government altogether.[3] Personalities apart, David Cameron always had to protect his political position by ensuring that his cabinet contained a sufficiently large number of committed Euro-sceptics. That said, most of a prime minister's difficulties under this heading concern the holders of the topmost positions in the government, positions likely to be held by political heavyweights. Otherwise, his control over ministerial appointments is all but total – and backbench MPs and junior ministers know it.

The British prime minister also possesses a little-noticed institutional resource, one replicated in few other liberal democracies. He can make, remake and unmake entire government departments at will. Under the terms of the Ministers of the Crown Act 1975 (which largely re-enacts provisions previously enacted in 1946):

> Her Majesty [i.e., the prime minister] may by Order in
> Council (a) provide for the transfer to any Minister of the
> Crown of any functions previously exercisable by any other
> Minister of the Crown; (b) provide for the dissolution of
> the government department in the charge of any Minister
> of the Crown and the transfer to or distribution among
> such other Minister or Ministers of the Crown as may
> be specified in the Order of any functions previously
> exercisable by the Minister in charge of that department;
> [and also] (c) direct that functions of any Minister of the
> Crown shall be exercisable concurrently with another
> Minister of the Crown, or shall cease to be so exercisable.

Thus, during the last quarter-century or so, ministerial responsibility for Britain's universities (and much else besides) has wandered from the Department for Education and Science to the Department for Education to the Department for Education and Employment to the Department for Education and Skills to the Department for Innovation, Universities and Skills and thence to the conglomerate Department for Business, Innovation and Skills. Not only do ministers and officials churn: so, frequently, do whole government departments. Sometimes the changes amount to little more than tinkering, but often they bear witness to a prime minister's priorities and at the same time to his ability to impose those priorities on his administration.

Yet another of the prime minister's institutional resources is his power of veto, a power that certainly exists in fact if not in form. In practice, it is all but impossible for other ministers to take important decisions or to pursue controversial objectives without the prime minister's active support or at least his tacit acquiescence. It was a clear indication of Margaret Thatcher's political weakness during 1989 and 1990 that she was finally forced to give way to John Major's insistence – with the foreign secretary's backing – that Britain should join the ERM. Even then, it took her colleagues a whole year to bring her round; and, until she was brought round, nothing could happen. To challenge a prime minister's veto is straightforwardly to challenge his personal authority, and such challenges are not undertaken lightly: they are almost certain to be career-threatening, if not career-terminating. Moreover, a successful challenge would in all probability require the active collaboration of a number of senior cabinet ministers, and any such collaboration, given ministers' differing departmental positions and their competing personal stakes, is most unlikely to be forthcoming. A good measure of the reality of the prime minister's power of veto is that it very seldom has to be exercised.

The prime minister benefits, too, from the fact that, as well as hiring and firing individual ministers, he is also in sole charge of organizing their collective activities. Although the best – i.e., the most authoritative – decisions in the British system are still collective cabinet decisions, the prime minister himself now determines the extent to which the cabinet as a whole will actually function as a collective decision-making body and how far it will merely meet once a week or thereabouts (and only when parliament is sitting) in order to ratify decisions taken elsewhere, to share information and to talk politics. In recent decades, the tilt has been steadily away from actual decision making towards information-sharing, consciousness-raising and (with luck) personal bonding. The fact that more and more people nowadays attend cabinet meetings is a sure sign that little or no real business is transacted at them. However, institutions resembling the cabinet certainly continue to function. Almost all of a government's business that cuts across departmental boundaries – that is, a large proportion of all government business – is discussed sooner or later by cabinet committees comprising cabinet ministers, non-cabinet ministers and often outsiders (for example, from the security services); and it is the prime minister who decides which cabinet committees will exist, who will chair them (including in some instances himself) and who will belong to them or attend their meetings. In other words, the prime minister decides who will decide – no mean source of institutional power in itself.

Another institutional advantage from the prime minister's point of view arises from the fact that the government of the United Kingdom, like the central government of any other large country, is highly departmentalized – which, in practice, means highly compartmentalized. Each department or agency has its own history, culture, way of working and well-defined spheres of operation. Most of the business every department transacts is with itself. It tends to resent outsiders, especially those whom it judges to have no legitimate reason for interfering in what it regards as its internal affairs. The home and justice secretaries know they have to do business with each other (and, alas, with the Treasury), but both of them would resent, and probably successfully resist, any attempt on the part of the health secretary or the transport secretary to give them advice, let alone participate in their internal decision making. But there is one minister who has the right to inquire into every department's affairs: the prime minister. By custom, practice and convention, he has an absolute right to patrol and police the whole of his Whitehall domain. Any efforts he makes to influence a department's or agency's decisions or policies may be resisted, quite possibly successfully, but they are unlikely to be regarded as illegitimate or inappropriate. The fact that, since the 1960s, the prime minister has been expected to answer questions in the House of Commons about anything and everything to do with the government has also entitled him, even more than previously, to ask his own questions about anything and everything that his ministers and officials are up to.

The prime minister thus appears, and is widely believed, to be in a truly commanding position: he or she who must be obeyed. But prime ministers themselves soon discover otherwise. Their power is not all it seems. Their reach almost invariably exceeds their grasp.

For one thing, apart from their ability to hire and fire and to distribute and redistribute departmental responsibilities, prime ministers have almost no executive power. There is almost no one to whom they can issue orders. Their ability to act depends overwhelmingly on the willingness of others to act. Absent that willingness, there is little that a prime minister can do. Most of his power is at second hand, or third, or fourth – or kth, where k is some very large number. His power is largely the power to persuade – and, if sufficiently determined, to nudge, wheedle, harry and cajole, all of which activities consume time and energy and may consume political capital as well. Immigration? That is a matter for the Home Office and its ministers and officials. Prisons? That is a matter for the Ministry of Justice and its ministers and officials. Pensions? That is a matter for the Department for Work and Pensions and the thousands of people who work there. Health? That is a matter for the Department for Health (and then only in relation to the NHS in England). Housing? That is a matter for countless departments and agencies. As for the Treasury, it is – and always has been – everywhere.

In his memoirs, the former chancellor Nigel Lawson recounts how he became involved with the reform of education. Margaret Thatcher established a cabinet committee to examine the issue. She took the chair, with Lawson as one of the committee's members along with the then education secretary, Kenneth Baker. According to Lawson:

> The process would start by Margaret putting forward various ideas . . . and there would then be a general discussion, to which I would contribute my fourpennyworth. At the end of it, Margaret would sum up and give Kenneth his marching orders. He would then return to the next meeting with a worked out proposal which bore little resemblance to what everyone else recalled as having been agreed

at the previous meeting, and owed rather more to his officials . . . After receiving a metaphorical handbagging for his pains, he would then come back with something that corresponded more closely to her ideas, but as often as not without any attempt by his Department to work them out properly.[4]

In that instance, Thatcher's persistence – she had been education secretary herself – eventually yielded results. More commonly, prime ministers are simply ground down. Tony Blair, for example, had only limited success in the field of education. A Department for Education and Skills official recalled: 'It is fair to say that the department was often able to see off the radical options that Number Ten really wanted. The department had the monopoly over information; when it came to understanding the impact of governance changes, the department just knew more than Number Ten did.'[5] Another official from the same department observed: 'The centre appears powerful because it makes announcements, but it then gets very frustrated because they are not turned into delivery.'[6] In almost every insider's account of the British prime ministership, the words 'frustrated' and 'frustration' constantly appear.

The ability of prime ministers to influence developments inside their own administration, let alone outside it, is also affected by their shortage of experienced and knowledgeable staff. Very few people in Whitehall work exclusively for the prime minister as distinct from other ministers. As a result, prime ministers often cannot ensure that their own initiatives are followed up. Similarly, they are not in a position to monitor carefully the progress – or lack of it – of others' initiatives. An aide to Harold Macmillan speculated that his boss must have 'ache[d] to collar a Department for himself' so that he was less reliant on his Downing Street few.[7] Harold Wilson installed in Number 10 a Policy Unit, which subsequent prime ministers perpetuated and which still exists. James Callaghan supplemented discussion in full cabinet (which he encouraged) with regular one-on-one meetings with individual departmental heads. Tony Blair, characteristically ambitious and not over-impressed by some of his ministers, not only retained the Policy Unit but added to it (and subtracted from it) at various points a Strategic Communications Unit, a Research and Information Unit, a Social Exclusion Unit, a Performance and Innovation Unit, a Strategy Unit and a Delivery Unit, the last-named with 'the personal authority of the prime minister'.[8] David Cameron, impressed by Blair as a politician but less impressed by him as prime minister, ditched the whole lot with the exception of the Policy Unit, which he nevertheless entirely revamped.

Certainly the British prime ministership is under-resourced compared with the headships of government of most other liberal democracies, which usually have what amount to prime ministers' departments. Australia and New Zealand each have a Department of the Prime Minister and Cabinet (with the emphasis in both cases on the former, not the latter). Canada's Privy Council Office is, in effect, the Canadian prime minister's department. Since 2001, the office of the German chancellor – the Bundeskanzleramt – has been housed in one of the largest government headquarters buildings in the world, one that dwarfs the White House, not to mention 10 Downing Street. The German chancellor's office functions almost as a government-in-parallel to the traditional government departments. Whether the British prime ministership should be more fully staffed along these lines is debatable; Jonathan Powell, having served as Tony Blair's chief of staff for a decade, believes there is an 'argument for more muscle inside Downing Street' but contrasts the 'small size, personal contact and nimbleness' of Number 10 with the 'ossified, slow and overly bureaucratic' nature of the German chancellor's office.[9] However, the fact remains that, for good or ill, Number 10's sheer institutional modesty helps guarantee that no British prime minister – not even Margaret Thatcher – could possibly hope to become a monarch in all but name.

There are other constraints on prime ministers' power. Although some prime ministers like to give the impression that they know it all – that they have an opinion worth listening to on every conceivable subject – none of them actually does. The prime minister is one person, doing one job, with no more hours in the day than anyone else. Some of them work astonishingly hard – Margaret Thatcher and Gordon Brown were notorious workaholics – but even they could not begin to be masters of every subject that required their attention. Prime ministers in the twenty-first century are frequently out of town, not because they choose to be, but because they have to be. A postwar prime minister seldom had to travel abroad. Modern prime ministers have no option but to attend EU summit meetings, G7 summit meetings, G20 summit meetings and biennial meetings of Commonwealth heads of government, to conduct bilateral negotiations on a wide range of topics – often on distant continents – with foreign ministers and heads of government and to visit British troops serving abroad. (Prime ministers know better than anyone else that foreigners are no longer in any meaningful sense foreign.) Modern prime ministers also have little option but to see the Queen almost every week, to meet and greet visiting foreign heads of state and to attend at least the occasional funeral, possibly including those of their more distinguished predecessors. Time spent in these ways may be time well spent; but it is time not spent on other things.

Prime ministers are also, whether they like it or not, full-time party politicians. Every prime minister is the leader of his party, and he is prime minister *because* he is leader of his party. If he ceases to be leader, he ceases to be prime minister. That means attending innumerable party gatherings, making a well-prepared (and often long-prepared) set-piece speech at his party's annual conference, fund-raising on the party's behalf, listening to (or pretending to listen to) the opinions and grievances of the party's members of parliament and, as we saw in Chapter 3, adjusting his government's rhetoric and possibly also its policies to accommodate the party faithful's more passionately held views.

Every prime minister is aware that his position is precarious or potentially so, and few prime ministers feel wholly secure throughout their time in office. Following the enforced devaluation of sterling in 1967, Harold Wilson's position was continually threatened, with widespread talk of a coup to replace him by Roy Jenkins, his chancellor. At one point, Wilson felt compelled to say, 'I know what is going on. *I* am going on.'[10] Edward Heath was – and felt – more secure because he had recently won an election and was universally expected (although wrongly, as it turned out) to win the next one. During his three years in office, James Callaghan, widely respected in any case, benefited from the fact that he had only just been elected leader of the Labour party. By contrast, Margaret Thatcher felt wholly secure in office only after Britain's victory in the Falklands War in 1982, and even as dominant a prime minister as her was ultimately ousted by a combination of alienated backbenchers, fearful of losing their seats, and unsupportive cabinet colleagues. It was a measure of how far she had lost touch with political reality that she alone was surprised by her fall. Despite having led the Conservatives to victory in 1992, John Major felt highly vulnerable – because he was – throughout his time in office. At one point, in desperation, he resigned the Conservative leadership in order to bolster his position by securing, as he did, re-election as leader of the party.

The position of Tony Blair, impregnable to begin with, looked less and less secure as time went on, especially in the aftermath of the calamitous Anglo-American invasion of Iraq in 2003. Gordon Brown and his allies eventually succeeded in undermining it completely, forcing Blair in 2006 to promise to leave office during the following year. As for Brown, calls from within his own party for his departure from Number 10 began within a few months of his arrival there. A series of high-profile ministerial resignations revealed how far and deep discontent with his leadership extended. As one minister remarked, 'We had our doubts, but he has performed at the lower end of our expectations.'[11] Had Brown not been ousted by the electorate in 2010, he would probably not have long survived in any case. His successor, David Cameron, little loved by many Conservatives, had a potential rival, Boris Johnson, looking over his shoulder – and at his job – right from the beginning. Fortunately for Cameron, Johnson to begin with was mayor of London and not an MP and therefore ineligible for either the party leadership or the premiership. 'Uneasy lies the head that wears a crown,' Henry IV famously complained. British prime ministers could say much the same, and most of them take precautions accordingly – with varying degrees of success.

Rivals and potential rivals apart, most prime ministers, though not all, find themselves trapped in a relationship with cabinet colleagues whom they cannot ignore even if they do not feel threatened by them. Conservatives used to call them 'the big beasts of the jungle': men (they were once always men) who are respected by their colleagues, whose views on a variety of subjects have to be listened to and taken into account and whose departure from the government, were it to happen for any reason, would be a serious embarrassment, not least to the prime minister. In Harold Macmillan's cabinet, R. A. Butler was one such. In Sir Alec Douglas-Home's, there were at least three: Butler himself, Edward Heath and Reginald Maudling. In Harold Wilson's 1964–70 cabinet, there were none to begin with, principally because Labour had been out of office for so long, but by the end Roy Jenkins had undoubtedly become one.

Edward Heath may well have suffered from the lack of a heavyweight but loyal lieutenant after the unexpected death of Iain Macleod, his first chancellor, in 1970. Both Harold Wilson during his second term in office and James Callaghan were surrounded by big beasts: Denis Healey, Tony Crosland (until his unexpected death in 1977), Michael Foot and Tony Benn, the latter two because of their standing in the Labour party. Margaret Thatcher leaned heavily during most of her time in office on the advice of William Whitelaw. 'Every prime minister', she famously said, 'needs a Willie' – but latterly made the mistake of not realizing that Nigel Lawson, her wilful chancellor, and Sir Geoffrey Howe, her soft-spoken chancellor, foreign secretary and finally nominal deputy, had become big beasts without her noticing it. In the end, Howe fatally mauled her. John Major's big beasts were Michael Heseltine and, latterly, Kenneth Clarke.

Tony Blair also had two big beasts, one of whom, John Prescott, was profoundly loyal to him and the other of whom, Gordon Brown, was profoundly not. Blair was far from being master in his own house. He had to share it with Brown, who took over some of the biggest policy rooms entirely for himself – in effect, every aspect of domestic policy that in any way involved money (which almost all of them did) – and chose to fight hand-to-hand with Blair over much of the territory that remained. In practice, Tony Blair's so-called government was a Blair–Brown duopoly. Gordon Brown then chose as his chancellor Alistair Darling, who, as we saw a moment ago, turned out to be a far more formidable beast than Brown had ever imagined. The biggest beast by far in David Cameron's administration was Nick Clegg, in this case not because of his personal qualities, but because of his leadership of the Liberal Democrats. Almost as important to

Cameron was his chancellor, George Osborne, a person his administration could not easily do without. As luck would have it, Cameron and Osborne trusted one another as implicitly as Blair and Brown had not.

The prime ministership is thus largely now what it has been for a long time: institutionalized, constrained, dependent on personalities and circumstances and less capable of being moulded to prime ministers' individual wishes than might be imagined. Nevertheless, there is still good sense in Asquith's dictum about the office being whatever its holder chooses to make of it. Different prime ministers choose to make of it very different things.

To put it crudely, most prime ministers are content to keep the show on the road. They want to *be* prime minister more than they want to *do* anything in particular with the office once they have acquired it. They reckon they can do a better job than any of their rivals; and, if there is a race going on, they want to win it. Contests for the leadership of Britain's political parties are seldom between people who differ profoundly in either ideology or the substance of government policy. They typically have much more to do with personality, competence and the candidates' ability to convince the party electors, whoever they are, that they are potential election-winners. The Labour contest between Michael Foot and Denis Healey in 1980 was one of the rare instances of two party leadership candidates competing along deep-seated ideological lines, although Conservative activists in more recent times have clearly been disinclined to back anyone thought to be pro-European.

Keeping the show on the road means a lot of things,

many of them time- and energy-consuming, some of them of enormous intrinsic importance: responding to crises (from unexpected ministerial resignations to floods, strikes by petrol-tanker drivers and attacks on the World Trade Center), chairing countless ministerial and other meetings, preparing for and answering parliamentary questions, reconciling the differences among cabinet colleagues, maintaining (or trying to maintain) the unity of the government, maintaining (or trying to maintain) party unity, pacifying (or refusing to pacify) backbench critics, appearing confident, well-informed and on top of the job in public, defending the government's record on radio and television, rebuffing assaults on one's position as prime minister and, not least, trying to maximize the chances of one's own party winning the next election. To say of a prime minister that he is not out to achieve great things does not mean that he is not a first-class prime minister. It means only that he is not overly ambitious in policy terms.

Harold Wilson, during both of his terms in office in the 1960s and 1970s, was preoccupied with crisis management, preserving party unity and keeping Britain out of the Vietnam War. His handling of the Labour party's internal difficulties over Britain's membership of the European Community was masterly. He saw off the threats to his leadership mentioned above and departed Downing Street at a time of his own choosing (apparently having realized that he was starting to suffer from a form of dementia). James Callaghan's preoccupations were similar: keeping the cabinet and the Labour party together while at the same negotiating a pact with the Liberals to keep both Labour and himself in office (Labour having lost its overall parliamentary majority). Few but Callaghan could have presided over the government's handling of Britain's dealings with the International Monetary Fund during the 1976 sterling crisis without precipitating cabinet resignations. His chancellor, Denis Healey, no great respecter of persons, described him as 'for most of his time, the best of Britain's postwar prime ministers after Attlee'.[12] John Major resembled both Wilson and Callaghan – although with less success than either – in devoting much of his time to trying to prevent a deeply divided party from falling apart. Gordon Brown, having spent most of his adult life seeking to become prime minister, evidently had little or no idea what to do with the office once he had it – beyond using the expertise he had acquired as chancellor to help dampen the international aftershocks of the 2008 financial crisis. Although unlike Brown in every other respect, David Cameron resembled him in seeming to want the office but in not having any great interest in doing much with it – beyond enjoying its prestige, perks and opportunities for foreign travel. The leading figure in a highly proactive administration, he himself was largely reactive in style, his government's public-relations chief rather than its guiding hand.

Against that background, three prime ministers stand out: Edward Heath, Margaret Thatcher (ironically, given that she and Heath came to loathe each other) and Tony Blair. All three aspired to do more than keep the show on the road. They wanted their governments to change Britain fundamentally, to leave it a different country from the one they found on taking office. At least to begin with, Heath wanted to break with the postwar economic consensus, to champion private enterprise and market forces and to curb trade-union power. All along, he wanted, even more, to anchor Britain securely in the European Community. He largely failed in the first effort. He triumphantly succeeded in the second. Intellectually and personally, and in the absence of rival big beasts, he was easily the dominant figure in his government. Thatcher shared Heath's broad economic aims but was far more dogged and successful than he had been in pursuing them. Britain's privatized industries and much-diminished trade unions are lasting monuments to her time in power. More than any premier since Attlee, she imparted to the whole of her administration a clear sense of purpose – a clearly signposted direction of travel. Once she had sacked the dissident 'wets', ministers and officials during her time in office knew what to do without having to be told.

Blair, a doer and activist by temperament, also had high ambitions. His direction of travel was broadly the same as Thatcher's – pro-business, pro-markets and anti-unions – but with significant deviations. His focus, more than hers, was on 'modernizing' the country (though that word meant more to him than to most people) and improving the quality of public services, searching for ways of making them more efficient and user-friendly. Like Thatcher, but unlike Heath, he greatly valued Britain's American connection. Like Heath, but unlike Thatcher, he was also pro-European. Unlike most prime ministers, Blair was someone who himself took initiatives, driving forward with considerable success competition-oriented reforms, especially in the fields of education and health. He would undoubtedly have accomplished more in his own terms – in other words, been more Thatcher-like – if he had not so often been harried and opposed by his rival and nemesis, Gordon Brown. Moreover, Blair's personal authority, as distinct from his authority as prime minister, substantially vanished in the years following the Iraq invasion. In the early days, the phrase 'Tony wants' coming down the phone line had the force of command. By the end, the same phrase amounted merely to a statement of fact.

Heath changed Britain's relationship with Europe. Thatcher permanently curbed trade-union power and established competition and profit-seeking at the forefront of British economic policy for decades to come. Blair's introduction of market forces into the delivery of public services is unlikely to be reversed any time soon. It is more likely to be extended. Any or all of these things might not have happened at all, or might have happened much later, had Heath, Thatcher and Blair not been in office when they were. Each was a transformative prime minister in that sense.

But they were unusual. The prime minister of the day is undoubtedly the single most powerful individual in the British political system (more powerful even than any of the Murdochs or the president of the European Commission); but, as this chapter should have shown, Britain's prime minister is not remotely all-powerful. Even Heath, Thatcher and Blair were not that. Prime ministers have useful – and often usable – power resources, but many others have power resources too, and every prime minister has only limited brain power, knowledge, time and energy. The fact that so much attention is focused on prime ministers – and that some of them manage to attract so much attention to themselves – helps to create the impression that prime ministers are somehow omnicompetent, even omnipotent; but pomp should never be confused with power, and celebrity is far from being capacity. Someone who worked for President Harry S. Truman reports that, as it became apparent during the summer of 1952 that General Dwight D. Eisenhower would probably succeed him in the Oval Office, Truman would remark, tapping his desk for emphasis, 'He'll sit here, and he'll say, "Do this! Do that!" *And nothing will happen.* Poor Ike – it won't be a bit like the Army. He'll find it very frustrating.'[13] The minority of British prime ministers who seek to accomplish more than merely keeping the show on the road know how that feels.

CHAPTER 12

MPs

Tens of thousands of tourists take photographs of Big Ben every year (as well as photographs of themselves gazing up at it), but that magnificent edifice, however physically imposing, is almost entirely misleading as a symbol of the British system of government as a whole. Parliament's position in the British system is paradoxical and far more complicated than Big Ben makes it appear. On closer inspection, parliament turns out to be simultaneously one of the most influential of Britain's governing institutions and also one of the feeblest. Whether it appears influential or feeble hinges largely on which of its aspects one chooses to inspect.

For MPs of all parties, but especially the governing party or parties, parliament – or at least the House of Commons – functions as a kind of high-class job centre or labour exchange. After all, in the British system the great majority of ministers are drawn from among the ranks of the MPs on the government side of the House, and their ability to perform in the House is one of the criteria by which they are judged. Performing tolerably well in the House is not a sufficient condition for becoming and remaining a minister, but it is a necessary condition. Someone who is inarticulate, ill-prepared or slow-witted is unlikely to find himself on the back seat of a ministerial car to begin with; and, even if he does achieve that eminence, he is unlikely to stay there for long. Prime ministers no longer spend much time in the House of Commons and therefore can seldom judge for themselves the quality of backbenchers' and junior ministers' performance there, but they have spies who can, mostly the government's whips. Somewhat bizarrely, Tony Blair, the most right-wing ever of Labour prime ministers, relied heavily on the judgement of Dennis Skinner, a Labour MP on the far left of the party, because Skinner had the advantage over him of spending most of his time on the green benches. The personal authority even of prime ministers is affected by how well they fare at the dispatch box. The unfortunate Gordon Brown did himself no favours in 2008 when, in the course of reporting to the House on his efforts to deal with that year's financial crisis, he began a sentence by saying, 'We not only saved the world . . .' and paused – too late – before going on to correct himself (he meant to say that his government had saved the banks). Labour MPs as well as Conservatives fell about: Brown 'was buried under a sudden, overwhelming, mountainous avalanche of laughter . . . and general mayhem filled the Chamber'.[1] In an instant, an unusually solemn prime minister secured his place as a permanent figure of fun.

Most conspicuously, the House of Commons is a partisan cockpit, the arena in which, week after week, the major political parties slug it out, mainly, though not only, at noon on Wednesdays during prime minister's questions. More than one party leader has expressed the hope that prime minister's questions could be turned into something more elevated than a Punch and Judy show. But they have hoped in vain, and prime minister's questions remains the purest expression of Britain's culture of adversarial politics. The party leaders hope to score off each other, partly in order to impress the public, but mainly in order to impress their own followers, especially their own party's MPs on the benches behind them. A prime minister who cannot dominate the leader of the opposition at question time, despite having the entire resources of the state at his disposal, is soon in trouble. John Major's personal authority suffered greatly from his inability to cope in the House of Commons with Tony Blair as leader of the opposition, just as Gordon Brown found it hard to deal with David Cameron. Thatcher and Blair almost never suffered in this way. Opinion polls suggest that, apart from enabling the prime minister, if he chooses, to keep his government as a whole on a tight rein, the principal effect of prime minister's questions – especially now that they are shown on television – is to arouse the ardour of the country's most avid partisans and to alienate almost everyone else. They certainly elicit little information.

In another familiar guise, parliament is a debating society, with MPs debating government and opposition motions in a stylized, ritualistic way. There was a time when parliamentary debates, whatever their impact on the government of the day, commanded a considerable amount of public attention. In the years immediately after the war, copies of *Hansard* – the substantially verbatim transcript of every speech made in both parliamentary houses – sold upward of 10,000 copies every week. As late as the 1960s, the main broadsheet newspapers still carried full accounts of every day's parliamentary debates, filed by what were called their 'parliamentary correspondents'. To this day, there is a Parliamentary Channel on BBC Television, and BBC Radio 4 regularly broadcasts reports of proceedings *Yesterday in Parliament*. However, although there is no reason to think that the quality of parliamentary debates has declined, outsiders' interest in them certainly has, and coverage of politics in the media nowadays concentrates almost exclusively on party politics rather than on the substance of the debates in either house of parliament. In the twenty-first century, public affairs are discussed and debated, not in parliament but overwhelmingly on broadcast and social media.

Strangely, however, although they receive much less public attention than they once did, set-piece parliamentary debates are probably just as important now as they were in the past, at least since voting along strict party lines in the House of Commons became the norm more than a century ago. Contrary to widespread belief, voting in the House of Commons is now less strictly along partisan lines than it was as recently as a generation ago. Not only has the party system as a whole become more fragmented: so have the parties themselves. Although a majority of career politicians may also be careerists, a significant minority are not; on the contrary, they are willing, even eager, to defy their party's whips whenever they feel sufficiently strongly about something. Professionalism in politics has brought with it a heightened wilfulness and assertiveness – an increased reluctance to be pushed around. In the nineteenth century, Walter Bagehot contemptuously dismissed Conservative backbenchers, especially those representing shire county constituencies, as 'the finest brute votes in Europe'.[2] Few today would be as dismissive of the present generation of Conservative MPs. It was a Labour member who, when asked about the power of the whips, replied, 'I call them not so much whips as feather dusters.'[3] During the 2010 parliament, roughly one-third of all the votes that took place in the House of Commons witnessed a rebellion of some sort by nominal supporters of the Cameron government. That parliament was the most rebellious since the Second World War, with well over half of all Conservative and Liberal Democrat MPs rebelling against the government at least once, some of them many times.[4] Far fewer MPs today than in the past are mere lobby fodder.

Already, long before the rumbustiousness of the current cohorts of MPs, debates in the House of Commons, and the discussions and arguments that swirled around them, often affected the behaviour of governments. Governments seldom feared outright defeat, but they did fear large-scale, embarrassing rebellions, and they were anxious, if at all possible, not to alienate substantial sections of their followers. In the continual give-and-take between ministers and government backbenchers, ministers gave almost as often as they took. The authority, energies and public standing of a government that constantly had to threaten and cajole its own parliamentary followers, as distinct from persuading them, would soon be sapped. Writing as long ago as the late 1960s, a percipient *Financial Times* journalist showed how, again and again, governments in the postwar decades had given way in the face of backbench pressure – often as a result of discussions and negotiations in ministers' offices and the corridors of the House of Commons – instead of running the risk of being embarrassed or humiliated on the floor of the House.[5] A rebellion in the division lobbies that does not take place may well be more significant than one that does: the government has already compromised. Furthermore, prime ministers and other cabinet ministers routinely factor their assessment of backbench opinion into their calculations *before* launching radical new initiatives. It is no accident that the government chief whip is, in effect, a full member of the cabinet. He is certainly someone the prime minister frequently consults.

The greater willingness of backbench MPs in recent decades to rebel against their party's whips has substantially increased their collective influence. More often than in the past, ministers run scared of backbenchers – and, despite their best efforts, are very occasionally caught up with. In the end, only fifty-one backbench Conservative MPs in 1988 voted openly in the Commons against the Thatcher government's poll tax; but widespread backbench unhappiness with the tax and Margaret Thatcher's handling of it contributed substantially, probably decisively, to her subsequent fall. In 1992, twenty-six Conservative backbenchers voted against the Major government's handling of the Maastricht Treaty despite John Major's insistence that, for him, this was a resigning issue. A few months later, twenty-seven Conservative backbenchers defied a three-line whip and actually caused the government to lose a key vote on the same treaty. The vote was reversed the next day only when the prime minister announced that the government proposed to treat the issue as a matter of confidence. Throughout his seven years as prime minister, Major ran scared of the Maastricht rebels and their allies; having only a minuscule parliamentary majority, he had no option. In 2003, Tony Blair, despite having a much larger majority, suffered a severe blow to his authority when 139 Labour MPs – nearly half of all the party's backbenchers – voted to oppose the impending Anglo-American invasion of Iraq. Most dramatically of all, in 2013 the House of Commons rebuffed by 285 votes to 272 the proposal of David Cameron and his coalition government that Britain should join the U.S. in taking military action against the Syrian regime, following its use of chemical weapons against its own people. The motion would have carried but for the defection of thirty-nine government backbenchers: thirty Conservatives and nine Liberal Democrats. On that occasion, parliament intervened – for the first time in well over a century – to change decisively the direction of British foreign policy. Like Major before him, David Cameron found himself under constant pressure from vociferous Conservative backbenchers on the issue of Europe, to which pressure he often gave way.

Debates in parliament occasionally have momentous consequences even if unaccompanied by formal votes. No vote took place in the House of Commons on 13 November 1990, but Sir Geoffrey Howe's resignation speech that day, reinforcing the discontent with Margaret Thatcher's leadership style that already existed on the Conservative benches, effectively destroyed her premiership. Not since the so-called Narvik debate on the lacklustre British campaign in Norway against Nazi Germany in the spring of 1940, which toppled Neville Chamberlain and made way for Churchill, had parliamentary proceedings resulted so precipitously in a change at the very top of British government. Members on all sides of the House gasped as Howe – once one of Thatcher's closest political allies – quietly, almost gently, rendered her position untenable:

> The conflict of loyalty, of loyalty to my Right Honourable friend the Prime Minister – and, after all, in two decades together that instinct of loyalty is still very real – and of loyalty to what I perceive to be the true interests of the nation, has become all too great. I no longer believe it possible to resolve that conflict from within this government. That is why I have resigned. In doing so, I have done what I believe to be right for my party and my country. The time has come for others to consider their own response to the tragic conflict of loyalties with which I have myself wrestled for perhaps too long.[6]

Within a fortnight, she was gone. Gordon Brown's saving-the-world gaffe a couple of decades later similarly cost him dear, though not quite so spectacularly.

Backbench MPs' greater willingness to rebel has been augmented in recent years by the increased activism of those obscurely named bodies, parliamentary select committees. There is nothing particularly 'select' about them. Instead, they comprise small groups of backbench MPs that specialize in monitoring the activities of individual Whitehall departments, so that, for example, the Commons Health Committee covers the Department of Health and the Transport Committee the Department for Transport. The arrangements linking select committees with individual departments were put in place in 1979, but initially their composition was effectively in the hands of the parties' whips, thereby limiting their capacity to function on a non-party basis, to produce unanimous reports and to be critical of the government of the day. Since 2010, however, chairmanships of the committees have been shared out among the parties and, more important, the chairs themselves have been elected by secret ballots of the House of Commons as a whole. The result has been the emergence of select committees considerably more independent-minded than in the past and readier to publish reports highly critical of the government of the day. Although the committees are routinely described as 'influential', their reports seldom exert that much influence. They are typically produced after the developments and events that they deal with; and although these committees are specialist, bizarrely they are not charged with examining legislative proposals emanating from the very departments whose work they are supposed to be monitoring. In other words, they have the least influence where they might be expected to have the most. The importance of the departmental select committees lies principally in the fact that their activities – which include holding public hearings – force both ministers and officials to pay far more attention than they otherwise would to the views of rank-and-file parliamentarians. Ministers and officials bear witness to the amount of time they spend preparing for their appearances before select committees and, even more, before the long-established Public Accounts Committee. The Public Accounts Committee, always tough, has latterly become ferocious.

It is worth adding that, although the media and the general public have largely lost interest in the substance – as distinct from the pure politics – of parliamentary proceedings, ministers and senior civil servants have not. Officials, in particular, are often close students of *Hansard*, at least in connection with subjects that they are professionally interested in. Speeches in parliament and the views expressed at select committee hearings often make serious substantive points, and they can warn of possible political trouble ahead. Ministers are seldom minded to ignore the prevailing mood at Westminster, not least because, in the British system, they themselves live much of their political lives at that location. Gossip in the Westminster village, as in all villages, can be cruel as well as kind. Gossip and fashionable opinion can often exert a kind of osmotic pressure.

Parliament – the House of Commons in particular – is thus a labour exchange, a partisan cockpit, a debating society, a maker and breaker of reputations and – to a modest extent, with the advent of departmental select committees – an investigative agency. But parliament is supposed also to be something else: a law-making body, a legislature. After all, the preamble to every Act of parliament solemnly intones:

> Be it enacted by the Queen's most Excellent Majesty, by
> and with the advice and consent of the Lords Spiritual
> and Temporal, and Commons, in this present Parliament
> assembled, and by the authority of the same, as follows . . .

Obviously, in passing any Act of parliament, parliament itself has given its consent to the Act, but has it also given its advice, whether wise or otherwise? Exactly how large parliament looms in the totality of Britain's governing arrangements depends largely – but not wholly – on how well or badly it performs its purely legislative functions. In this connection, parliament has changed scarcely at all since the classic era of postwar government described in Chapter 1.

The government still controls the vast bulk of the parliamentary timetable and introduces the vast bulk of proposed legislation. The first reading of a bill is a mere formality, and the outcome of the second-reading debate, given the government's majority in the House of Commons, is still normally a foregone conclusion. The committee stage on most bills still serves mainly to give ministers a chance, by way of amendments, to correct mistakes that they turn out to have made themselves in the original versions of their bills. The report stage and the third reading, both in the full House, are also largely formalities. However, the incumbent government does not invariably get its way. In 2006, and again in 2008, the Blair and Brown governments were forced to abandon efforts to extend the period during which terrorism suspects could be held without charge; in 2012, the Cameron government was similarly forced to abandon its proposals for reform of the House of Lords. On these occasions, the government faced strenuous opposition from among its own backbenchers and in the House of Lords. But such setbacks are rare. Most of the time, the government of the day gets its way on what it believes to be the essentials of its bills. Considered as a legislative assembly, parliament typically plays only a peripheral role. In this respect, the British system is very nearly as government-centred and power-hoarding as it ever was.

A number of features of this largely unreformed legislative process stand out. One is the hard-and-fast distinction between departmental select committees and what are called public bill committees. The select committees specialize in health, transport, education or whatever. The public bill committees – which used to be called standing committees – do not specialize in anything. The select committees, as we noted a moment ago, are not charged with examining legislation falling within their subject area, indeed are not allowed to go anywhere near legislation of any kind. Instead, the parties' whips decide who will sit on the various public bill committees, which are created ad hoc to deal with individual bills, and their decisions owe more to members' record of party loyalty and their availability to serve on any given committee than on their knowledge – which they usually lack – of the details, or even the broad field, of the bill's subject matter. Substantive knowledge and expertise are at a discount, especially on the government side: experts (or self-proclaimed experts) are liable to make trouble.

Public bill committees are highly partisan in both composition and spirit, and they look like and function like mini-parliaments, with the government and opposition benches facing each other. Opposition MPs oppose. Government ministers and backbenchers are there simply to ensure that the bill under consideration passes. The vast majority of the amendments accepted by public bill committees are government amendments. Government supporters on these committees – some bored out of their minds – frequently snooze or deal surreptitiously with their constituency correspondence (or sign their Christmas cards). Very often the government lays down a timetable for the progress of a government bill, with the result that large parts of it, especially if the bill is long and complicated, go unexamined and undiscussed. Members of the public may submit written evidence to public bill committees, and the committees themselves are empowered to summon witnesses. However, the committees receive any written and oral evidence (if they receive any at all) only after a bill has been read a second time in the full House – that is, only after the House as a whole has accepted the bill's broad outline. There is little evidence to suggest that the committees' evidence-taking powers, to the extent that they are used, make any significant difference to anything. Public bill committees thus mostly go through the motions. They are not desperately dignified, and they are certainly not efficient.

Elements missing from the legislative process, thus described, are legion. Apart from private members' bills, which seldom deal with matters of great significance and which in any case almost always require government support to have any chance of being enacted, parliament plays little or no part in the gestation of legislation. Neither select committees nor their individual members initiate legislation; public bill committees deal only with legislation that is already on track. In other words, the government acts: parliament and its committees react. The government is active, parliament and its committees passive. Interested parties lobby the government in the course of its gestation of legislation, and ministers frequently go through the largely cosmetic process of public consultation; but there are few parliamentary forums for head-scratching, evidence-taking and extensive discussion and debate. Civil servants are allowed to advise ministers, but are not allowed to advise members of parliament except on behalf of ministers and effectively as their mouthpieces. The entire process is stifling and stifled.

Both in the full House and in public bill committees, party competition and antagonisms are almost invariably to the fore. Relations between government and opposition are formally correct and may even on occasion be friendly, but governments seldom reach out to the opposition with a view to establishing cross-party agreement. The leader of the opposition may be a potential future prime minister, but so long as he remains leader of the opposition his capacity to influence legislation is minimal to the point of non-existence. During one leadership contest being conducted by the then main opposition party, a parliamentary sketch writer rightly pointed out that 'a lot of effort was being expended in pursuit of a job that will confer on the winner . . . roughly as much raw power as the Hon. Sec. of a crown green bowling club'.[7] In a large number of democratic legislatures – in the German Bundestag, for example – members wear two hats. They are partisans, of course, often ardently so, but they also see themselves as legislators, in the business of trying to improve the quality of legislation even if that legislation is being promoted by a party or parties other than their own. By contrast, the UK parliament's procedures encourage MPs to wear only one hat, adorned with their party's colours.

There is, however, an exception to that general rule – not as yet an important exception, but one that might in time become so. It is the procedural device known somewhat clumsily as 'pre-legislative scrutiny'. Under this procedure, originally introduced with little fanfare during the 1990s, the government of the day still takes the initiative; but, instead of formally introducing a fully worked-out bill of its own, it publishes instead a draft bill, which may be quite rudimentary, which it then invites one of the departmental select committees, or a joint committee of MPs and peers, to consider in detail. The committee in question can then accept some of the government's draft clauses, reject others and, if it wants to, propose new clauses of its own. The committee is expected to function on a non-partisan, Bundestag-like basis. On that basis, a joint Commons–Lords committee developed the Communications Act 2003, generally thought (including by the government) to have been a substantial improvement on the government's original proposals. If a draft bill is referred to a committee for pre-legislative scrutiny, the committee is free to seek advice wherever it can, to hold hearings and to elicit written comments. Unfortunately, although successive governments since the 1990s have published draft bills in considerable numbers, a large proportion of them have been minor (e.g., the Draft Groceries Code Adjudicator Bill 2011), by no means all have been subjected to detailed scrutiny and the recommendations contained in several scrutiny committee reports have been rejected so summarily as to raise questions about why the relevant draft bill was made available for scrutiny in the first place. For instance, a House of Commons scrutiny committee had this to say about the coalition government's Draft Local Audit Bill 2012:

> We have a number of serious concerns regarding the practicability, workability and completeness of the proposals outlined in the draft Bill.

The draft Bill fails to provide adequate safeguards to guarantee the independence of audit, it falls short in addressing many of the technical aspects of audit and is silent on how high quality statutory local audit will be obtained and reviewed in the new regime.[8]

But the government chose to press on regardless. The truth is that, despite the existence of the new procedure, the government of the day remains – at least for the time being – fully in charge. It decides whether or not to publish draft bills and typically decides not to publish drafts of its most important bills, and it alone decides whether or not to pay any attention to what parliament's scrutineers may have said. Pre-legislative scrutiny has not become routine. Successful – that is, effective – scrutiny remains a special event.

This chapter has concentrated so far on the House of Commons. That is because the power of the House of Commons, whatever its limitations, far outstrips that of the House of Lords. The Lords are bound by the loss of their absolute veto more than a century ago, by the terms of the Salisbury convention referred to in Chapter 1 and by their consciousness that, in the end, they lack legitimacy and therefore have no option but to defer ultimately to the democratically elected lower house. The most important government ministers seldom sit in the Lords, where in any case there are few ministers (with the result that those few are grossly overworked, given that they are responsible for taking through the House all government legislation). The debates in the House of Lords are frequently of higher quality than those in the Commons, being less partisan in character and with men and women of great knowledge and practical experience often taking part. But the House of Lords' influence, while not negligible, is largely confined to using its delaying power to force government ministers to think again, or even to back down, rather than see their legislative timetable disrupted. The Lords can be a nuisance, and people likely to be a nuisance can often, up to a point, get their way. But the House of Lords is an essentially auxiliary body, not a politically or governmentally crucial one. Its members stand the best chance of getting their way when they are in league, deliberately or not, with like-minded and potentially rebellious backbenchers on the government side in the Commons. Even then, it is from the Commons that the real power emanates.

The weakness of the House of Commons as a legislative body has consequences. One is to make it easy for governments to commit blunders: parliament collectively is seldom in a position to stop them. In order to stop them, backbench and opposition MPs and peers would need far more in the way of time, resources and procedural opportunities than they currently possess. They would need to be able to force ministers to deliberate more fully and carefully before acting and to act less often with precipitous haste. Modern ministers are typically in a hurry, and people in a hurry often fall over their own feet. Parliament in the form of Conservative MPs and ministers destroyed Margaret Thatcher, but parliament collectively failed to forestall the introduction of the preposterous poll tax. As a result of parliament's collective inattention to detail, the unfortunate Child Support Act 1991 reached the statute book, inflicting misery on hundreds of thousands. The government's Learning and Skills Act reached the statute book in 2000, and was then implemented, without anyone in parliament seeming to notice that it effectively handed crooks a licence to commit fraud, which they did on a large scale. The legislation providing for the creation of a grotesquely ill-conceived private-finance-initiative scheme for refurbishing and upgrading the London Underground – one that probably in the end cost taxpayers in the region of £20 billion–£30 billion (at early 2000s prices) – was inserted towards the end of the bill that in 1999–2000 established the Greater London Authority. The bill was enormous, one of the most voluminous in history, MPs' attention was distracted and almost none of them noticed the implications of what was being proposed. Even if more of them had noticed, they would almost certainly have been unable to halt the government's juggernaut. Parliament – in the form of the Lords as well as the Commons – was more successful towards the end of the 2000s in delaying the introduction of universal ID cards; but, even then, an Identity Cards Act, although much amended, did reach the statute book in 2006, and it was left to a new government, with a differently constituted parliamentary majority, to repeal it in 2010. Overall, parliament's record in the vitally important field of blunder-prevention has not been impressive.

More generally, and by common consent, the deeply flawed manner in which many laws are made in the UK can result, and often does, in deeply flawed laws. Ministers often want something, but are not entirely clear what they want. Even so, they are keen that whatever laws they do want are enacted at speed. They therefore insist that these laws, on which they are so keen, are drafted at speed. As most ministers are like-minded in this regard, the parliamentary timetable becomes hopelessly overcrowded. Because of this overcrowding – that is, the sheer volume of new legislation – the House of Commons, whose legislative procedures are flawed in any case, is given insufficient time in which to examine in detail the government's proposals. Bills thereupon arrive in the House of Lords having not been properly considered in the House of Commons. The Lords then have too little time in which to consider them themselves. Meanwhile, ministers, having acted at speed, begin to repent. However, they do not repent at leisure. On the contrary, they repent at even greater speed, introducing dozens upon dozens of amendments, some of which amend previous amendments. Many government bills, already convoluted, sometimes because of their technical nature, have become even more convoluted by the time they reach the statute book. Secondary legislation, introduced to give effect to all this primary legislation, is also put in place at high speed. As a Hansard Society report put it succinctly, 'There is currently a serious mismatch between the scrutiny mission of Parliament and its capacity to carry out that mission.'[9]

The cumulative outcome is a bloated statute book and innumerable volumes of secondary legislation replete with laws, rules and regulations that are – again by common consent – ill-drafted, over-complicated, totally incomprehensible, internally inconsistent, only loosely related to one another and in imminent danger of resulting in wholly unintended consequences. Provisions relating to the same matter are often scattered over a number of separate statutes. One exasperated judge was echoing the sentiments of many of his colleagues when he complained vehemently in court:

[1] Section 174(1)(b)(i) of the Criminal Justice Act 2003 requires a court passing sentence to explain to an offender in ordinary language the effect of the sentence. This requirement has been in place since 1991. These proceedings show that, in relation to perfectly ordinary consecutive sentences imposed since the coming into force of much of the Criminal Justice Act 2003, this task is impossible. Indeed, so impossible that it has taken from 12 noon until 12 minutes to five, with a slightly lengthier short adjournment than usual for reading purposes, to explain the relevant statutory provisions to me, a professional judge.

[2] The position at which I have arrived and which I will explain in detail in a moment is one of which I despair. It is simply unacceptable in a society governed by the rule of law for it to be well nigh impossible to discern from statutory provisions what a sentence means in practice. That is the effect here.[10]

In the course of giving evidence to the House of Commons Political and Constitutional Reform Committee, someone who had previously served as a parliamentary counsel but had gone on to work for a City law firm vented his frustration at having to watch from outside as the government and parliament made a mess of writing new statutes:

When I was Parliamentary Counsel, I used to think that I was working away writing an Act and there were clever lawyers in the City waiting to tear it to pieces and cunningly find holes in it. One of the most eye-opening experiences I have had as part of the parliamentary team in Berwin Leighton Paisner [his new law firm] has been seeing that lawyers are not there waiting to pick holes in it. They are mostly sitting there waiting to make it work, and the frustrating thing – and we had this with the Localism Bill, for example – is that sometimes you have expertise sitting there wanting to help, being able to see that this is not going to work, being able to watch it go wrong, and not being able to play a real part in controlling it and helping to make it work.[11]

His view was that informed outsiders should be fully engaged in the initial drafting of a bill and, subsequently, in a more thoroughgoing process of pre-legislative scrutiny. Pressed to say whom he believed was responsible for this currently unsatisfactory state of affairs, the witness pointed the finger of blame squarely at the House of Commons itself. 'That question I do not need to duck,' he replied. 'You are responsible.'[12]

As a political institution, parliament – especially the House of Commons – is thus clearly close to the heart of Britain's governing arrangements. As a legislative assembly, it is evidently less so. The towering presence of Big Ben gives a benign impression, but also a misleading one.

CHAPTER 13

Judges

It would never have occurred to anyone writing a book about British government and politics during the postwar period to include a chapter devoted to Britain's judges and courts. They were of no political consequence. If judges and lawyers became newsworthy, it was usually because they had made fools of themselves. On one occasion, Mr Justice Harman, a leading figure in the aged-and-eccentric school of judging, emerged from his house to hear a case that had suddenly arisen only to find himself surrounded by a scrum of journalists and photographers. He aimed a kick at one of them but connected instead with his own taxi driver. A caption in the *Sun* the next day read: 'It's me nuts, m'Lord.'[1] During the trial for obscenity of *Lady Chatterley's Lover* in 1960, Mervyn Griffith-Jones, prosecuting for the crown, caused much hilarity by asking members of the jury whether the novel was the kind of book 'you would even wish your wife or your servants to read'. His reputation seemingly intact, he was promoted to the judicial bench soon afterwards.

That era now seems very long ago. Today, judges, courts and the judgments of courts are constantly in the news, as are the sometimes profound disagreements between judges, who, apart from handing down their judgments, usually maintain a dignified silence, and elected politicians, who frequently think it their duty to do the opposite, with tabloid newspapers always eager to wade in. Because so many contentious cases involve issues such as immigration, asylum, penal policy and human rights, home secretaries have often been among the first to castigate the judiciary. The courts frequently overturned decisions made by Michael Howard, home secretary between 1993 and 1997; on one occasion Howard used an interview on BBC Radio 4's *Today* programme to slag off, without naming, one of his judicial tormentors. The home secretary's contemptuous comments would probably have been ruled out of order had they been made in the House of Commons. When the same minister repeatedly insisted that prison 'worked', a senior law lord publicly begged to differ. One of Howard's successors at the Home Office, David Blunkett, was especially combative. When a judge ruled that a newly enacted piece of legislation violated the European Convention on Human Rights, Blunkett told the BBC, 'Frankly, I'm personally fed up with having to deal with a situation where parliament debates issues and the judges then overturn them.'[2] One of Blunkett's successors, Theresa May, was visibly and audibly irritated by the judiciary's repeated refusal to allow her to deport to Jordan an alleged terrorist called Abu Qatada. (She succeeded only when the Jordanian government undertook not to use evidence obtained by torture in the course of Qatada's trial on terrorism charges.) No less than the prime minister, David Cameron, sounded remarkably like Blunkett in his condemnation of the European Court of Human Rights' repeated insistence that the UK should no longer deprive all prisoners serving custodial sentences of the right to vote. 'If Parliament decides that prisoners should not get the vote,' he told workers at a tea factory in Stockton-on-Tees, 'then I think they damn well shouldn't. It should be a national decision taken by our Parliament.' He reckoned the court's wings should be clipped.[3]

The judges' unexpected (including by them) rise to political prominence began during the late 1950s and 1960s with the arrival on the scene of a new and more confident generation of judges serving in the Court of Appeal and on the Judicial Committee of the House of Lords, the predecessor to today's Supreme Court. Whereas previous judicial generations had been brought up to believe that it was British judges' duty to remain in the background and always, when in doubt, to defer to parliament and ministers, many of the newcomers – led by Lords Reid, Diplock, Wilberforce and Scarman – believed that citizens in a democracy had certain rights and that it was the courts' duty to protect those rights even if it meant overruling individual ministers and conceivably even parliament itself. Legal education in the UK began to be permeated by ideas of checks and balances and the separation of powers, with the courts, even in Britain, having a duty to be one of those 'powers'. A substantial proportion of British judges travelled to judicial conferences abroad, especially elsewhere in the Commonwealth, where they encountered the idea that a proper liberal democracy should have a constitution, whether written or not, and that that constitution, embodying the basic principles of the rule of law, should take precedence over ordinary law. Judges in Britain were also aware of the active role being played by the

U.S. Supreme Court in promoting social change, especially civil rights; the Supreme Court's ruling in *Brown v. Board of Education* in 1954, when the court unanimously struck down the principle of racially segregated public education, was almost as familiar to British lawyers as to Americans. Moreover, judges in Britain from an early date were aware of, and influenced by, developments in jurisprudence emanating from the continent of Europe. Altogether, the judges were becoming increasingly restive.

Their restlessness showed itself in a variety of ways. The law lords decided that they should no longer be bound absolutely by precedent. Later they decided that, when interpreting a statute, they should be prepared, if need be, to consult relevant parliamentary proceedings and ministerial statements and should no longer limit themselves to trying to construe the statute's words as they were set down on the printed page. Above all, the judges increasingly made use of their long-established power of judicial review, a power that, although never abandoned in principle, had substantially fallen into abeyance in practice. Not so long ago, few non-lawyers had ever heard the phrase 'judicial review'. Nowadays there is scarcely a non-lawyer who is *not* familiar with it – even if he or she may not be quite sure what it means.

In essence, the judges' power of judicial review is – and was – straightforward. Judges have always had the power under the common law to declare null and void actions by ministers, civil servants and other persons in public authority that either exceeded their powers under the law or else violated some basic principle of the rule of law (for instance, actions taken in a manifestly unfair manner). Beginning in the 1960s, the judges began to exercise that traditional power more often and robustly. But they also expanded it substantially – indeed, in the words of two eminent authorities, 'in spectacular fashion'.[4] They began by deciding that the actions of public officials must not only be in strict accordance with the law: if challenged, the public officials in question must be able to produce strong evidence or give good reasons for acting as they did. In one case, the House of Lords in its then judicial capacity ruled that, just because a certain statute gave a government minister the power to decide whether or not to refer a citizen's complaint to an independent committee, the minister was not entitled, in making his decision, to do so on any ground that suited his purposes or just happened to occur to him. If he decided not to refer the citizen's complaint to the committee, his grounds for doing so must be appropriate to the circumstances of the specific case. Successive governments sought to make judicial review more difficult or impossible by writing into statutes provisions – so-called 'ouster clauses' – designed to achieve that effect. But the courts increasingly found ways around those clauses, including, in effect, by simply ignoring them. Judges, not ministers or their minions, would decide what were proper ways of proceeding.

Quite soon, by the standards of the law's stately progress, they went further. They began to take an interest, not merely in administrative procedures (often called 'due process') but in the intrinsic reasonableness of the decisions that ministers and other public officials arrived at. In a 1985 case, Lord Diplock, speaking on behalf of the law lords, defined an unreasonable decision – or, as he put it, an 'irrational' decision – as one 'so outrageous in its defiance of logic or of accepted moral standards that no sensible person who had applied his mind to the question to be decided could have arrived at it'.[5] A decade later, the Court of Appeal expanded on even that elastic definition when it struck down a rule introduced by a prison governor empowering him or her to censor correspondence between prisoners and their solicitors. The court's language was significant. It held that incarcerated prisoners had a 'constitutional right', no less, to communicate confidentially with their legal advisers, a right that could be impinged upon only if the authorities could show that there was some 'pressing need' to do so.[6] Soon after that, the House of Lords declared that the then home secretary – Michael Howard again – had no legal right retrospectively to increase the length of a prisoner's sentence beyond that imposed by the original trial judge. In his judgment at the conclusion of the case, Lord Steyn was vehement:

> Parliament does not legislate in a vacuum. Parliament legislates for a European liberal democracy based upon the principles and traditions of the common law . . . and . . . unless there is the clearest provision to the contrary, Parliament must be presumed not to legislate contrary to the rule of law.[7]

Lord Steyn did not go on to say, at least on that occasion, how he would respond if parliament did lay down 'the clearest provision to the contrary'.

Needless to say, ministers and civil servants find judicial

review irksome, especially since it is now resorted to on an almost industrial scale (although subject in its initial stages to a fast-track procedure). A booklet entitled *The Judge Over Your Shoulder*, published by the government for the guidance of officials, has gone through multiple editions, and efforts have been made to limit access to judicial review by, for example, increasing some of the fees charged and imposing tighter time-limits on applications for review. But judicial review is now woven into the fabric of the British constitution and seems all but certain to remain there – a direct consequence of the judges' new-found confidence and assertiveness.

The judges thus brought the burden of judicial review upon themselves, but the burden of administering European Union law in the UK was landed upon them. They had no choice in the matter. In passing the European Communities Act in 1972, parliament in effect – if unwittingly, at least on the part of some MPs – ensured that henceforth the law of the European Community would trump British law whenever the two came into conflict. A number of years before Britain joined the European Economic Community (as it then was), that body's supreme court, the European Court of Justice, had determined that from now on Community law was to take precedence over the domestic laws of the member states. The court's language in coming to that conclusion was forthright:

> The transfer by the States from their domestic legal
> systems to the Community legal system of rights and
> obligations arising under the Treaty [of Rome] carries with

it a permanent limitation of their sovereign rights, against which a subsequent unilateral act incompatible with the concept of the Community cannot prevail.[8]

In case any doubt remained, the British House of Lords in its judicial capacity later determined in a landmark judgment that it would go so far as to 'disapply' an Act of the UK parliament – the Merchant Shipping Act 1988 – solely on the ground that its terms contradicted those of relevant European Community legislation.

The European Court of Justice, in its wisdom, imposed further tasks on the UK's courts – on all of them, not just the House of Lords or, later, the Supreme Court. The European court came to realize early on that, if the developing body of Community law were to be given practical effect throughout the Community, then the courts and judges of the member states would need to be involved. A task on that mammoth scale could not possibly be undertaken by the European court alone: it would soon be overwhelmed, especially as the Community grew. In any case, the member states' courts and judges, in the court's view, had the great advantages of being 'sufficiently numerous and proximate and familiar to citizens'.[9] Thus, at the very moment Britain joined the European Community, British judges found themselves saddled with the task of enforcing European law within the UK. Moreover, the law in question was not only law that related to the rarefied relations between the institutions of the Community and the governments of the member states. On the contrary, from now on all manner of ordinary individuals and organizations could use the British courts to assert their rights under European law, including against the British government. Whether they liked it or not – and not all judges did like it – Britain's courts were now also, in effect, European courts.

These new responsibilities of Britain's courts undoubtedly emanated from a place called 'Europe' – in this case, in the form of what is now the European Union. More recently, the British courts have acquired yet more heavy responsibilities, and these responsibilities, too, have associations with 'Europe' – but they have nothing whatsoever to do with either the European Union or its bureaucracy in Brussels. Britain's courts would be involved even if the EU did not exist. In this connection, the multipurpose adjective 'European' is merely confusing.

Shortly after the Second World War, Britain and a number of other European countries created a body called the Council of Europe in the interests of furthering co-operation among European governments and safeguarding Europe's common culture and heritage. Its principal early achievements included the adoption of a European Convention on Human Rights – one of whose principal authors was the Conservative MP Sir David Maxwell Fyfe, whom we encountered in Chapter 4 – and, soon afterwards, the creation of the European Court of Human Rights, composed of jurists from all over Europe and based in the French city of Strasbourg (hence frequent references to it as 'the Strasbourg court'). More than forty assorted states, including Russia and Azerbaijan, are members of the Council of Europe. Fewer than thirty states, all of them democracies, belong to the European Union, a completely different entity (even if, to confuse matters further, the European Union's parliament also meets in Strasbourg).

Clement Attlee's postwar government ratified the Council of Europe's human-rights convention; later, in 1966, another Labour government, that of Harold Wilson, granted British citizens the right to appeal directly to the court. The Wilson government went further and explicitly acknowledged the jurisdiction of the European Court of Human Rights in respect of cases brought by individuals against the UK government and other UK public authorities. The results were far-reaching. Large numbers of British cases – some of them affecting important matters such as the inhuman treatment of terrorist suspects in Northern Ireland, the use of corporal punishment in schools, access to legal aid and the deportation of individuals to countries where they might be tortured – found their way to Strasbourg and were decided there. The English courts, followed after some delay by those in Scotland, responded by taking the Strasbourg court's judgments seriously, by permitting articles of the European convention to be cited in court proceedings and by taking the view that the courts had a special duty to scrutinize the decisions of ministers and civil servants whenever issues of human rights arose. For their part, UK ministers also took the European court's decisions seriously and almost invariably abided by them, including by amending statutes and introducing new ones where necessary. They often took the trouble, when drafting legislation, to make sure that it was compatible with the convention, even if the Strasbourg court had not yet pronounced on the matter at hand.

It was only a matter of time before judges and politicians

in Britain began to wonder why, if the Strasbourg court was such a good thing and if its judgments were being taken so seriously by the courts in Britain, the UK did not have a Human Rights Act of its own. In particular, they wondered why the European Convention on Human Rights – which, after all, a British Conservative politician had helped to draft – should not simply be written, with suitable provisos, into British domestic law. They were conscious that, while most British judges took the convention and the Strasbourg court's rulings seriously, not all of them did. They were even more conscious that there was something absurd about a situation in which British people had to go all the way to Strasbourg – to what was, in effect, a foreign court – to obtain British justice. Sir Thomas ('Tom') Bingham, one of England's most senior judges, readily acknowledged that writing the European convention into UK law would not usher in the New Jerusalem:

> But the change would over time stifle the insidious and damaging belief that it is necessary to go abroad to obtain justice. It would restore this country to its former place as an international standard-bearer of liberty and justice. It would help to reinvigorate the faith, which our eighteenth and nineteenth century forebears would not for an instant have doubted, that these were fields in which Britain was the world's teacher, not its pupil.[10]

The Blair government duly obliged, and Britain's own Human Rights Act – with the European convention included word for word in a schedule at the end of the Act – came into force near the end of the millennium. In order to preserve intact the long-established doctrine of the ultimate sovereignty of parliament, the Act contained a provision to the effect that, if a court declared an Act of the British parliament to be incompatible with the convention, then parliament could – and, by implication, should – make use of a fast-track procedure to amend the Act in question in order to render it compatible. Regarding judgments handed down by the Strasbourg court, the Human Rights Act was Delphic. In Section 2, it said that 'a court or tribunal determining a question which has arisen in connection with a Convention right must take into account any judgment, decision, declaration or advisory opinion of the European Court of Human Rights'. On the one hand, the phrase 'any judgment, decision, declaration or advisory opinion' was sweeping. On the other hand, the phrase 'must take into account' left judges a good deal of leeway. So long as they took Strasbourg's rulings into account, they did not have to abide by them. They were free to take other factors into account.

During its first decade, the Human Rights Act remained relatively uncontroversial. On occasion, the courts quashed ministerial decisions they judged to violate the terms of the Act, and in 2002 the Court of Appeal held an important provision of the Mental Health Act 1983 to be incompatible with the European convention and therefore with the Human Rights Act. The government at once amended the Act. However, at the same time, the courts – especially after the 2001 terrorist attacks on the World Trade Center in New York – tended to tread warily in matters relating to national security. Regarding national security, they were inclined to defer to ministers, as they had done in the distant past.

Nevertheless, the Human Rights Act, and its very presence on the UK statute book, gradually became more controversial as time went on, largely because of attacks by the tabloid press on some of the judgments handed down under it and also because it inevitably became a focus for a growing section of the Conservative party's dislike of the character of Britain's various relationships with the rest of Europe – 'Europe' for these purposes including the European Court of Human Rights as well as the EU. The Conservatives gradually committed themselves to replacing the Human Rights Act 1998, with its explicit nods in the direction of Strasbourg, with a British bill of rights, one that presumably would enshrine broadly the same rights as the original European declaration but not draw on the Strasbourg jurisprudence. How all that could be achieved – and whether it could be achieved – was unclear, given that by the mid-2010s the UK courts had effectively embedded much of Strasbourg's jurisprudence in the common law, and given also that people in Britain would still have the right to appeal to Strasbourg unless Britain withdrew its backing entirely from the European court and from its association with the European declaration.

Also at issue in the minds of many Conservatives – and not just Conservatives – were the tensions between the claims to ultimate authority of a democratically elected parliament on the one hand, and, on the other, the widespread belief, embodied in the European convention, that a number of fundamental human rights – for example, the right to a fair trial – should be regarded as inviolable and should on no account and on no occasion be violated. Which rights, if any, were fundamental in this sense? And who should decide which of them were? The people and their elected representatives in parliament? Or judges, whether in Strasbourg, in the UK's Supreme Court in London, or anywhere else? Which principle should take precedence, the principle of unfettered democracy or the principle that the actions of governments should be checked by means of constitutional guarantees? Questions as profound as these underlay the quarrel mentioned earlier between the courts and parliament – and specifically between the Strasbourg court and David Cameron – over whether some or all incarcerated prisoners should be accorded the right to vote.

For their part, the great majority of Britain's judges have all along simply wanted to judge. They have not been legally ambitious and have even seen the increased use of judicial review as no more than a revival in the application of well-established principles. Above all, most of them have seen themselves as lawyers, applying and trying to make sense of the law, not as legal innovators. In so far as they have been innovators, it is because they have seen gaps in the law that needed to be filled and flaws that needed to be rectified. Even someone as radical as Lord Bingham (as he became) saw himself as building on ancient traditions, not as establishing new ones. For centuries, the development of the common law has been a process of judges gradually adapting the law to suit changing circumstances. Judges have been reluctant to be drawn into party-political controversy and have been surprised and dismayed when they have been. They have never challenged head-on the doctrine of parliamentary sovereignty and, given half a chance, have been inclined to render unto parliament the things that are parliament's.

A case decided by the Supreme Court in 2014 illustrates the point. It concerned whether a British statute that made it a criminal offence for someone to assist another in committing suicide did or did not contravene the European Convention on Human Rights and the decisions by the Strasbourg court arising out of it. The nine justices who heard the appeals in the case wrote nine judgments. On only one point were they unanimous: that the final decision on the issue rested with authorities here in the UK and not with Strasbourg or anyone else. The question they had to ask themselves, therefore, was whether the decision rested with the Supreme Court or with the UK parliament. Only two of the nine concluded both (1) that denying individuals the right to assist other individuals in committing suicide did contravene the European Convention on Human Rights and therefore the UK Human Rights Act and also (2) that, being that that was so, the Supreme Court should issue a formal declaration of incompatibility between the terms of the Human Rights Act and the terms of the British statute denying people the right to assist others in committing suicide. The other seven justices, while sympathizing with the appellants in the case, refused to go that far. Three of the seven took the view that, although the court was indeed legally entitled to issue a declaration of incompatibility, it should refrain from doing so, at least for the time being, and should instead allow parliament to give the matter further consideration. Lord Neuberger, one of the three, noted in his judgment, among other things, that the question of amending the British statute raised 'a difficult, controversial and sensitive issue, with moral and religious dimensions, which undoubtedly justified a relatively cautious approach from the courts'. The courts 'should, as it were, take matters relatively slowly'.[11] The remaining four of the seven justices were more categorical, arguing in effect that it would be contrary to the British constitution for any court, including the Supreme Court, to usurp parliament's prerogative to deal with a moral issue of such difficulty and one that had such broad social ramifications. As Lord Sumption, one of the four, put it:

> The question whether relaxing or qualifying the current absolute prohibition on assisted suicide would involve unacceptable risks to vulnerable people is in my view a classic example of the kind of issue which should be decided by Parliament . . . [As] I have suggested, the issue involves a choice between two fundamental but mutually inconsistent moral values, upon which there is at present no consensus in our society. Such choices are inherently legislative in nature. The decision cannot fail to be strongly influenced by the decision-makers' personal opinions about the moral case for assisted suicide. This is entirely appropriate if the decision-makers are those who represent the community at large. It is not appropriate for professional judges. The imposition of their personal opinions on matters of this kind would lack all constitutional legitimacy.[12]

The Supreme Court's decision in this case, binding on all the UK's lower courts, was taken by a majority of seven to two.

So much for the notion that Britain's judges, aided and abetted by the Strasbourg court, have become rapacious seekers after power.

Undoubtedly, Britain's judges and courts have come over the past half-century to play a significantly larger role in the British system of government than they did before. The senior judges are now players in the system and not merely bystanders. They and their immediate predecessors were to some extent responsible for enlarging their role in this way. The revival of judicial review was almost entirely a judge-driven phenomenon. But British judges played no part, except a wholly passive one, in importing European Union law into this country: the European Communities Act 1972, enacted by parliament, left them no option except to do that. The same was true of the Human Rights Act 1998: parliament enacted it; and parliament expected the courts to give effect to it. If the position of the courts has become controversial, it is overwhelmingly because parliament has invited judges to make controversial decisions. Parliament, in the persons of successive governments, has chosen to outsource to the courts a good deal of its power. Parliament remains sovereign in the purely legal sense, but in practical terms its sovereignty is strictly limited – in this as in so many other respects.

Who Governs?

There is something surreal about the way in which British politicians comport themselves at the moment – and the way in which they have comported themselves for several decades past. Few British politicians are liars, but most of them are living a lie – or, if not an outright lie, then at least a bizarre fantasy. They behave as though they imagine that Britain's place in the world has not changed and that the capacity of Her Majesty's Government to influence both the lives of Britons and the world beyond Britain's shores is now as great as it ever was. It may be that their delusion stems from the fact that so much of Britain's political architecture and furniture has changed so little; the world has changed utterly, but the great bell of Big Ben still chimes, the door of Number 10 still swings open and the chancellor of the exchequer still holds aloft his red box on budget day. It may also be that millions of Britons' undoubted alienation from those in power owes something to a sense, strongly felt but seldom articulated, that the United Kingdom's political leaders – and would-be leaders – are living in a world that is not only remote but also unreal. The rules of the game have changed, but Britain's political players play on regardless, as though nothing had happened.

As we have noted in previous chapters, the changes in the rules – some of them widely noticed, some hardly noticed at all – have been momentous. The old two-party system has crumbled, enormously increasing the chances that coalition and minority governments will have to be formed. The influence of party activists has increased while their numbers have dwindled. Despite its name, the UK government, as a consequence of its devolution of wide-ranging powers to Scotland, Wales and Northern Ireland, is no longer, for many practical purposes, the government of the UK. Instead, the grand-sounding government of the United Kingdom of Great Britain and Northern Ireland is merely, under many headings, the government of England. Thus, the UK's governing arrangements are no longer nearly as centralized as they once were. In other ways, the capacity of UK ministers to influence events is also newly trammelled. Events in the outside world intrude into Britain's domestic affairs even more than they used to, not least, though by no means only, as a result of Britain's membership of the European Union. Judges, whether in London, Luxembourg or Strasbourg, increasingly make a nuisance of themselves, as do outspoken and uppity backbench members of parliament. Journalists and broadcasters, more assertive and better educated than in the past, function as a kind of anti-government, probing and critical even when not positively disparaging.

The system is certainly less establishmentarian than it was. No politician in the twenty-first century would dream of saying – or probably even thinking – that 'the gentleman in Whitehall really does know better what is good for people than the people know themselves'.[1] The people were once expected to defer to their betters. Now the people are more likely to be on the receiving end of what little deference is going. Politicians in the twenty-first century, far more than their predecessors, give the impression that they believe that the people's wishes have not merely a prudential claim on their attention but also a moral claim – that they have a right to be listened to not merely as voters, people to be feared, but also as citizens, people to be respected. In their backgrounds, schooling and wealth, leading figures in the Conservative party today resemble their upper-class antecedents, but that fact is widely assumed to be a liability rather than an asset to the party. Even within that party's own ranks, the old-fashioned high social status of several of its leaders is resented. In 2012, a backbench Conservative MP went so far as to dismiss her own prime minister and chancellor as 'two arrogant posh boys'.[2] The phrase, cutting as it was, had many of her fellow Conservative MPs nodding in agreement. More significant is the fact that popular referendums, although by no means a regularized and institutionalized feature of the British system, are now an accepted and acceptable feature of it, used to determine everything from whether Hartlepool and Newham should have directly elected mayors to whether Scotland should become an independent nation. Not so long ago, the thought of holding popular referendums was anathema to the entire British political elite. Now referendums are regarded as exceptional, to be sure, but also as an integral part of the UK's political repertoire.

The closed-off world of Whitehall is also far more open than it was. Senior officials appear routinely before parliamentary select committees, leaks abound and – although its effects have not been as dramatic as its proponents hoped and its opponents feared – the Freedom of Information Act has made it substantially harder than in the past for ministers and officials to keep potentially embarrassing data secret. Those same ministers and officials, who once did their business largely in private, are now open to – and subject to – influences and pressures from well beyond Whitehall, from diverse think tanks as well as 'the interests' (or at least some of them). There are now far more participants than there used to be in the on-going Whitehall conversation. Unfortunately, not much is publicly known about some of them or about what they have to say. No one seems to have investigated the influence of professional multi-client lobbying organizations such as Bell Pottinger and Weber Shandwick.

An identifiable political class has emerged, and the costs of its emergence undoubtedly outweigh its benefits. Although members of the class are mostly well educated and politically savvy, few have acquired useful pre-political or pre-ministerial experience. In most cases, they are jacks of all trades and not really masters of any – except the specifically political trade of using, or seeking to use, words to advantage. The philosopher Bertrand Russell is said to have remarked that 'metaphysicians, like savages, think words are things'. Members of the political class often give the same impression. Under some circumstances, words are indeed things – useful things, as Abraham Lincoln, the two Roosevelts and Winston Churchill demonstrated – but their importance can be overrated as compared with solid and enduring accomplishments. Great political leaders are remembered for their deeds, not their words. Few today would bother to quote even Winston Churchill's magnificent speeches if Britain had lost the war.

Defying the age-old adage that one should make haste slowly, the corporate culture of today's political class seems to require that ministers, in particular, should make haste quickly. A large proportion of in-a-hurry, activist ministers are self-starters, like testosterone-fuelled young drivers who spin their wheels on their way out of the car park, but most ministers at some time or another – and in some cases all the time – are under pressure from others to do or say something and to do or say whatever that something is in time for the six o'clock news. The pressure can emanate from the prime minister, backbench MPs, special advisers, party stalwarts in the constituencies, social media or one or more of the traditional mass media; but, wherever it comes from, it can be intense, and more often than not ministers are reluctant to say, 'Hang on a moment, we need time to think about this.' As we noted in Chapter 10, officials are often reluctant to say the same, even to their ministerial bosses. The result is that activity can easily trump genuine action, orotund pronouncements morph into a substitute for careful planning.

During the decades following the last war, the UK was continually beset by economic and financial crises, and the world was an even more dangerous place then than it is now; but at that time Britain's governing arrangements themselves were remarkably settled. Harold Wilson, a civil servant during the war and a cabinet minister soon after it, moved comfortably into 10 Downing Street when he arrived there two decades later. Although the issues had changed, the system had not; he occupied familiar territory. Since then, as we have seen, the system has changed a great deal, and, remarkably, systemic change, once rare, now shows every sign of becoming self-perpetuating. For the first time in history, UK parliaments are meant to have fixed terms. The future of the country's principal media organization, the BBC, is constantly called in question. Some would like to see the position of ministers vis-à-vis officials strengthened even further than it has been already. Some would like to see the judges' expanded powers curbed. The recall of errant MPs by their constituents is widely mooted. A big question-mark continues to hang over Britain's future within, or possibly without, the EU. Not least, the precise terms of the relationships among the governments of the UK, England, Scotland, Wales and Northern Ireland remain to be sorted out – and may never be sorted out to general satisfaction. Wise in this, as in so much else, Walter Bagehot wrote more than a century ago:

> In well-framed polities, innovation – great innovation
> that is – can only be occasional. If you are always altering
> your house, it is a sign either that you have a bad house, or
> that you have an excessively restless disposition – there is
> something wrong somewhere.[3]

In a polity in which constant alterations have become commonplace, two significant elements of non-change are conspicuous and are also, partly for that reason, anomalous. One is that, despite the increased openness and permeability of the government of the United Kingdom, that polity's government is still, in essence, every bit as much a power-hoarding arrangement as it ever was. The government of the UK is still meant to govern – full stop. It is not meant to, and does not, share power with others, certainly not with opposition parties. On almost every issue that arises, the government of the day is expected to take the initiative. The government of the day acts. Others react. Ministers decide. No one else does. The political parties in coalition governments certainly share power between or among themselves, but they do not share it with anyone else. Just as with one-party governments, coalition governments are seldom in the business of dealing with organizations and bodies of opinion outside government on a basis of rough equality. Reforms to the NHS in England or to English schools are not negotiated painstakingly with stakeholders. They are handed down from above by governments, like gifts from heaven. Full-on power-sharing within the UK is strictly for Northern Ireland.

Party politics is also as adversarial as it ever was (if not quite as hyperbolic as the postwar period, when, as we saw in Chapter 1, Churchill threatened the country with a Labour Gestapo and Nye Bevan reviled the Conservatives as 'lower than vermin'). When John Major at prime minister's questions reminded Tony Blair, the leader of the opposition, that both major parties were divided over Europe, Blair retorted that there was a difference between them: 'I lead my party. He follows his.'[4] When Gordon Brown's government executed a U-turn and brought its policy on inheritance tax more in line with the Conservatives', David Cameron as leader of the opposition mocked Brown across the dispatch box: 'The difference between our policy and your policy is that we thought of it and you stole it.'[5] Exchanges like that are the stuff of political contestation across the democratic world, but there are probably few other countries in which party-political point-scoring is so incessant. It carries on during the years between election campaigns. It features prominently in almost every parliamentary set-piece debate. Scarcely a television or a radio discussion programme with a politician on it is devoid of it. Television and radio interviews involving politicians are almost invariably punctuated by it. Opposition spokespersons naturally oppose – that is their job – but ministers for their part evidently feel obliged to blame all the country's ills, whatever they currently happen to be, on mistakes perpetrated by the previous administration. As often as not, prime minister's questions topples over the border into self-parody. The spectacle is one of members of the political class constantly fighting an internecine war with other members of the political class.

In the early decades of the twenty-first century, popular alienation from the whole of a country's political class is by no means confined to Britain. The fact that it can be found in this country cannot conceivably be ascribed solely to the failings and foibles of Britain's politicians. It is probably owing to politicians' failure to prevent or mitigate the effects of the post-2008 economic downturn, to the palpable injustices wrought by that downturn, with many of the rich getting richer and most of the poor getting poorer, and to a sense of helplessness in the face of seemingly out-of-control economic forces. Going further back in time, it is probably also rooted in the breakup of the old class-centred politics and to the feeling, felt in almost all countries (though probably less strongly in Germany than elsewhere), that politicians are focused exclusively on playing political games, games only loosely related to the lives and interests of non-political citizens – a phenomenon that an astute Frenchman long ago called *la politique politicienne*. Rightly or wrongly, it seems to millions to matter little which political party or parties are in power. The consequent mixture of apathy and anger has resulted across most of the liberal-democratic world in declining voter turnout and the rise of populist political parties, parties that are impossible to place securely anywhere on the traditional right–left spectrum.

In Britain, perhaps more than in most other countries, this widespread mixture of apathy and anger has been fuelled by the ritualized and irrelevant-seeming adversarialism of the main political parties and by the fact that successive governments have seemed to screw up so often, scoring own goals and making unforced errors. The British were once used to quiet, boring competence. Instead, today they all too often get noisy, unsettling incompetence, with almost everyone in the land able to draw personal attention to some nonsensical new rule or to some exciting new government initiative that threatens to cause an immense amount of disruption and probably waste at least as much money as it saves. A thick volume published in the early 2010s was called *The Blunders of Our Governments*, and everyone who read it thought there would need to be at least one more volume.[6] A Labour government presided over the late-2000s banking disaster. A Conservative-led coalition administration promised to cut net immigration to below 100,000 a year by the year 2015 only to see it remain (utterly predictably) at roughly double that number. The phrase 'trust in government' used to refer to ministers' and officials' honesty and integrity. Now it refers just as often, possibly even more often, to whether or not they can be trusted actually to deliver, on their promises or on anything else. Alexander Pope famously declared:

> For forms of government, let fools contest;
> Whate'er is best administered is best.

Ministers in the twenty-first century continually contest our forms of government while at the same time administering the UK's affairs with diminished competence – an unfortunate combination.

There may well be another factor in play, the one referred to in the very first paragraph of this chapter. Against the background of Britain's imperial greatness – still made manifest in the Palace of Westminster and the towering height of Big Ben – British political leaders constantly contrive to give the impression that they still think they can move mountains, that they still have it within their power to exert great influence on the world stage and to alter fundamentally Britain's social and economic order. Tony Blair's Labour party offers the electorate a vision 'of national renewal, a country with drive, purpose and energy'.[7] David Cameron, on behalf of the Conservatives, undertakes to build a 'Big Society'. But it is not within any British government's power either to fashion 'a country with drive, purpose and energy' or to transform Britain's complex existing social structure into any sort of 'Big Society'. Modern British governments can nudge, goad, incentivize and encourage, but they can seldom, if ever, bring about radical economic and social change, certainly not in the foreshortened time scales that they allow themselves; and they can certainly not begin to exert on the world stage the kind of influence that their Victorian predecessors did.

In other words, British party leaders' high-flown rhetoric – and the way they typically present themselves to the public – is out of phase with the modern world. They present themselves as more important than they are, or could possibly be, and in the process wind up looking faintly absurd. The opinion polls often report that British voters believe that British politicians break their promises (plural) the whole time; but perhaps what they break the whole time is, in reality, only one promise (singular), one that they constantly hold out: namely, that they can influence world events and effect change at home on a far larger scale than in fact they can. The continuing gap between promise and performance is almost certainly one reason why British citizens and voters so often feel powerless and defrauded.

Who, then, does govern Britain today? The short answer is: no one institution and certainly no one individual. Governments of the United Kingdom, like the governments of other liberal democracies, are multiply hobbled and constrained, even more in the twenty-first century than in the past. Much is expected of them – and they themselves, or their leaders, fuel such expectations. But many of those expectations are bound to be disappointed, and it is not always governments' fault. British governments are constrained by global market forces, by international and supranational institutions and also, far more than is commonly recognized, by the preferences of voters. Politicians are not brilliantly original intellectuals, and they are no better placed than anyone else to escape the prevailing intellectual climate. Today's British governments are more constrained than in the past by the courts, and they also pay more heed than in the past to the wishes of their own most partisan supporters. Perhaps more than is strictly necessary, they also heed the views of sections of the press. Ministers can never ignore – and never could ignore – the views of their own parliamentary supporters. Nowadays, United Kingdom ministers simply have to live with the fact that, for a wide range of purposes, their writ does not run in substantial parts of the United Kingdom – and looks like running less and less there as time goes on.

A common image of government is that of an ordered hierarchy, with a chain of command stretching down from above, possibly from the government as a whole, possibly from the prime minister. That is certainly the way in which many in government would like government to operate, and occasionally it does operate that way. If a government decides to privatize or outsource this or that, it usually can. If it decides to raise or lower the duty on petrol, it can usually do that too. But, most of the time, the business of government is more complicated. Ministers are dependent on each other and on groups and individuals – and forces – beyond their capacity to control or even influence. A government may decide to reduce the size of the regular army and to recruit reservists instead. Reducing the size of the army is something it can do on its own. Recruiting reservists is another matter. In reality, government is less like a pyramid, more like a sprawling city with crowded pavements, multiple traffic jams and a sequence of dangerous crossing points.

Governing is a difficult business, a fact that ministers – not typically a humble lot – are reluctant to concede.

If the UK is not as well governed as it should be, by whomever is in power, what should be done? Comprehensive constitutional change of the kind widely advocated during the 1970s and 1980s is simply not going to happen. The people at large are not much interested in it (witness the outcome of the 2011 Alternative Vote referendum), and there is no appetite for it among those prominent members of the political class who would have to initiate it. In any case, they have other, more pressing matters to deal with. But there are a number of more modest changes to our existing governing arrangements that might be worth considering. Some relate to the structure of institutions. Some are more cultural in character.

Although the notion that the UK would gain effective independence – that is, effective control over almost the totality of its own affairs – by departing from the European Union is a chimera, there is a lot to be said for the idea that the EU's institutions have a tendency to overextend themselves. The launching of the euro, when it was launched, was probably not a good idea. The inclusion of Greece in the eurozone was – and was known at the time to be – a very bad idea. State universities in the fifty states of the United States can still charge in-state students lower fees than out-of-state students. By contrast, EU rules require all EU universities to charge students from all EU countries whatever fees they charge home students. That seems at best unnecessary and at worst a way of forcing countries with good universities to subsidize the education of students from countries with less good universities, thereby freeing the governments of those countries from the obligation of providing their own citizens with better, and probably more, institutions of higher education. From the beginning, the building of a more united Europe has been a largely top-down exercise. There is something to be said for a more bottom-up approach or, at the very least, for a pause in the building works. There is, after all, no great hurry.

A more intractable problem concerns the exaggerated role that party members and activists play in the affairs of the British state. As we saw in Chapter 3, although there are occasional up-ticks in the parties' enrolment of new members, especially among smaller parties such as the Scottish National Party and UKIP, the long-term trend among political parties as a whole is downward, with their aggregate memberships today numbered in the few hundreds of thousands rather than the millions of yesteryear. Yet those tiny bands of party members have far more lethal political weaponry in their hands than ever they did before. Not only do they continue to select parliamentary candidates (and, in effect, elect the local MP in a majority of parliamentary constituencies), but they now elect the leaders of their parties – that is, decide which two or three people will be in a position to become prime minister. They absolutely determine the choice of prime minister offered to the people. If the views and outlook of party members, taken collectively, approximated to that of the electorate as a whole, the mere arithmetic might not matter; but there are good reasons – and some hard evidence – for believing that party members' views and the views of a majority of voters diverge quite sharply, with practical consequences for the pressures brought to bear on governments and the decisions they take. But it is not easy to see what, practically, could be done about that.

A marginally more tractable problem concerns the quality of ministers, in the sense of individual ministers who are doing specific jobs being able to do those jobs to a high standard. An unknown but possibly considerable proportion of ministers do not answer that description at the moment. A lot of ministers are not very bright and/or know very little about the matters with which they are dealing (and with which they may have been dealing for only a few weeks or months). The best ministers are very capable: they possess good political antennae and are, among other things, what the Americans call 'quick studies' – that is, able to ingest and understand the implications of large amounts of new material very quickly. But the best, in practice as well as by definition, are not all that numerous. Aides to prime ministers often complain, although strictly in private, about the quality of the people their bosses have to appoint to ministerial office.

A certain amount could be achieved (and may already have been) by dint of party headquarters leaning on their members in the constituencies, when they have a number of aspirant MPs in front of them, to keep an eye out for ministerial potential – and, even better, to do that beforehand, when drawing up shortlists. A certain amount could also be achieved by means of pre-ministerial training, such as that offered to parties in opposition by the non-partisan Institute for Government. But it would be even better if prime ministers could break with long-standing tradition and appoint to ministerial posts – possibly at subcabinet level to begin with – a considerably larger proportion of men and women from outside parliament with relevant extra-political experience and aptitudes. The prime minister of the day could do that without any need to amend old legislation or pass new. Some of the appointments made in this way would, of course, not work out well (history affords well-known instances); but some of the appointments made from among sitting MPs do not work out well either (the present day affords numerous instances). One of the most formidable ministers of the twentieth century, Ernest Bevin, had never been an MP when Churchill appointed him minister of labour in 1940. He worked out very well – in that office and as postwar foreign secretary.

A decision would inevitably have to be made about whether these more numerous outside appointees would need to become, as they do at present, members of either the House of Commons or the House of Lords, or whether they could remain neither MPs nor peers. Whatever the outcome of that decision, all those appointed from outside would, of course, have to be enabled, indeed required, to play a full part in any parliamentary proceedings involving their department or portfolio – answering questions, participating in debates and so forth. That is what happens in other countries that do not require, or even allow, ministers also to be parliamentarians. Members of Britain's ancient parliament would need to be persuaded of the desirability of departing in such a radical way from their long-established and deeply cherished practice. Beyond doubt, they would need a lot of persuading.

Another advantage of appointing more ministers from outside would be to enable prime ministers to decrease the rate of turnover among holders of ministerial office. People could be brought in from outside, probably at a rather junior level, instead of so many existing ministers having to be moved around. A career ladder could even be created within departments, with people being promoted more easily to more senior posts within a department, instead of being moved on and up elsewhere. A further advantage, easily overlooked, is that a smaller number of MP-ministers would mean a larger number of MPs free to function as government critics and proper legislators. One serious disadvantage of reducing the size of the House of Commons, as is frequently advocated, is that, unless the number of MP-ministers were also greatly reduced, it would almost certainly mean a reduction in the number of MPs on the government side of the House available to perform non-ministerial duties such as improving the quality of the government's own legislative proposals.

Parliament as a legislative assembly – or, rather, as a seriously underfunctioning legislative assembly – is a problem. It passes, usually without close examination, too many bad laws (as well as too many laws altogether). A large part of the problem lies with ministers who, for reasons of their own, introduce too many bills – too many of which are inadequately drafted – and who then force the parliamentary pace by timetabling almost every one on an exceedingly tight schedule. But part of the problem also lies with MPs' willingness to accept such a substantial degree of ministerial control and with the curious organizational structure of the House of Commons, whereby its investigative committees are not allowed to participate in legislation and its legislative committees are scarcely allowed to investigate. The House of Commons certainly needs, along with more time, a more efficient and effective committee system. It also needs more MPs on both sides of the House committed to playing a more constructive legislative role. The only hard-to-surmount difficulty – and it certainly is one – is the modern-day expectation that every MP will have a close association with his or her constituency and will function as that constituency's advocate, booster, social worker and shoulder to cry on. For backbench MPs, as for ministers and prime ministers, there are only so many hours in the day. It is not entirely clear how the conflicting roles of legislator and 'good constituency member', which every MP is supposed to be, can be reconciled.

Another awkward issue concerns the relationship between ministers and officials. Although at a personal level this relationship is beyond anyone's capacity to control, it is evident that the old duopoly between ministers and officials – which had much to be said for it – could only be restored if officials had not only the intelligence and commitment but also the subject-specific knowledge and expertise (and the institutional memory) that they once possessed. If ministers are to lean on their officials, then they must be confident, both that those same officials will not attempt to use any means to obstruct them, and also that, if they do lean on them, they, the ministers, will not fall over. Officials, including senior officials, have been drastically reduced in numbers in recent years, and that may in itself be no bad thing; but the officials who survive need to be able to speak truth to power in the knowledge – on the part of both themselves and their ministers – that they actually do have truths to speak. The currently rapid rate of turnover of officials as well as ministers appears on the face of it not to be conducive to that end. Individual officials' career advancement seems for the time being to outweigh the more consequential cause of policy development. No one yet seems to have worked out how to strike a balance between the desirability of having a substantial cadre of first-class career officials – the permanent civil service – and the equal but opposite desirability of importing outsiders who can bring relevant non-governmental knowledge and experience to bear.

The dominant role in government played nowadays by Britain's pan-party-political class is almost certainly a bad thing, but what to do about it is something else again. Its very existence deters some people from seeking a political career, and the fact that politicians collectively have such a bad name has the same effect. Although egalitarian sensibilities are offended by the very thought of substantially raising MPs' and ministers' salaries, it probably is the case that considerable numbers of men and women who have established successful careers in business or one of the better paid professions are put off seeking political careers because of the financial sacrifices they would have to make. The salaries that MPs are paid today undoubtedly strike those on low incomes as positively munificent; they do not look nearly so good to people already making – and whose way of life has come to rely on their making – very good money. If MPs' salaries were raised substantially, an MP who thought that he or she was being paid too much could always give the money away. (Communist members of the postwar French national assembly were required to live on a manual-worker's wage and to hand over the rest of their salary to their party.) However, in the end it is probably up to whomever selects parliamentary candidates to tilt the balance of advantage away from incipient members of the political class in favour of people who have hitherto done 'real jobs', ideally for a considerable period of time. The dominance of the political class can survive only as long as those who select parliamentary candidates allow it to.

All of those are more or less institutional possibilities, but political culture – the mind-set that individuals bring to the business of doing politics and arriving at governmental decisions – is probably even more important. And the mind-set that most British politicians bring to their task is almost certainly not the one that is most appropriate to the circumstances of the United Kingdom in the early twenty-first century.

Britain is not a country whose citizens are deeply divided along ideological lines. Nor are the main political parties as deeply divided ideologically as they once were. To be sure, there are still deep divisions of opinion within the country – concerning Europe, immigration, high-speed rail, wind farms, the location of airports, the desirability of overseas humanitarian intervention and much else besides – but those divisions are as much within the various parties as between them. The old arguments over nationalization and privatization have largely been settled. 'Socialism', whatever that word ever meant, is no longer on the agenda. The

Conservative and Labour parties differ over questions of equality, taxation, income redistribution and how public services should be provided, but all parties except the Greens agree on the desirability of economic growth as well as on the desirability of high rates of employment and low rates of inflation. By no means all, but a very large proportion, of political arguments in the twenty-first century turn on issues of means rather than ends. Only a minority on the Conservative side want to see the postwar welfare state totally dismantled. One of the very few issues that deeply divides millions of Britons is the issue of independence for Scotland, and that is an issue almost entirely for the Scots. Yet UK governments persist in hoarding power, and the national political style remains peculiarly adversarial.

An alternative and potentially more productive way of proceeding suggests itself and is available. Call it, for simplicity's sake, 'the Nordic style'. Party competition is fierce in the five Nordic countries, and it is by no means always pretty to look at. No Mary Poppins ever flies in magically to put everything right. But there is a common understanding in all those countries – and to a large extent in the Netherlands and Germany as well – that there are matters on which it is preferable for a number of parties, occasionally for all of them, not to bury their differences but instead to try to find some way round them. The more serious the matter, the more strongly is felt the need to find some form of accommodation. That way of operating is by no means unknown in the United Kingdom: it brought majorities in all the main political parties together during the 1914–18 Great War and again during the Second World War, and it informed the manner in which the Conservatives and Liberal Democrats formed their governing coalition in 2010. But that way of operating has never become part of the genetic makeup, so to speak, of this country's political elites; and in practice the Conservative–Liberal Democrat coalition after May 2010 proceeded to govern in very much a business-as-usual way.

Formal or even informal inter-party coalitions are not essential. What is essential is a mind-set, a disposition on the part of politicians, especially party leaders, to continue to differ about matters on which their differences are irreconcilable but to seek as wide a body of agreement as they can on everything else – in other words, to fight on about the issues that deeply divide them along partisan lines but in effect to call truces about everything else. In some circumstances, the parties do that already. They did so during the 'troubles' in Northern Ireland, when the Conservatives and Labour respected each other's right to negotiate secretly over the future of the province. In early 2015, all three main party leaders signed a concordat on climate change. But such circumstances are rare. There is no good reason why they should be.

Such an approach to governing would have five inter-related advantages.

In the first place, it would encourage politicians and officials to engage in a process of due deliberation before finally deciding. It would encourage them to consider all the available options and to weigh them up carefully – and perhaps, in the course of doing that, to identify options that always were available but that had not previously occurred to them. It would also encourage them to take their time, not to act over-hastily. Some decisions need to be taken very quickly (for example, when a big bank threatens to collapse), but very few do. It is telling that, whereas British ministers always seem eager to grasp nettles, the Dutch have a saying, 'If you have a hot potato, put it in the fridge.' Not least, a proper process of deliberation would entail reaching out to all the interested parties as well as to knowledgeable individuals. It would encourage them to take counsel, to draw in all those with advice to give and all those on whose assent, or at least acquiescence, the success of the policy might depend. Had a process of due deliberation taken place, a large proportion of the many blunders perpetrated by modern British governments would never have been committed. The poll tax, for one, would never have come anywhere near the statute book.

Second, a more Nordic, deliberative approach would increase the chances that those involved would consider not only the abstract merits of proposed courses of action but also what would be involved, in practical terms, in giving effect to them. A policy is not what ministers announce in the House of Commons or at their party conference: it is what eventually happens on the ground. Unfortunately, experience suggests that a common characteristic of British policy making is that ministers' bright ideas – and their manifesto commitments – are never properly reality-tested. The question, 'What would we like to do? is asked and answered; but the related question, 'How would we actually do it?' is too often not even asked – and often, when asked, is answered by, in effect, 'It'll be all right on the night.' But government policies, as well as plays, are frequently not all right on the night. Reports from the House of Commons Public Accounts Committee, over many years, attest to that sad fact.

Third, a feature of government in the Nordic countries is how seldom government policies are radically changed. The process of making policy is frequently slow, sometimes frustratingly so, but once a policy has been decided upon it typically remains in place for years, often for generations. Because all, or almost all, the stakeholders have been involved in developing the policy, whatever has been decided upon usually sticks, either because the stakeholders have all agreed on it or at least because they have been properly consulted. In most cases, their fingerprints are on it. They are committed to it. By contrast, it is common in Britain for incoming governments to be committed to repealing or radically amending the policies adopted by their predecessors – and, not infrequently, to performing U-turns in connection with policies that they themselves have adopted. Governments in the UK are notoriously stable, certainly compared with governments in other countries (including, for example, the Netherlands), but British governments' policies – regarding taxation, for instance – tend to be far less stable.

Fourth, a more leisurely deliberative approach makes it easier for the Nordic countries to tackle what were referred to earlier in this book as 'the wicked issues', the ones lodged in what is sometimes called a government's 'too difficult' box. As we noted in Chapter 5, precisely because British governments hoard power rather than sharing it with others, they expose themselves electorally; and, precisely because they expose themselves electorally, they are often reluctant to tackle issues that run the risk of causing them electoral pain, and successive governments can go on being reluctant for the same reason. The more power-sharing style of government in the Nordic countries enables their governments to implicate more parties and party leaders in the taking of difficult decisions and the tackling of difficult issues. The fingerprints of more people are on the policy. More people have, as one politician put it, dipped their fingers in the blood.

Fifth, and finally, the adoption of a more consensual, less confrontational governing style – and the confining of political disagreement to those issues on which full agreement really is impossible – increases the chances that the general public will retain at least a degree of respect for the political class. Not everyone can be satisfied all the time; democracy has been described as 'institutionalized disappointment'. But opinion surveys taken in the Nordic countries suggest that levels of satisfaction with their democracies and their political leaderships are considerably higher than in the UK. A number of factors undoubtedly account for those findings, but those countries' modes of politicking and governing are almost certainly among them.

The United Kingdom is a far better governed country than many others, including many other members of the European Union. Britons can count their blessings. But anyone looking dispassionately at the way in which the UK is governed today, as distinct from in years gone by, is bound to say, perhaps a trifle wistfully: 'Could do better.'

GOVERNMENTS AND
PRIME MINISTERS, 1945–2015

GOVERNMENTS		PRIME MINISTERS	
Labour	1945–51	Clement Attlee	1945–51
Conservative	1951–64	Winston Churchill	1951–5
		Anthony Eden	1955–7
		Harold Macmillan	1957–63
		Alec Douglas-Home	1963–4
Labour	1964–70	Harold Wilson	1964–70
Conservative	1970–74	Edward Heath	1970–74
Labour	1974–79	Harold Wilson	1974–6
		James Callaghan	1976–9
Conservative	1979–97	Margaret Thatcher	1979–90
		John Major	1990–97
Labour	1997–2010	Tony Blair	1997–2007
		Gordon Brown	2007–10
Conservative–Liberal Democrat coalition	2010–15	David Cameron	2010–15

A SHORT GUIDE TO
Further Reading

The following list is by no means comprehensive. It is meant to be merely suggestive. For those requiring more basic knowledge of the British system than is provided by this book, four solid textbooks are:

- Ian Budge, David McKay, John Bartle and Kenneth Newton, *The New British Politics*, 4th edn (Harlow: Pearson Education, 2007)
- Bill Jones and Philip Norton, *Politics UK*, 8th edn (Abingdon: Routledge, 2014)
- Dennis Kavanagh, David Richards, Martin Smith and Andrew Geddes, *British Politics*, 5th edn (Oxford: Oxford University Press, 2006)
- Michael Moran, *Politics and Governance in the UK*, 2nd edn (Basingstoke: Palgrave, 2011)

Three useful books specifically on Britain's constitution are:

- Vernon Bogdanor, *The New British Constitution* (Oxford: Hart, 2009)
- Jeffrey Jowell and Dawn Oliver, eds, *The Changing Constitution*, 7th edn (Oxford: Oxford University Press, 2011)
- Anthony King, *The British Constitution* (Oxford: Oxford University Press, 2007)

FURTHER READING

PARTISANS

- Alistair Clark, *Political Parties in the UK* (Basingstoke: Palgrave, 2012)
- Thomas Quinn, *Electing and Ejecting Party Leaders in Britain* (Basingstoke: Palgrave, 2012)

POLITICIANS

- Peter Oborne, *The Triumph of the Political Class* (London: Simon & Schuster, 2007)
- Jeremy Paxman, *The Political Animal: An Anatomy* (London: Penguin Michael Joseph, 2002)
- Peter Riddell, *Honest Opportunism: The Rise of the Career Politician* (London: Hamish Hamilton, 1993)
- Peter Riddell, *In Defence of Politicians (In Spite of Themselves)* (London: Biteback, 2011)

IDEAS

- David Marquand and Anthony Seldon, eds, *The Ideas That Shaped Post-War Britain* (London: Fontana, 1996)
- Richard Wade, *Conservative Party Economic Policy: From Heath in Opposition to Cameron in Coalition* (Basingstoke: Palgrave, 2013)

INTERESTS

- Wyn Grant, *Pressure Groups and British Politics* (Basingstoke: Macmillan, 2000)

MEDIA

- Nick Davies, *Hack Attack: How the Truth Caught up with Rupert Murdoch* (London: Chatto & Windus, 2014)
- Malcolm Dean, *Democracy under Attack: How the Media Distort Policy and Politics* (Bristol: Policy Press, 2013)

MINISTERS, OFFICIALS

- Colin Campbell and Graham K. Wilson, *The End of Whitehall: Death of a Paradigm?* (Oxford: Blackwell, 1995)

- John Hutton and Leigh Lewis, *How to Be a Minister: A 21st-Century Guide* (London: Biteback, 2014)
- R. A. W. Rhodes, *Everyday Life in British Government* (Oxford: Oxford University Press, 2011)
- Ben Yong and Robert Hazell, *Special Advisers: Who They Are, What They Do and Why They Matter* (Oxford: Hart, 2014)

PRIME MINISTERS

- Patrick Diamond, *Governing Britain: Power, Politics and the Prime Minister* (London: I. B. Tauris, 2014)
- Jonathan Powell, *The New Machiavelli: How to Wield Power in the Modern World* (London: Bodley Head, 2010)

MPs

- Paul Flynn, *How To Be an MP*, 2nd edn (London: Biteback, 2012)
- Philip Norton, *Parliament in British Politics*, 2nd edn (Basingstoke: Palgrave, 2013)

JUDGES

- Jeffrey Jowell and Dawn Oliver, eds, *The Changing Constitution*, 7th edn (Oxford: Oxford University Press, 2011)
- Alan Paterson, *Final Judgment: The Last Law Lords and the Supreme Court* (Oxford: Hart, 2013)

WHO GOVERNS?

- Rudy B. Andeweg and Galen A. Irwin, *Governance and Politics of the Netherlands*, 3rd edn (Basingstoke: Palgrave, 2009)
- Charles Clarke, ed., *The 'Too Difficult' Box: The Big Issues Politicians Can't Crack* (London: Biteback, 2014)
- Philip Johnston, *Bad Laws* (London: Constable, 2010)
- Anthony King and Ivor Crewe, *The Blunders of Our Governments*, 2nd edn (London: Oneworld, 2014)

References

CHAPTER 1: INHERITANCE

1. André Mathiot, *The British Political System*, translated by Jennifer S. Hines (London: Hogarth Press, 1958), p. 335.
2. Herman Finer, *The Major Governments of Modern Europe* (Evanston, IL: Row, Peterson, 1960), p. 67.
3. Walter Bagehot, *The English Constitution* (London: Chapman & Hall, 1867), p. 5.
4. Richard E. Neustadt, 'White House and Whitehall', reprinted in Anthony King, ed., *The British Prime Minister*, 2nd edn (London: Macmillan, 1985), p. 159.
5. Ibid.
6. See Richard Crossman, *The Diaries of a Cabinet Minister*, Vol. 1, *Minister of Housing 1964–66* (London: Hamish Hamilton and Jonathan Cape, 1975). On one occasion – reported on p. 25 of this volume of Crossman's diaries – Sharp fought and won an exhausting intra-Whitehall battle in defence of a position taken up by his and her Ministry of Housing and Local Government. At a subsequent meeting, when Crossman turned to her and said, 'Well, Dame Evelyn, you've won,' she replied briskly, 'Of course, I always win.'
7. J. A. G. Griffith, an academic lawyer, quoted in Jeffrey Jowell, 'Administrative Law', in Vernon Bogdanor, ed., *The British Constitution in the Twentieth Century* (Oxford: Oxford University Press for the British Academy, 2003), p. 385.
8. Sir Hartley Shawcross, the attorney-general, is often quoted as having said 'We are the masters now.' What in fact he said was, 'We are the masters at the moment'; adding, 'and not only at the moment, but for a very long time to come.' See Antony Jay, ed., *The Oxford Dictionary of Political Quotations*, 3rd edn (Oxford: Oxford University Press, 2006), pp. 274, 361.

REFERENCES

9. Norman Fowler, *Ministers Decide: A Personal Memoir of the Thatcher Years* (London: Chapmans, 1991).

10. Quoted in Vernon Bogdanor, 'Western Europe', in David Butler and Austin Ranney, eds, *Referendums Around the World: The Growing Use of Direct Democracy* (Washington, DC: AEI Press, 1994), p. 36.

11. L. S. Amery, *Thoughts on the Constitution*, 2nd edn (London: Oxford University Press, 1964), pp. 20–1.

12. Quoted in Roy Jenkins, *Churchill* (London: Macmillan, 2001), p. 792.

13. Quoted in Jay, *Oxford Dictionary of Political Quotations*, p. 38.

CHAPTER 2: FOREIGNERS

1. *Outside and Inside: Norway's Agreements with the European Union*, Official Norwegian Reports NOU 2012: 2, p. 23.

2. Ibid., p. 36.

3. Public Accounts Committee, *HM Revenue & Customs: Annual Report and Accounts 2011–12* (HC 2012–13, 716), p. 3.

CHAPTER 3: PARTISANS

1. A Conservative backbencher, Nigel Birch, quoted Browning's poem 'The Lost Leader' (1845) in the course of a vitriolic attack in the House of Commons on his own leader, Harold Macmillan, for his handling of the Profumo affair in 1963. The relevant passage of the poem is spelt out in Antony Jay, ed., *The Oxford Dictionary of Political Quotations*, 3rd edn (Oxford: Oxford University Press, 2006), p. 59.

2. John Ramsden, *An Appetite for Power: A History of the Conservative Party since 1830* (London: HarperCollins, 1999).

CHAPTER 4: POLITICIANS

1. *From Max Weber: Essays in Sociology*, translated and edited by H. H. Gerth and C. Wright Mills (London: Routledge & Kegan Paul, 1948), pp. 84–6.

2. W. Gore Allen, *The Reluctant Politician: Derick Heathcoat Amory* (London: Christopher Johnson, 1958).

3. Quoted in Susan Barnes, *Behind the Image* (London: Jonathan Cape, 1974), p. 68

4. Richard Marsh, *Off the Rails: An Autobiography* (London: Weidenfeld and Nicolson, 1978), pp. 156–7.

5. The books in the Nuffield College series of election studies always contain a detailed demographic breakdown of the membership of the House of Commons just elected. The figures in the text have been calculated from D. E. Butler, *The British General Election of 1955* (London: Macmillan, 1955), pp. 42–3; and Byron Criddle, 'More Diverse, Yet More Uniform: MPs and Candidates', in Dennis Kavanagh and Philip Cowley, *The British General Election of 2010* (Basingstoke: Palgrave Macmillan, 2010), pp. 326–7.

6. *From Max Weber*, p. 95.

7. See the account of Roy Jenkins's life as a backbencher in John Campbell, *Roy Jenkins: A Well-Rounded Life* (London: Jonathan Cape, 2014), p. 145. A younger colleague of Jenkins, Roy Hattersley, recalls a newly elected Sheffield MP in 1950 promising to visit his constituency every three months – and that promise being gratefully received. See Roy Hattersley, *Who Goes Home? Scenes from a Political Life* (London: Little, Brown, 1995), p. 11.

8. Quoted in David Marquand, *Ramsay MacDonald* (London: Jonathan Cape, 1977), p. 491.

9. Quoted in the *Guardian*, 1 December 2014. In view of several of Brown's budget speeches as chancellor, his critics may have felt entitled to say that this was a case of the kettle calling the pot black.

CHAPTER 5: VOTERS

1. F. W. S. Craig, ed., *British General Election Manifestos 1959–1987, 3rd edn* (Aldershot: Dartmouth, 1990), p. 123.

2. *Hansard*, HC Deb 16 November 1961, col. 799.

3. Sam Silkin, a Labour MP, quoted in Anthony King, *The British Constitution* (Oxford: Oxford University Press, 2007), p. 56.

4. Geoffrey Filkin, 'Ready for Ageing', in Charles Clarke, ed., *The 'Too Difficult' Box: The Big Issues Politicians Can't Crack* (London: Biteback, 2014), p. 81.

5. L. S. Amery, *Thoughts on the Constitution*, 2nd edn (London: Oxford University Press, 1964), pp 20–1. Although this later edition of *Thoughts* was

published in 1964, Amery's remarks were originally made in the course of a lecture delivered in 1947.

CHAPTER 6: IDEAS

1. John Maynard Keynes, *The General Theory of Employment, Interest and Money* (London: Macmillan, 1936), p. 383.
2. John Maynard Keynes, *The End of Laissez-Faire* (London: Hogarth, 1926), p. 16.
3. National Audit Office, *The Role of Major Contractors in the Delivery of Public Services*, HC 810 (London: Stationery Office, 2014), p. 10.
4. Anthony King, *The British Constitution* (Oxford: Oxford University Press, 2007), p. 67. The phrase 'romantic revolt' was coined by the Harvard political scientist Samuel H. Beer. See his *Britain against Itself: The Political Contradictions of Collectivism* (New York: W. W. Norton, 1982), Chap. 4.

CHAPTER 7: INTERESTS

1. David Butler and Dennis Kavanagh, *The British General Election of February 1974* (London: Macmillan, 1974), p. 29.
2. John Rentoul, *Tony Blair: Prime Minister* (London: Little, Brown, 2001), p. 173.
3. Quoted in Wyn Grant, *Pressure Groups and British Politics* (Basingstoke: Macmillan, 2000), p. 3.
4. Ibid., p. 33.
5. John Cridland, in the *Daily Telegraph*, 26 October 2014.
6. Public Accounts Committee, *Tax Avoidance: The Role of Large Accountancy Firms* (HC 2012–13, 870), p. 4.
7. *Guardian*, 2 July 2014. According to the *Guardian*'s account, those attending the dinner donated £5 million to the party in the course of the following year, £1.1 million of it during the week immediately after the event.
8. Kiran Stacey, 'The Explosion of Hedge Fund Donations to the Tories', *Financial Times Westminster Blog*, 8 December 2011, quoted in Owen Jones, *The Establishment: And How They Get Away with It* (London: Allen Lane, 2014), p. 55. The *FT* itself commented on the same day, 'Even donors admit

that Tory MPs' desire to cut the top 50p rate of income tax is because these rich City donors are so close to the party.'

CHAPTER 8: MEDIA

1. 'It's the *Sun* wot really runs the country!' (*Guardian*, 30 October 1997), reprinted in Hugo Young, *Supping with the Devils: Political Writing from Thatcher to Blair* (London: Atlantic, 2003), p. 60.

2. Lance Price quoted in Malcolm Dean, *Democracy under Attack: How the Media Distort Policy and Politics* (Bristol: Policy Press, 2013), p. 6.

3. Nick Davies, *Hack Attack: How the Truth Caught up with Rupert Murdoch* (London: Chatto & Windus, 2014), p. 164.

4. Peter Oborne, *Alastair Campbell: New Labour and the Rise of the Media Class* (London: Aurum, 1999), p. 177.

5. 'Dacre receives the highest praises', *Press Gazette*, 14 March 2003.

6. Quoted in Margaret Scammell and Charlie Beckett, 'Labour No More: The Press', in Dennis Kavanagh and Philip Cowley, *The British General Election of 2010* (Basingstoke: Palgrave Macmillan, 2010), p. 285.

7. Francis Elliott and James Hanning, *Cameron: The Rise of the New Conservative* (London: Fourth Estate, 2007), p. 261.

8. Blair's speech is summarized and quoted at length in Dean, *Democracy under Attack*, pp. 23–6.

9. Adam Boulton quoted in Dean, *Democracy under Attack*, p. 26.

10. Adam Price and Tom Watson, speaking on the Channel 4 *Dispatches* programme on 4 October 2010, quoted in Alan Rusbridger, *Play It Again: An Amateur against the Impossible* (London: Jonathan Cape, 2013), pp. 68–9.

11. Davies, *Hack Attack*, p. 216. According to that line of thinking, Blair desperately wanted Britain to draw ever closer to the EU, perhaps even to the point of joining the single currency, but he feared that, if he crossed Murdoch over Iraq and sided with the French and Germans instead of the Americans, 'the anti-EU Murdoch papers would throw all available ammunition at him' (p. 216).

12. Quoted in Anthony King, *Britain Says Yes: The 1975 Referendum on the Common Market* (Washington, DC: American Enterprise Institute, 1977), p. 134.

13. *Daily Express*, 21 October 2003. In fact, the closing of children's playgrounds had little, if anything, to do with the EU and was mostly in

response to home-grown British regulations. The stories about bananas and cucumbers were largely inventions.

14. See Dean, *Democracy under Attack*, pp. 231, 234–5.

15. Lance Price, *Where Power Lies: Prime Ministers v the Media* (London: Simon & Schuster, 2010), p. 349.

16. Quoted in Dean, *Democracy under Attack*, p. 163.

17. Anonymous official quoted in Davies, *Hack Attack*, p. 223.

18. Reprinted in *The Times Guide to the House of Commons April 1992* (London: Times Books, 1992), p. 340.

19. Quoted in Roy Jenkins, *Baldwin* (London: Collins, 1987), p. 120. There was more in the same vein in the same speech:

> The papers conducted by Lord Rothermere and Lord Beaverbrook [the *Daily Mail* and the *Daily Express*] are not newspapers in the ordinary acceptance of the term. They are engines of propaganda for the constantly changing policies, desires, personal wishes, personal likes and dislikes of two men. What are their methods? Their methods are direct falsehood, misrepresentation, half-truths, the alteration of the speaker's meaning by publishing a sentence apart from the context . . . [p. 120].

CHAPTER 9: MINISTERS

1. The phrase 'gene pool' in this context seems to have been introduced by Sir Andrew Turnbull, the cabinet secretary between 2002 and 2005. See his and others' evidence given to the House of Commons Public Administration Select Committee, *Goats and Tsars: Ministerial and other Appointments from outside Parliament* (HC 2009–10, 330), Ev. 1–14.

2. Amanda H. Goodall and Agnes Bäker, 'A Theory Exploring How Expert Leaders Influence Performance in Knowledge-Intensive Organizations', in Isabell M. Welpe, Jutta Wollersheim, Stefanie Ringelhan and Margit Osterloh, eds, *Incentives and Performance: Governance of Research Organizations* (Cham, Switzerland: Springer, 2015), p. 49. See also Amanda H. Goodall, *Socrates in the Boardroom: Why Research Universities Should Be Led by Top Scholars* (Princeton, NJ: Princeton University Press, 2009).

3. John Major quoted in R. K. Alderman, 'A Defence of Frequent Ministerial Turnover', *Public Administration* 73 (1995), p. 497; and Jack Straw, *Last*

Man Standing: Memoirs of a Political Survivor (London: Macmillan, 2012), pp. 549–50.

4. Straw, *Last Man Standing*, p. 549.

5. Peter Riddell, Zoe Gruhn and Liz Carolan, *The Challenge of Being a Minister: Defining and Developing Ministerial Effectiveness* (London: Institute for Government, 2011), p. 15.

6. Ibid., p. 20.

7. Charles Moore, *Margaret Thatcher*, Vol. 1, *Not for Turning* (London: Allen Lane, 2013), pp. 420, 422.

8. Interview with Robert Armstrong (Lord Armstrong of Ilminster) quoted in Moore, *Margaret Thatcher*, p. 521.

9. Margaret Thatcher, *The Downing Street Years* (London: HarperCollins, 1993), p. 48.

10. One of Margaret Thatcher's innovators quoted anonymously in Anthony King and Ivor Crewe, *The Blunders of Our Governments* (London: Oneworld, 2013), p. 336.

CHAPTER 10: OFFICIALS

1. Samuel Brittan, *The Treasury under the Tories 1951–1964* (Harmondsworth: Penguin, 1964), p. 208.

2. L. S. Amery, *Thoughts on the Constitution*, 2nd edn (London: Oxford University Press, 1964), p. 29.

3. Bridges' essay is summarized and quoted by R. A. W. Rhodes in *Everyday Life in British Government* (Oxford: Oxford University Press, 2011), pp. 59–60.

4. Quoted, among many other places, in David Marsh, David Richards and Martin J. Smith, *Changing Patterns of Governance in the United Kingdom: Reinventing Whitehall?* (Basingstoke: Palgrave, 2001), p. 39.

5. Margaret Thatcher, *The Downing Street Years* (London: HarperCollins, 1993), p. 48.

6. Peter Riddell, Zoe Gruhn and Liz Carolan, *The Challenge of Being a Minister: Defining and Developing Ministerial Effectiveness* (London: Institute for Government, 2011), p. 23.

7. Anonymous official quoted in Marsh, Richards and Smith, *Changing Patterns of Governance*, pp. 87–8.

8. John Hutton and Leigh Lewis, *How to Be a Minister: A 21st-Century Guide* (London: Biteback, 2014), p. 102.

9. Anonymous official quoted in Anthony King and Ivor Crewe, *The Blunders of Our Governments* (London: Oneworld, 2013), p. 337.

10. Anonymous official quoted in King and Crewe, *Blunders of Our Governments*, p. 342.

11. Anonymous official quoted in Marsh, Richards and Smith, *Changing Patterns of Governance*, p. 54.

12. Anonymous official quoted in King and Crewe, *Blunders of Our Governments*, p. 382.

13. Public Accounts Committee, *Reforming the UK Border and Immigration System* (HC 2014–15, 584), p. 3.

14. David Blunkett, *The Blunkett Tapes: My Life in the Bear Pit* (London: Bloomsbury, 2006), p. 400. See also Edward C. Page and Bill Jenkins, *Policy Bureaucracy: Government with a Cast of Thousands* (Oxford: Oxford University Press, 2005), especially Chap. 2. Page and Jenkins remark at one point: 'Subject specialization [among middle-ranking officials] is neither generally encouraged nor frequently developed' (p. 47).

15. *Report of the Laidlaw Inquiry into the Lessons Learned for the Department for Transport from the InterCity West Coast Competition* (HC 2012, 809), p. 71.

16. Ibid., p. 62.

17. Vernon Bogdanor quoted in Anthony King, *The British Constitution* (Oxford: Oxford University Press, 2007), p. 217.

CHAPTER 11: PRIME MINISTERS

1. Quoted, among many other places, in Antony Jay, ed., *The Oxford Dictionary of Political Quotations*, 3rd edn (Oxford: Oxford University Press, 2006), p. 16.

2. Quoted in John Major, *The Autobiography* (London: HarperCollins, 1999), p. 343. Neither Major nor the journalist realized that a microphone in the studio, which had been left behind after an earlier interview, was still switched on.

3. Alistair Darling, *Back from the Brink* (London: Atlantic, 2011), p. 250.

4. Nigel Lawson, *The View from No. 11: Memoirs of a Tory Radical* (London: Bantam, 1992), pp. 609–10.

5. Anonymous official quoted in Patrick Diamond, *Governing Britain: Power, Politics and the Prime Minister* (London: I. B. Tauris, 2014), p. 154.

6. Will Paxton quoted in Diamond, *Governing Britain*, p. 154.

7. Lord Egremont (John Wyndham), *Wyndham and Children First* (London: Macmillan, 1968), p. 167.

8. Jonathan Powell, *The New Machiavelli: How to Wield Power in the Modern World* (London: Bodley Head, 2010), p. 75.

9. Ibid., p. 81.

10. Quoted in Ben Pimlott, *Harold Wilson* (London: HarperCollins, 1992), p. 538.

11. Anonymous minister quoted in Dennis Kavanagh and Philip Cowley, *The British General Election of 2010* (Basingstoke: Palgrave Macmillan, 2010), p. 56.

12. Denis Healey, *The Time of My Life* (London: Michael Joseph, 1989), p. 447.

13. Richard E. Neustadt, *Presidential Power: The Politics of Leadership* (New York: John Wiley, 1960), p. 9.

CHAPTER 12: MPs

1. Simon Hoggart, *House of Fun: 20 Glorious Years in Parliament* (London: Faber and Faber, 2014), p. 246. It did not help that a year before, when Brown was conspicuously mishandling a scandal involving the Labour party, the Liberal Democrat Vince Cable had observed: 'The House has noticed the prime minister's remarkable transformation in the past few weeks – from Stalin to Mr Bean' (ibid., p. 235).

2. Actually, Bagehot was quoting someone whom he described only as 'a cynical politician', but he evidently agreed with him. See Walter Bagehot, *The English Constitution* (London: Chapman & Hall, 1867), p. 175.

3. Anonymous backbench MP quoted in Anthony King, *British Members of Parliament: A Self-Portrait* (London: Macmillan in association with Granada Television, 1974), p. 59.

4. Philip Cowley and colleagues at the University of Nottingham monitor the numbers and rates of rebellion among nominal government supporters in the House of Commons. See their website at revolts.co.uk. The figures in the text are drawn from, and where necessary extrapolated from, the data presented in their report on the 2013–14 parliamentary session, 'The Four Year Itch', pp. 2–3 (available via their website at revolts.co.uk/?p=829).

5. Ronald Butt, *The Power of Parliament*, 2nd edn (London: Constable, 1969).

6. Quoted in Geoffrey Howe, *Conflict of Loyalty* (London: Macmillan, 1994), p. 667.

7. Hoggart, *House of Fun*, p. 87.

8. House of Commons Draft Local Audit Bill ad hoc Committee, *Draft Local Audit Bill: Pre-legislative Scrutiny* (HC 2012–13, 696), p. 3.

9. Ruth Fox and Matt Korris, *Making Better Law: Reform of the Legislative Process from Policy to Act* (London: Hansard Society, 2010), p. 14.

10. Mr Justice Mitting quoted in J. R. Spencer, 'The Drafting of Criminal Legislation: Need It Be So Impenetrable?', *Cambridge Law Journal* 67 (2008), p. 585.

11. Daniel Greenberg, giving evidence to the House of Commons Political and Constitutional Reform Committee, *Ensuring Standards in the Quality of Legislation* (HC 2013–14, 85), Ev. 2.

12. Ibid., Ev. 3.

CHAPTER 13: JUDGES

1. Story told in Anthony King, *The British Constitution* (Oxford: Oxford University Press, 2007), p. 138.

2. Blunkett was speaking on BBC Radio 4's *The World at One*, 20 February 2003.

3. Quoted in the *Daily Telegraph*, 13 December 2013.

4. Lord Woolf and Jeffrey Jowell, *Judicial Review of Administrative Action*, 5th edn (London: Sweet & Maxwell, 1995), p. 3.

5. Quoted in Joshua Rozenberg, *The Search for Justice: An Anatomy of the Law* (London: Hodder & Stoughton, 1994), p. 197.

6. Lord Steyn quoted in Jeffrey Jowell, 'Administrative Law', in Vernon Bogdanor, ed., *The British Constitution in the Twentieth Century* (Oxford: Oxford University Press for the British Academy, 2003), p. 392.

7. Ibid., p. 393.

8. Quoted in Ian Loveland, 'Britain and Europe', in Bogdanor, *British Constitution in the Twentieth Century*, pp. 666–7.

9. Ibid., p. 677.

10. Quoted in Rozenberg, *The Search for Justice*, p. 214.

11. *R (on the application of Nicklinson and another) v. Ministry of Justice*, 25 June 2014, para. 116.

12. Ibid., para. 230.

CHAPTER 14: WHO GOVERNS?

1. Douglas Jay, a once prominent Labour politician, quoted in Antony Jay (no relation), ed., *The Oxford Dictionary of Political Quotations*, 3rd edn (Oxford: Oxford University Press, 2006), p. 197. Jay was writing in 1939, but that cast of mind lived on in Whitehall until at least the 1960s, possibly the 1970s.

2. Nadine Dorries, the maverick member of parliament for Mid Bedfordshire, interviewed on the BBC *Daily Politics* show, quoted in the *Daily Telegraph*. 24 April 2012.

3. Walter Bagehot, 'The Chances for a Long Conservative Régime in England' (1878), in *The Works and Life of Walter Bagehot*, edited by Mrs Russell Barrington, 10 vols (London: Longmans, Green & Co., 1915), vol. 7, p. 74.

4. Quoted in John Rentoul, *Tony Blair: Prime Minister* (London: Little, Brown, 2001), p. 262.

5. Quoted in the *Guardian*, 7 November 2007.

6. Co-authored by Anthony King and Ivor Crewe (London: Oneworld, 2013).

7. Labour party's 1997 election manifesto, reprinted in *The Times Guide to the House of Commons May 1997* (London: Times Books, 1997), p. 307.

Index

N

O

Classical
Literature
Richard Jenkyns

**What makes
Greek and Roman
literature great?**

**How has
classical literature
influenced
Western culture?**

**What did Greek
and Roman
authors learn
from each other?**

Richard Jenkyns is emeritus
Professor of the Classical
Tradition and the Public
Orator at the University of
Oxford. His books include
Virgil's Experience and *The
Victorians and Ancient Greece*,
acclaimed as 'masterly' by
History Today.

A PELICAN
INTRODUCTION

Economics:
The User's Guide
Ha-Joon Chang

What is economics?

What can – and can't – it explain about the world?

Why does it matter?

Ha-Joon Chang teaches economics at Cambridge University and writes a column for the *Guardian*. The *Observer* called his book 23 *Things They Don't Tell You About Capitalism*, which was a no.1 best-seller, 'a witty and timely debunking of some of the biggest myths surrounding the global economy'. He won the Wassily Leontief Prize for advancing the frontiers of economic thought and is a vocal critic of the failures of our current economic system.

A PELICAN
INTRODUCTION

Greek and Roman Political Ideas

Melissa Lane

Where do our ideas about politics come from?

What can we learn from the Greeks and Romans?

How should we exercise power?

Melissa Lane teaches politics at Princeton University, and previously taught for fifteen years at Cambridge University, where she also studied as a Marshall and Truman scholar. The historian Richard Tuck called her book *Eco-Republic* 'a virtuoso performance by one of our best scholars of ancient philosophy'.

A PELICAN
INTRODUCTION

Human Evolution
Robin Dunbar

What makes us human?

How did we develop language, thought and culture?

Why did we survive, and other human species fail?

Robin Dunbar is an evolutionary anthropologist and Director of the Institute of Cognitive and Evolutionary Anthropology at Oxford University. His acclaimed books include *How Many Friends Does One Person Need?* and *Grooming, Gossip and the Evolution of Language*, described by Malcolm Gladwell as 'a marvellous work of popular science'.

A PELICAN INTRODUCTION

Revolutionary Russia, 1891–1991
Orlando Figes

What caused the Russian Revolution?

Did it succeed or fail?

Do we still live with its consequences?

Orlando Figes teaches history at Birkbeck, University of London and is the author of many acclaimed books on Russian history, including *A People's Tragedy*, which *The Times Literary Supplement* named as one of the '100 most influential books since the war', *Natasha's Dance*, *The Whisperers*, *Crimea* and *Just Send Me Word*. The *Financial Times* called him 'the greatest storyteller of modern Russian historians'.

A PELICAN
INTRODUCTION

The
Domesticated
Brain
Bruce Hood

**Why do we
care what
others think?**

**What keeps
us bound
together?**

**How does the
brain shape
our behaviour?**

Bruce Hood is an award-winning
psychologist who has taught
and researched at Cambridge
and Harvard universities and
is currently Director of the
Cognitive Development Centre
at the University of Bristol. He
delivered the Royal Institution's
Christmas Lectures in 2011 and
is the author of *The Self Illusion*
and *Supersense*, described by *New
Scientist* as 'important, crystal
clear and utterly engaging'.

A PELICAN
INTRODUCTION